W9-BVQ-538

# MEDIEVAL CULTURE

## The Image and the City

## The Cultures of Mankind

GREEK CULTURE: The Adventure of the Human Spirit
*Edited by Alice von Hildebrand*

ROMAN CULTURE: Weapons and the Man
*Edited by Garry Wills*

MEDIEVAL CULTURE: The Image and the City
*Edited by Ruth Brantl*

RENAISSANCE CULTURE: A New Sense of Order
*Edited by Julian Mates and Eugene Cantelupe*

THE AGE OF REASON: The Culture of the Seventeenth Century
*Edited by Leo Weinstein*

THE ENLIGHTENMENT: The Culture of the Eighteenth Century
*Edited by Isidor Schneider*

ROMANTICISM: The Culture of the Nineteenth Century
*Edited by Morse Peckham*

TWENTIETH-CENTURY CULTURE: The Breaking Up
*Edited by Robert Phelps*

# Medieval Culture

## *The Image and the City*

Edited by Ruth Brantl

George Braziller · New York

Published simultaneously in Canada by Ambassador Books, Ltd., Toronto



For information, address the publisher,
George Braziller, Inc.
One Park Avenue, New York, N.Y.

Library of Congress Catalog Card Number: 66-15758

First Printing

Printed in the United States of America

DESIGN BY JULIUS PERLMUTTER

## ACKNOWLEDGMENTS

The editor and publisher have made every effort to determine and credit the holders of copyrights of the selections in this book. Any errors or omissions may be rectified in future editions. The editor and publisher wish to thank the following for permission to reprint the material included in this anthology:

Appleton-Century-Crofts—for selections from *The Statesman's Book of John of Salisbury,* translated by John Dickinson. Copyright 1927, by Alfred A. Knopf, Inc. Reprinted by permission of Appleton-Century-Crofts.

Burns & Oates Ltd.—for selections from *The Journey of the Mind to God* by St. Bonaventure. Reprinted by permission of the publisher.

Chatto and Windus Ltd.—for selections from *The Rule of St. Benedict,* translated by Cardinal Gasquet, 1936.

Columbia University Press—for selections from *The Two Cities* by Bishop Otto of Freising, translated by C. C. Mierow, copyright 1928 by Columbia University Press.

Curtis Brown Ltd., New York and Helen Waddell—for selections from *Medieval Latin Lyrics,* translated by Helen Waddell.

## ACKNOWLEDGMENTS

E. P. Dutton & Co., Inc. and J. M. Dent & Sons Ltd.—for selections from *The Divine Comedy* by Dante, translated by Carlyle, Okay and Wickstead. Temple Classics Edition; and Chapman & Hall Ltd. for selections from *The Song of Roland,* translated by C. K. Scott Moncrieff. All selections reprinted by permission of the publishers.

Angel Flores—for "I am Eve, wife of Adam" translated by Marian Robinson from *Medieval Age,* edited by Angel Flores, copyright © 1963 by Angel Flores. Published by Dell Publishing Co., Inc., 1963.

Franciscan Herald Press—for a selection from the "Chronicle" of Salimbene degli Adami in *XIII Century Chronicles,* translated by Placid Hermann, 1961.

The Franciscan Institute—for a selection from *De Reductione Artium ad Theologiam* (*Retracing the Arts to Theology*) by St. Bonaventure, translated by Sister E. T. Healy, 1955. Originally published by St. Anthony Guild Press, 1940.

Harper & Row, Publishers, Inc. and William Collins Sons & Co., Ltd.—for a selection from *The Phenomenon of Man* by Teilhard de Chardin. Copyright © 1959 by Harper & Row, Publishers. Reprinted by permission of the publishers.

Harvard University Press—for a selection from "First Sermon" from "Nineteen Sermons on Ecclesiastes" by Hugh of St. Victor, translated by Henry O. Taylor in his *The Medieval Mind,* Vol. II.

Thomas Nelson & Sons Ltd.—for a selection from *Theophilus: De Diversis Artibus* (*The Various Arts*) edited by C. R. Dodwell; and Oxford University Press, New York for a selection from *John of Salisbury's Memoirs of the Papal Court,* translated and edited by Marjorie Chibnall.

Oxford University Press—for "Charm for Unfruitful Land," translated by Charles W. Kennedy from his *An Anthology of Old English Poetry.* Copyright © 1960 by Oxford University Press, Inc. Reprinted by permission of the publisher.

Penguin Books Ltd.—for "The Wolf of Gubbio" from *The Little Flowers of St. Francis,* translated by Leo Shirley-Price, 1959.

Random House, Inc. and Burns & Oates Ltd.—for selections from *The Basic Writings of St. Thomas Aquinas,* edited by Anton C. Pegis, copyright 1945 by Random House, Inc. Reprinted by permission of the publishers.

The University of Michigan Press—for a selection from *The Life of Charlemagne* by Einhard, translated by S. E. Turner.

University of Minnesota Press—for a selection, "On Marriage," by John of Salisbury, translated by Joseph B. Pike from his *Frivolities of Courtiers,* 1938.

The Viking Press, Inc.—for a selection from *Giotto* by Lorenzo Ghiberti, translated by J. B. Ross and "Letter of Peter the Venerable to Heloise concerning Abelard," translated by Mary Martin McLaughlin, both selections from *The Portable Medieval Reader,* edited by James Bruce Ross and Mary Martin McLaughlin. Copyright 1949 by The Viking Press, Inc. Reprinted by permission of the publisher.

# Contents



## I THE IMAGE

### The Divine Center



### A Way of Seeing

## The Universal Church



## The Church and Society



# II SERVICE

## The Structure of Service



## Chivalry

## The Service of Woman



# III THE JOURNEY

## The Pilgrim



## The Merchant



## The Crusader



## The Artist

## The Scholar



## The Philosopher



# IV THE CITY



## The Social Image

CONTENTS

## The Literary Image

# List of Illustrations

Illustrations for frontispiece and part titles are leaves from an illuminated *Antiphonary* (in the Library of the Museum). Italian manuscript, XV century. New York, The Metropolitan Museum of Art, Gift of Louis L. Lorillard, 1896.

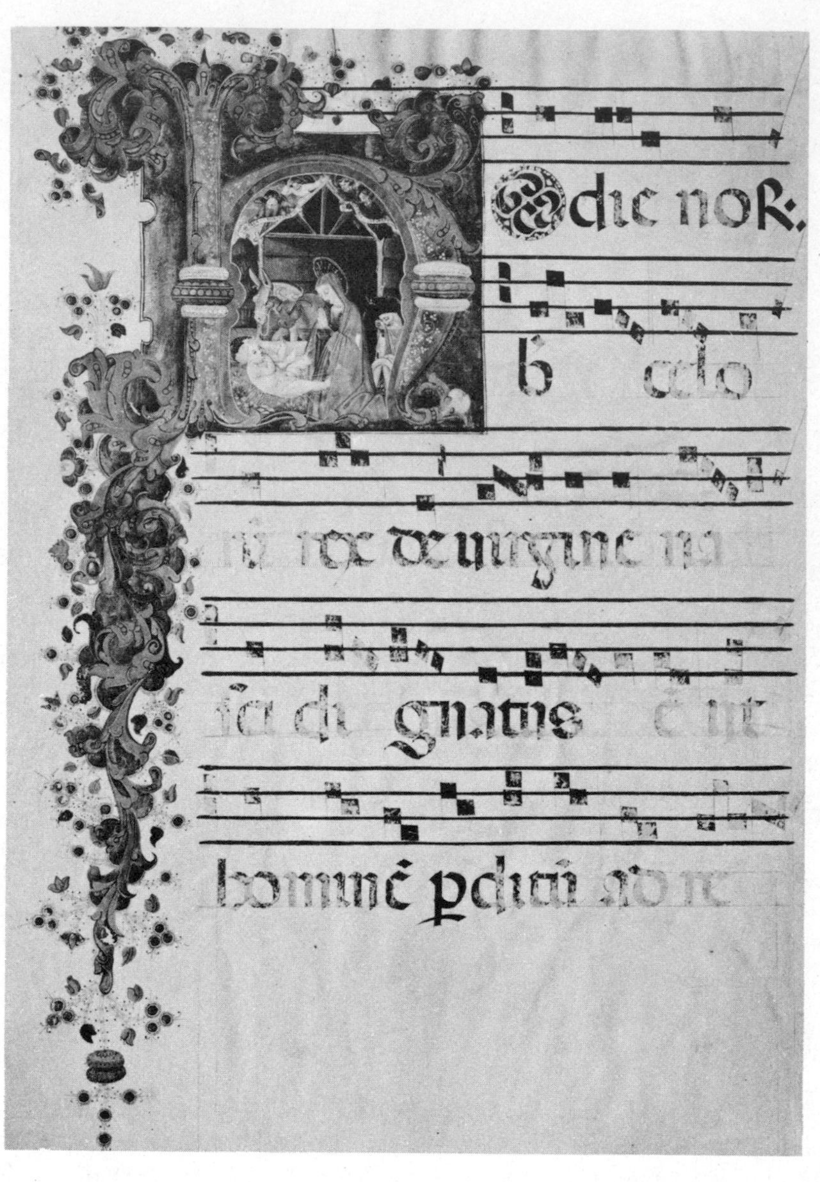

dic nob
rex de uirgine na
gnatus
hominē pditū

# INTRODUCTION

1. Cathedral of Mont-Saint Michel.

The Middle Ages saw the first and greatest attempt to build a society upon the basic commitments of the Christian faith. In this age when Western man sought to Christianize the human community in all of its aspects, medieval culture became both the consequence of Christian humanism and the test of its viability.

At the beginning of every great cultural period may be found a new affirmation of human transcendence, a confident commitment to the ideal vision which this culture hopes to realize in the immanent affairs of men. In a sense, each culture rediscovers man, redefines him and recommits man to his own ideal possibilities as embodied in his definition. Each such affirmation is a faith, and from this faith evolve those elements which are normative values for a culture. It is this faith which gives spirit and passion to man's activities and determines the form or structure which the global view of his culture will manifest. In this sense, the development of a culture exemplifies the principle which was widespread in the medieval period: *faith seeking understanding.* Although this phrase is generally interpreted in the limited terms of faith and reason as intellectual repositories, its implications are far richer. "Faith" is the commitment of man to the ultimate values by which he will live and die. "Understanding" may be interpreted as the embodiment or articulation of this commitment in act or in structures, whether of reason, moral endeavor or institutions. If faith is the spirit of a culture, understanding is its body.

Certainly "faith seeking understanding" aptly describes and summarizes the medieval experience. For the Christian faith contained a startling new affirmation of transcendence, of destiny, of human responsibility—in fact, rarely has a faith been more inclusive in its claims on the totality of human experience. Arising at a time when the decline of the Roman Empire had left the Western world a wasteland, it found men ripe for its affirmations and its implied possibilities. It seemed to offer the longed-for new chance for man to gain Man. The medieval experience was the attempt to incarnate this faith by institutionalizing it, to "understand" it in the totality of men's affairs and thus to Christianize human society in its intellectual, scientific, economic and social activities. And in giving form to the developing civilization, it gave birth to a Christian culture in all its manifestations.

No period of history is all of a piece. Always there exists the stubborn reality of human choice: the distinction between the values men profess and society demands, on the one hand, and those that are affirmed in their behavior. If we refer to the medieval period as one of great Christian humanism, we must remember that it was never fully Christian nor fully humanistic. Too, every value-commitment entails a choice which from its very nature excludes other possibilities of choice. When dealing with a mystery-faith like Christianity, there is even less likelihood of finding homogeneity. For when such a faith is culturally institutionalized, mystery is secularized; but mystery, by its very nature, is paradoxical. Constantly, then, there arise in such cases dualities, countertrends, heresies—each claiming closer adherence to the common faith, each asserting greater fidelity to the mystery.

The medieval period, for example, begins with a central mystery, the fact of Christ, God-incarnate. In the cultural institutionalization of this faith, emphasis is placed on the immanence or incarnational aspect of the God-man—the value of hereness, of time, of human potentiality, of matter; thus, on the value of building society here and now into a city of God among men. But, in the Christ-figure there is polarity: He is always more than man and his teachings always imply that fulfillment is beyond time, that the Christian must ever keep himself detached from total immersion in the world. "My kingdom is not of this world." This approach, that of transcendence, is reflected sharply in the "two laws" of St. Paul, the polarity between good and evil, which from this viewpoint are irreconcilable. Consequently, the development of medieval culture, which was dominated by the image of incarnation—of the redeeming of flesh and matter and the recognition of its intrinsic value—saw at the same time the frequent reaffirmation of separation, other-worldliness, purity, immateriality. In their several aspects, these were the origins of the various great religious heresies of the period, all of which had deep social as well as religious roots. The major medieval heresies centered upon the mystery of the Incarnation, the identity-in-distinction of the human and divine in the one person, Christ. This mystery signifies the

2. Tympanum, south portal. Chartres Cathedral.

polar co-inherence of transcendence/immanence. Heretical emphasis on transcendence implied the sundering of the incarnational reality, while the institutionalization of the faith in holding to incarnation stressed immanence. As over-immanence can lead to the total secularization of a faith, the medieval experience led ultimately to the momentous reaffirmation of transcendence which characterizes the Protestant Reformation. Consequently, although the prevailing cultural force in the medieval period was the unity of the Christian faith embodied in the institutions of men, still this was a direction only, a movement; within this framework of cultural unity there was intense diversity, heterodoxy. Barbarism existed side by side with charity, sin with sanctity, heresy with orthodoxy.

## Origins

Great cultural changes—new faiths and new commitments—wait upon time and the social, political and economic conditions which make them not only possible but urgent. Through the centuries there have been historic periods when elements of diverse civilizations met and fused organically into a new cultural entity and from this new burst of creative energy originated a cultural renaissance. Such a period was the Middle Ages. For, out of the Dark Ages with its gloom and anarchy rose an iridescent culture, brilliant in its intellectual and artistic contributions, vivid in its complexity, continuity and change; a culture of striking organic wholeness, offering an uncommon example of the development, fruition and decline of a human experience.

The elements of this culture were in the making over several centuries. The fall of the Roman Empire had been more cataclysmic than is generally realized. Agricultural though it was, its structure was based on the cities; even in the provinces it worked through town outposts. With the sacking of the cities by marauding barbarians, the destruction of Roman civilization was total. Its decadent remains were no match for the conquerors and a new order began to rise.

The fortuitous mixture of races in Europe was an important factor in the new development. In northern Europe the Celts were an intelligent, quick-witted, fey and progressive people. Their Druidical culture held learning in high esteem: their priests were trained for twenty years to be the teachers as well as the diviners of their clans. They believed in the prophetic role of women and rejoiced in romance and heroic adventure —their epic hero, Cuchulain, is a hyperbolic Achilles. Here Christianity

3. Jeweled book cover of Codex Aureus of St. Emmeram, made for Reims or St. Denis. West Frankish, IX century.

4. Oak statuette of angel. Reims School. France, XII century.

found fertile soil and numerous monastic foundations came to be repositories for classic learning. In England the Celts were overrun and absorbed by the Angles and Saxons, rude, restless people of tremendous hardihood, the folk of Beowulf. To the East the Teutonic tribes were a blunt, tactless, calm people, characterized by purpose and vigor. Weak in political arts, their basic unit of folk was based on blood ties while their tribal king was advised by a witan, a council of companions who fought for him in time of war. Their institutions and traditions were few, but they were quick to admire the civilization of their Roman conquerors. From the North meanwhile, the Vikings roamed the seas, ravaging the coastline, restrained by no boundaries.*

All these people had been touched by the Roman conquest. After the fall of Rome, however, civilization retreated before hordes of barbarians. Except for a glow of learning in the Irish monasteries, all was dark. The period from the fifth to the eighth centuries was largely a clearing away of wreckage. Northward, out of Monte Cassino, came the monks of St. Benedict, teaching methods of agriculture, clearing away forests, raising cattle, then endeavoring to Christianize the barbarians. Missionaries generally combined the two efforts, finding that a gentler faith and a settled life complemented each other.

The ninth century opened hopefully with the coronation of Charlemagne as Emperor of the Franks. This man of enormous strength purposed to rebuild the Roman Empire as the City of God on earth, and by pure force of personality he sought to establish a common culture. In the cathedral schools begun during his reign he laid the base for a common scholarship; from England he brought the famous teacher, Alcuin, heir of Irish monastic learning. This was, however, less a creative culture than a revival of the Latin Fathers of the Church, of Roman classicists and of the Latin language. Largely an improvisation, it was still a dynamic culture of great momentum so that within its narrow compass man stood on the verge of an educational breakthrough. But with Charlemagne's death his empire divided under weaker men who had not shared his dream of a Holy Roman Empire. Even when it came to be rebuilt in future time, it would never be holy nor Roman, nor even truly empire. Little of its cultural gain was lasting, for there was no

* Not only do runes show their penetration of America as far as Minnesota, but they are probably responsible for the Shawnee Indian legend of white men with iron weapons in the Chesapeake area centuries before the coming of the English.

machinery to keep it in motion; north of Italy educated men were too rare to maintain a general culture.

The most lasting cultural contribution of Charlemagne's period was the cathedral school which had been required of every bishopric in the realm. These schools, as well as those of the monasteries, became workshops of the arts and, as a result, art developed in an orderly fashion. It was the small art common to migratory peoples: illuminations rather than large painting, ivory carving in preference to sculpture. The classics were preserved by skilled copyists who laboriously wrote page upon page and had no thought of finishing in a lifetime for this was the work of a monastery rather than of a man. From Ireland came the minuscule script which became the handwriting of Europe; the gorgeously colored Book of Kells, fashioned by Irish monks in the late eighth century, has never been surpassed in style or color.

Outside of the monastery and cathedral centers disorder prevailed, and when for security a man placed himself and his land under a stronger sword, there occurred the essential change from tribalism to the territorialism of the feudal system. However faulty feudalism appears from the vantage of democratic centuries, it was the salvation of Europe—what else could have functioned? For this Teutonic style of companions was better suited to the maintenance of order than were the earlier clans. Rewards of land-grants established a class of men obligated to their lord, and in a moneyless society each lord's domain became independent of the outside world. From these oases of stability, order began to radiate.

The establishment of feudal order permitted economic growth which was a vital factor in the medieval rebirth. Town life developed, a condition for social revolution: along the trade routes, by rivers and harbors, medieval towns were growing and by A.D. 1100 were making their mark. With some semblance of safety in travel, merchants carried their wares farther overland. When the western Crusaders came into Constantinople, they were amazed at the comfort and luxurious living there and rapidly acquired a taste for the spices, silks and steels of the East. Such contacts spurred on the growth of trade, the interest in navigation and improved methods of transportation. Thus, economic growth complemented the rising political stability: the merchant class supported the growing monarchies against rapacious nobles, the new kings offering the merchants safety and status. And the growing prosperity of the merchant class made it possible for them to become patrons of the arts.

Even as commercial contacts were developing between East and West, a flood of intellectual wealth was entering Europe by way of Spain and Sicily. A century earlier, Norman pilgrims returning from Jerusalem had settled in Sicily and made it a center of far-reaching cultural activity, a curious mixture of Moslem and Christian. Known as the "baptized Sultan," Roger II, King of Sicily in the early twelfth century, became one of the great patrons of learning. Roman law was revived with Norman overtones; students of geography, mathematics and astronomy gathered; Aristippus, translator of Plato and Aristotle, lived at court. The Moslems, in conquering Syria, had gained custody of the Greek classics, and now by way of Sicily and, similarly, Spain, the world of Greek knowledge became part of the European heritage. The great medieval renaissance became a reality.

## An Age of Faith

The fusing element, the catalyst for all these diverse, heterogeneous elements, was the humanism in the deposit of the Christian faith. In its early years the Christian Church had been totally occupied with the struggles against persecution and heresy, while later its missionary and monastic efforts were directed toward the education and religious training of the barbarian peoples. Now, freed from these pressures, there was the opportunity to cultivate the deeper human and spiritual resources of the faith. At every point, indeed, it seemed to fit the needs and aspirations of medieval man: from the Good Shepherd of the peasant to the Blessed Sacrament of the theologian, Christ became a living reality and a central figure of the medieval experience. From the peasant and the craftsman to Dante and the cathedral architects, this faith would now give organic unity to a vast cultural endeavor.

The Nicene Creed provides an introduction to this far reaching activity. Propounded in A.D. 325 at the Church Council of Nicaea, it states the basic tenets of the Christian faith.

> I believe in one God,
> The Father almighty, maker of heaven and earth, and of all things visible and invisible.
> And in one Lord Jesus Christ, the only begotten Son of God,
> Born of the Father before all ages.
> God of God, light of light, true God of true God.

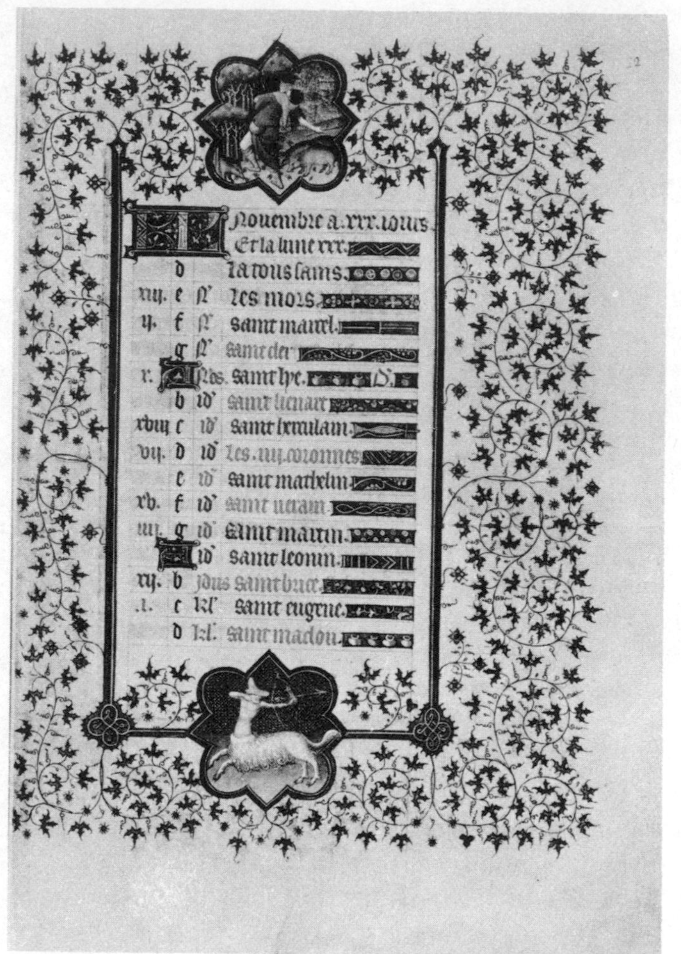

5 Calendar of November from *The Book of Hours of Jean, Duke of Berry,* Limbourg Brothers. French manuscript, XV century.

6. Ivory rosary from Germany, XVI century.

Begotten, not made; being of one substance with the Father; by whom all things were made.

Who for us men, and for our salvation, came down from heaven.

And was incarnate by the Holy Spirit of the Virgin Mary: and was made man.

He was crucified also for us, suffered under Pontius Pilate, and was buried.

And the third day He rose again according to the Scriptures.

And ascended into heaven. He sitteth at the right hand of the Father.

And He shall come again with glory to judge both the living and the dead; of whose kingdom there shall be no end.

And I believe in the Holy Spirit, the Lord and giver of life:

Who proceedeth from the Father and the Son.

Who together with the Father and the Son is adored and glorified.

Who spake by the Prophets.

And in one, holy, catholic and apostolic Church.

I confess one baptism for the remission of sins.

And I look for the resurrection of the dead.

And the life of the world to come. Amen.

These beliefs were later subject to interpretation and theoretical systematization; a Christian philosophy and a theology came into being. The basic source of the elements of belief as well as of many of the ambiguities which arose in their interpretation was to be found in the Scriptures. But to these were joined several other important influences. The tradition of Christian Platonism, originating in St. Augustine and in the Pseudo-Dionysus, contributed a sense of divine imagery as a cosmic principle, a vision of the hierarchical structure of the universe and the eschatological theory of history which later governed medieval thought. There was, too, the influence of Jewish and Arabic scholars who, by introducing Aristotle into the Western world, made possible the last stages of medieval intellectualism with its stress on rational nature and a universe governed by moral-natural law. Together they constituted a rich, highly developed world-view which gave both structure and polarity to medieval culture.

Four general characteristics or principles in this world view will serve as the divisions of this book. A brief description of each follows.

1. *The Universe as Image.* In Genesis it is said that when God came to make man, He created him *in His image.* This phrase, central to Christian Platonism, implied not only a view of man in relation to God, but a theory of universal becoming and a cultural dynamic. The being and development of the universe, of man and of community will be "true" insofar as it images God—insofar, that is, as its development is an "othering" of God. If the divine "idea" of things is the divine Nature as the immanent law of things, how much more of man who as person can most perfectly image God. But, if man was made in the image of God, by sin he limited his likeness. His restoration to grace and his spiritual life become a process of restoring the image—a second creation.

The image, in fact, is rather an imaging. Creatures reflect God and in their development they image in time the fulness of perfection which is eternally God. Therefore, man's vocation is to build the image of God in his life while he recognizes the imaging of God in nature about him. The universe then becomes a vast process of divine "othering" which in its fidelity constitutes the glory of God.

This theory of imagery implied as well a scale of beings from the lowest to the highest, from amoeba to angel, each in itself complete, but representing hierarchical degrees of approximation to the perfection of God. To fulfill the will of God is then to fulfill or incarnate the Idea which is the law of one's development as well as one's mode of imaging God; and this in relationship to one's position in the scale of beings as defined by divine creation.

In this world man is highest on the scale of beings. He, among creatures, is made uniquely to image God. And the supreme exemplar of human imaging or perfection is to be found in Christ: "I have given you an example." To become like Christ is then to become man in the fullest sense. "I am the vine, you are the branches." And insofar as the Christian community finds its organic unity in Christ, it is that community of men (ideally, all men) which will ultimately embody the spirit of Christ and thus most fully image God.

2. *Service.* The Christian universe of imagery is governed by divine law, which promulgated in nature is natural law. Man is called to obey the law, to be, in the Scriptural phrase, a "doer of the word." St. Anselm, quoting St. John, expressed the same thought in his exhortation, "Do the truth." The image of God, what men "are," is what they are called to be.

7. Fourth tone of music, east capital. Autun Cathedral.

To image God is to act according to the law of God immanent in nature. Image is law: to image "truly" (to be) is to act the truth (morally)

In man's obedience to law is his service. As there is a hierarchy of forms, a scale of being, so there are degrees of service, from the "obedience" of physical necessity in nature through degrees of human servile obedience to the free service of love. The ultimate reaches of service are embodied in Augustine's phrase, "Love and do what thou wilt": when God is loved, man's will so identifies with the will of God that the Law of God becomes man's desire. Finally, if every man is called to service according to his degree, the supreme act of service is that of the entire Christian community to God.

3. *The Journey*. In creating, God calls all things from nothingness. The great adventure of life is the return to God while salvation is man's

8. Bronze *Crucifixion Plaque* (from a book cover?). Ireland, VIII century.

escape—actually his redemption—from nothingness. God or nothingness—this cosmic struggle dominates the Christian mind and constitutes the adventure of the medieval spirit.

Frequently Thomas Aquinas writes that "all things desire God," their desire is their very nature. This desire produces an endless movement of creatures toward God, a movement which incarnates God in nature. Man, then, is a viator, a pilgrim on a journey toward God. In whatever he does, he is either returning to God by seeking fulfillment or rejecting God as he turns aside to other goals. In every medieval endeavor this sense of pilgrimage was dominant. History is the universal journey back to God; faith, its dynamic principle, seeks understanding but moves back upon itself and onward toward ultimate vision. To live is to journey; to journey, to risk: all life is an adventure.

4. *The City of God.* The ultimate goal towards which things of this earth progress is the City of God. Not man in isolation, but all men building a community made up of all who attempt to incarnate Christ in themselves, a community which in itself will be the most apt imaging of that Community which is the inner life of God.

Under the social dualism of Augustine, humanity from all time has been divided into two cities: men whose goals are material and carnal make up the terrestrial city; men of good will seeking the things of the spirit comprise the heavenly city. These latter are pilgrims, inhabiting the earthly city as strangers, living by faith in their journey through the world. Neither city actually corresponds to any existing institution, although there was often a tendency to equate the earthly city with the state and the heavenly city with the church. While the Church functions as the visible organ of the Eternal City, the City itself is an organism growing through the interaction of God and the individual souls of men. This is the true Church, which will give place, at the end of time, to the "kingdom not of this world."

PART I

# The Image

*Medieval man inhabited a universe filled with God. It was a world of confidence, of adventure and newness, freed of the divine indifference and the consequent pessimism which medievals found in the classical world. Christ, God-made-man, was a radical turning point in history for medieval man, where God not only showed the value of man in His divine economy but gave fresh value to the world of matter and of human history. The second Adam, in redeeming man, had renewed humanity.*

*While the God of Aristotle had been an absolute eternal Prime-Mover under whom history was a closed system, the God of Christians was a providential co-worker with men, for whom history became an intensely personal drama of human salvation. While the absolute values in Plato had seemed relegated to a world apart, the values of the Christian world were incarnate in nature, traces of God in things. Nature had become truly Christian, the becoming of things in their god-likeness. All things reflect God, image His perfection in obeying His law. And in Man is to be found the ultimate natural image of God, heightened beyond imagination by the supernatural calling which Christ restored in the very fact of redemption.*

## *The Divine Center*

*If the task of medieval man was to Christianize the social order, he would find his guiding principle in the presence of God to nature, to man and to human history. Imagery would give him direction: God working in all things as they are moved and motivated to reach their perfection, which is their imitation of the perfection of God.*

*This belief in imagery entailed several important considerations for the medieval mind: (1) that nature is a divine mirror for man to contemplate; (2) that man is a co-worker in building the image of God in nature and society; (3) that the fact of religious belief is an all-pervasive, totally inclusive element in experience; and (4) that this universality and primacy of the religious factor is embodied in the Church of Christ which not only represents the law of God but symbolizes His presence among men.*

## NATURE AS IMAGE

### St. Augustine

Not with uncertain, but with assured consciousness do I love Thee O Lord. Thou hast stricken my heart with Thy sword, and I loved Thee. And also the heaven, and earth, and all that is therein, behold, on every side they say that I should love Thee; nor do they cease to speak unto all, so that they are without excuse. But more profoundly wilt Thou have mercy on whom Thou wilt have mercy, and compassion on whom Thou wilt have compassion, otherwise do both heaven and earth tell forth Thy praises to deaf ears. But what is it that I love in loving Thee? Not corporeal beauty, nor the splendor of time, nor the radiance of the light, so pleasant to our eyes, nor the sweet melodies of songs of all kinds, nor the fragrant smell of flowers, and ointments, and spices, not manna and honey, not limbs pleasant to the embracements of flesh. I love not these things when I love my God; and yet I love a certain kind of light, and sound, and fragrance, and food, and embracement in loving my God, who is the light, sound, fragrance, food and embracement of my inner man—where that light shineth unto my soul which no place can contain, where that soundeth which time snatcheth not away, where there is a fragrance which no breeze disperseth, where there is a food which no eating can diminish, and where that clingeth which no satiety can sunder. This is what I love, when I love my God.

And what is this? I asked the earth; and it answered, "I am not He;" and whatsoever are therein made the same confession. I asked the sea and the deeps, and the creeping things that lived and they replied, "We are not thy God, seek higher than we." I asked the breezy air and the universal air with its inhabitants answered, "Anaximenes was deceived, I am not God." I asked the heavens, the sun, moon and stars: "Neither," say they, "are we the God whom thou seekest." And I answered unto all these things which stand about the door of my flesh, "Ye have told me concerning my God that ye are not He; tell me something about Him." And with a loud voice they exclaimed, "He made us." My questioning was my observing of them; and their beauty was their reply. And I directed my thought to myself and said, "Who art thou?" And I answered, "A man." And lo, in me there appear both body and soul, the one without, the other within. By which of these should I seek my God, whom I had sought through the body from earth to heaven, as far as I was able to send messengers—the beams of mine eyes? But the better part is that which is inner; for to it, as both president and judge, did all my corporeal messengers render the answers of heaven and earth and all things therein, who said, "We are not God, but He made us." These things my inner man knew by the ministry of the outer; I, the inner man, knew all this—I, the soul, through the senses of my body. I asked the vast bulk of the earth of my God, and it answered me, "I am not He, but He made me."

Is not this beauty visible to all whose senses are unimpaired? Why, then, doth it not speak the same things unto all? Animals, the very small and the great, see it, but they are unable to question it, because their senses are not endowed with reason to enable them to judge on what they report. But men can question it, so that the invisible things of Him . . . are clearly seen, being understood by the things that are made. (X, 6)

. . .

Behold, the heaven and earth are; they proclaim that they were made for they are changed and varied. Whereas whatsoever has not been made, and yet has being, has nothing in it which there was not before; this is what it is to be changed and varied. They also proclaim that they made not themselves; "therefore we are, because we have been made; we were not therefore before we were, so that we could have been made ourselves." And the voice of those that speak is itself an evidence. Thou, therefore, Lord, didst make these things; Thou who art beautiful, for they are beautiful; Thou who art good, for they are good; Thou who art,

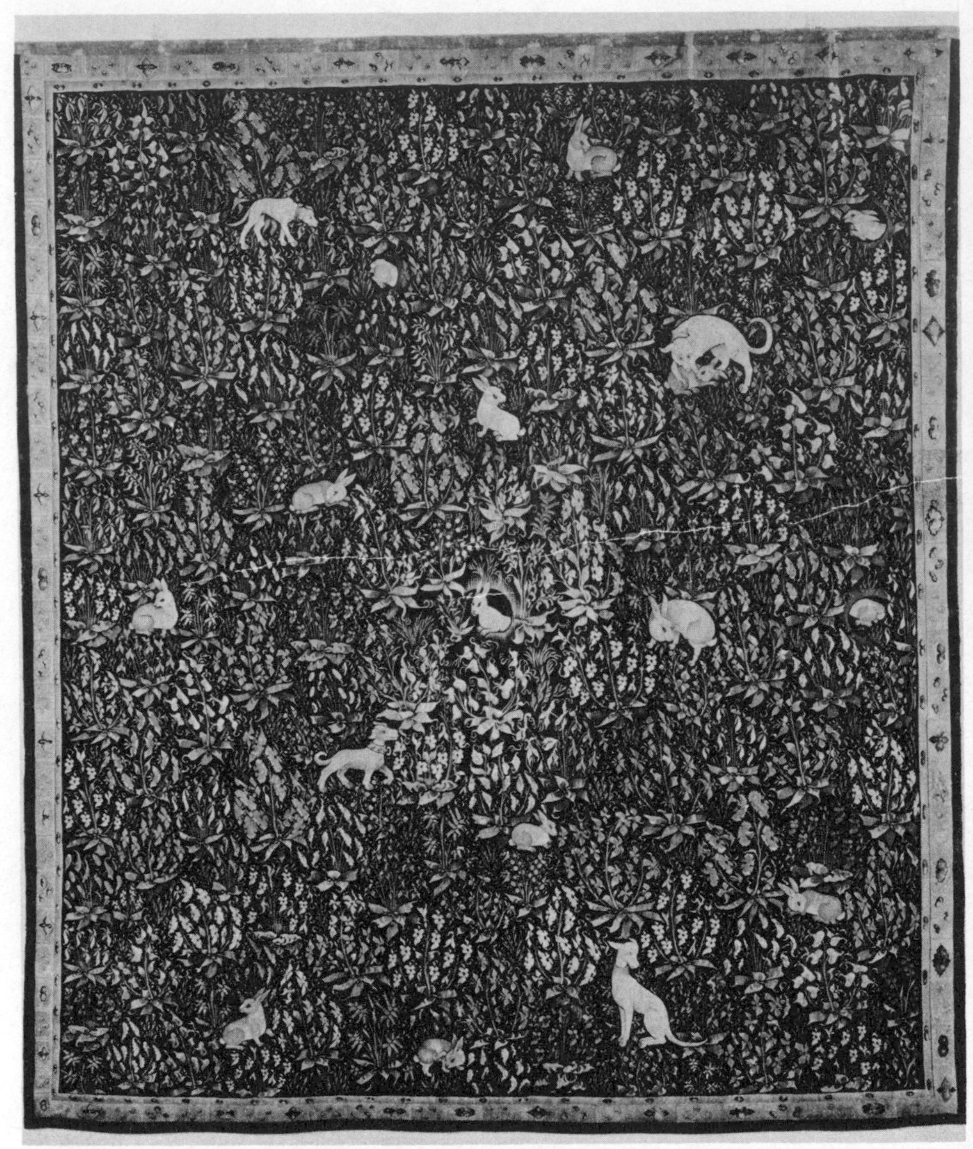

9. *Millefleurs* tapestry. Franco-Flemish, c. 1500.

for they are. Nor even so are they beautiful, nor good, nor are they, as Thou their Creator art; compared with whom they are neither beautiful, nor good nor are at all. These things we know, thanks be to Thee. And our knowledge, compared with Thy knowledge, is ignorance. (XI, 4)

. . .

Which of us understands the Almighty Trinity? And yet which speaks not of It, if indeed it be It? Rare is that soul which, while it speaks of It, knows what it speaks of. And they contend and strive, but no one without peace sees that vision. I could wish that men would consider these three things that are in themselves. These three are far other than the Trinity; but I speak of things in which they may exercise and prove themselves, and feel how far other they be. But the three things I speak of are, to Be, to Know, and to Will. For I Am, and I Know, and I Will; I Am Knowing and Willing; and I Know myself to Be and to Will; and I Will to Be and to Know. In these three, therefore, let him who can see how inseparable a life there is—even one life, one mind, and one essence; finally, how inseparable is the distinction, and yet a distinction. Surely a man has it before him; let him look into himself, and see, and tell me. But when he discovers and can say anything of these, let him not then think that he has discovered that which is above these Unchangeable, which Is unchangeably, and Knows unchangeably, and Wills unchangeably. And whether on account of these three there is also, where they are, a Trinity; or whether these three be in Each, so that the three belong to Each; or whether both ways at once, wondrously, simply, and yet diversely, in Itself a limit unto Itself, yet illimitable; whereby It is, and is known unto Itself, and suffices to Itself, unchangeably the Selfsame, by the abundant magnitude of its Unity—who can readily conceive? Who in any wise express It? Who in any way rashly pronounce on It? (XIII, 11)

. . .

Thus, O Lord, thus I beseech Thee, let there arise, as Thou makest, as Thou givest joy and ability—let truth spring out of the earth, and righteousness look down from heaven, and let there be lights in the firmament. Let us break our bread to the hungry, and let us bring the houseless poor to our house. Let us clothe the naked, and despise not those of our own flesh. These fruits having sprung forth from the earth, behold, because it is good; and let our temporary light burst forth; and let us, from this inferior fruit of action, possessing the delights of contemplation and of the Word of Life above, let us appear as lights in the world, clinging to the firmament of Thy Scripture. For therein Thou makest it plain unto us, that we may distinguish between things intelligible and things of sense, as if between the day and the night; or between souls, given, some to things intellectual, others to things of sense; so that now not Thou only in the secret of Thy judgment, as before the firmament was made, dividest between the light and the darkness, but Thy spiritual children also, placed and ranked in the same firmament (Thy grace being manifest throughout the world) may give light upon the earth and divide between the day and night, and be for signs of times; because old things have passed away and behold all things are become new; and because our salvation is nearer than when we believed; and because the night is far spent, the day is at hand; and because Thou wilt crown Thy year with blessing, sending the laborers of Thy goodness into Thy harvest, in the sowing of which others have labored, sending also into another field, whose harvest shall be in the end. Thus Thou grantest the prayers of him that asketh, and blessest the years of the just; but Thou art the same, and in Thy years fail not; Thou preparest a garner for our passing years. For by an eternal counsel Thou dost in their proper seasons bestow upon the earth heavenly blessings.

For, indeed, to one is given by the Spirit the word of wisdom, as if the greater light, on account of those who are delighted with the light of manifest truth, as in the beginning of the day; but to another the word of knowledge by the same Spirit, as if the lesser light; to another faith; to another the gift of healing; to another the working of miracles; to another prophecy; to another the discerning of spirits; to another divers kinds of tongues. And all these as stars. For all these worketh the one and self-same Spirit dividing to every man his own as He willeth; and making stars appear manifestly, to profit withal. But the word of knowledge, wherein are contained all sacraments, which are varied in their periods like the moon and the other conceptions of gifts, which are successively reckoned up as stars, inasmuch as they come short of that splendor of wisdom in which the fore-mentioned day rejoices, are only for the beginning of the night. For they are necessary to such as he Thy most prudent servant could not speak unto as unto spiritual, but as unto carnal—even he who speaketh wisdom among those that are perfect.

But the natural man, as a babe in Christ—and a drinker of milk—until he be strengthened in solid meat, and his eye be enabled to look upon the Sun, let him not dwell in his own deserted night, but let him be contented with the light of the moon and the stars. Thou reasonest these things with us, our All-wise God, in Thy Book, Thy firmament, that we may discern all things in an admirable contemplation, although as yet in signs, and in times, and in days, and in years. (XIII, 18)

. . .

For behold O Lord our God, our Creator, when our affections have been restrained from the love of the world, by which we died by living ill and began to be a living soul by living well; and Thy word which Thou spakest by Thy apostle is made good in us, "Be not conformed to this world," next also follows that which Thou presently subjoinest, saying "But be ye transformed by the renewing of your mind"—not now after your kind, as if following your neighbor who went before you, nor as if living after the example of a better man (for Thou hast not said, "Let man be made after his kind," but "Let us make man in our image, after our likeness"), that we may prove what Thy will is. For to this purpose said that dispenser of Thine—begetting babies by the gospel—that he might not always have them babes, whom he would feed on milk and cherish as a nurse; "Be ye transformed," saith he, "by the renewing of your mind, that he may prove what is that good, and acceptable, and perfect will of God. Therefore Thou sayest not, "Let man be made," but "Let us make man." Nor sayest Thou, "after his kind," but, after "our image" and "likeness." Because, being renewed in his mind, and beholding and apprehending Thy truth, man needeth not man as his director that he may imitate his kind; but by Thy direction proveth what is that good, and acceptable and perfect will of Thine. And Thou teachest him, now made capable, to perceive the Trinity of the Unity, and the Unity of the Trinity. And therefore this being said in the plural, "Let us make man," it is yet subjoined in the singular, "and God made man;" and this being said in the plural, "after our likeness," is subjoined in the singular, "after the image of God." Thus is man renewed in the knowledge of God, after the image of Him that created him; and being made spiritual, he judgeth all things—all things that are to be judged—yet he himself is judged of no man. (XIII, 22)

(from *The Confessions*)

# MAN AS IMAGE

## St. Augustine

And we indeed recognize in ourselves the image of God, that is, of the supreme Trinity, an image which, though it be not equal to God, or rather, though it be very far removed from Him—being neither co-eternal, nor, to say all in a word, consubstantial with Him—is yet nearer to Him in nature than any other of His works, and is destined to be yet restored, that it may bear a still closer resemblance. For we both are, and know that we are, and delight in our being, and our knowledge of it. Moreover, in these three things no true-seeming illusion disturbs us; for we do not come into contact with these by some bodily sense, as we perceive the things outside of us—colors, e.g., by seeing, sounds by hearing, smells by smelling, tastes by tasting, hard and soft objects by touching—of all which sensible objects it is the images resembling them, but not themselves which we perceive in the mind and hold in the memory and which excite us to desire the objects. But, without any delusive representation of images or phantasms, I am most certain that I am, and that I know and delight in this. In respect of these truths, I am not at all afraid of the arguments of the Academicians, who say, "What if you are deceived?" For if I am deceived, I am. For he who is not, cannot be deceived; and if I am deceived, by this same token, I am. And since I am if I am deceived, how am I deceived in believing that I am? for it is certain that I am if I am deceived. Since therefore I, the person deceived, should be, even if I were deceived, certainly I am not deceived in this knowledge that I am. And, consequently, neither am I deceived in knowing that I know. For, as I know that I am, so I know this also, that I know. (XI, 26)

(from *The City of God*)

# THE FOOTPRINTS OF GOD

## St. Bonaventure

### Degrees of the Soul's Ascent: God's Footprints in Creation

"Happy the man whose help is from Thee, when he hath set pilgrimages in his heart through the Valley of Tears, to the goal he hath fixed."

Since happiness is nothing else but the enjoyment of the Supreme Good, and the Supreme Good is above us, no one can be happy who does not rise beyond himself. This raising up of man is to be understood, of course, of mind and heart and not of body, and since there is question of reaching above himself on the part of man, he must be helped by supernatural strength and be lifted up by a higher power that stoops to raise him. However much then a man's inward steps are ordered and progress made, it is of no avail unless accompanied by help from on high. But divine aid is at hand for those who seek it with a devout and humble heart, and sigh for it in this Valley of Tears; this is done by fervent prayer. Prayer is, therefore, the source and origin of every upward progress that has God for goal. Wherefore, Dionysius in his "Mystical Theology," wishing to instruct us in these transcendent workings of the soul sets down prayer as the first condition. Let us each, therefore, have recourse to prayer and say to our Lord God: "Lead me, O Lord, on Thy path, that I may walk in Thy truth. Let my heart rejoice that it feareth Thy name."

By so praying we are led to discern the degrees of the soul's ascent to God. For, inasmuch as, in our present condition, this universe of things is a ladder whereby we may ascend to God, since among these things some are God's footprints, some God's image, some corporeal, some spiritual, some temporal, some eternal, and, hence, some outside of us, and some inside, it follows that if we are to attain to the contemplation of the First Principle and Source of all things, in Himself altogether spiritual, eternal, and above us, we must begin with God's footprints which are corporeal, temporal and outside us and so enter on the Way that leads to God. We enter in within our own souls, which are images of the eternal God, spiritual and interior to us, and this is to enter into the Truth of God. Finally, we must reach out beyond and above ourselves to the region of the eternal and supereminently spiritual and look to the First Principle of all, and that is to enjoy the knowledge of God in reverential contemplation of His Majesty. . . .

In direct relation with this threefold progress of the soul to God, the human mind has three fundamental attitudes or outlooks. The first is towards corporeal things without, and in this respect it is designated as animal or simply sensual; the next is where it enters in within itself to contemplate itself, and here it ranks as spirit; the third is where its upward glance is beyond itself, and then it is designated "mens" or mind. In all three ways the human soul must prepare to raise itself to God so that it may love Him with the whole mind, with all its heart, and with its whole soul, for in this consists the fullness of the Law and the highest Christian Wisdom.

But since every one of the aforesaid modes is doubled, according as we come to consider God as Alpha, and as Omega, or according as we come to contemplate God in each as in and through a mirror, or because each of these modes of contemplation may be joined with another, or operative simply and purely in itself, so it is necessary that these three primary grades should be raised to the number six; whence, as God completed the universal world in six days, and rested on the seventh, so the smaller world of man is led in the most orderly way, by six successive grades of illumination, to the quiet of contemplation. A symbol of this may be seen in the six steps that led to the throne of Solomon; in the six-winged Seraphim which Isaiah beheld in vision; in the six days after which God called Moses from the midst of darkness; and in the six days after which, as we read in Matthew, Christ led His disciples up into a mountain, and was transfigured before them.

Corresponding to the six degrees of the soul's ascent to God there are within the soul six kinds of faculties or powers by which we rise from depths to the heights, from external to things internal, from things of time to those of eternity, to wit, sense, imagination, reason, intellect, intelligence, and the fine point or apex of the soul. These powers we have implanted in us by nature; by sin deformed, they are reformed through grace; and they must be purified by justice, exercised by knowledge, and made perfect by wisdom.

In his primitive constitution man was created by God capable of untroubled contemplation, and for that reason was placed by God in a "garden of delights." But, turning his back on the true light in order to pursue the mutable good, he found himself, through his own fault, diminished and removed from his pristine stature. With him the whole human race, through original sin, was afflicted in a twofold manner: the human mind by ignorance and the human body by concupiscence. As a result man, blinded and bent down, sits in darkness and sees not the light of heaven, unless he be strengthened against concupiscence by grace with justice, and against ignorance by knowledge with wisdom. All this is done by Jesus Christ, "who of God is made unto us wisdom and justice and sanctification and redemption." He, being the Power and Wisdom of God, the Incarnate Word full of grace and truth, is the Author of both grace and truth. He it is who infuses the grace of charity which, when it comes "from a pure heart, and a good conscience, and an unfeigned faith," is capable of ordering the whole soul according to the threefold aspect above mentioned. He also taught the knowledge of truth according to the triple mode of theology: by symbolic theology in which He teaches us how we might rightly use sensible things, by theology properly so called wherein we learn the use of things intelligible, and by mystical theology through contact with which we may be raised aloft to things unspeakable.

Whoso, therefore, would set out in quest of God must leave aside such sins as deform nature, and engage in the exercise of the aforesaid powers of his soul. By prayer he may hope for grace which will readjust his powers in harmony; in a holy life he must seek for purifying justice; in meditation he will seek that knowledge which enlighteneth; in contemplation he will acquire perfecting wisdom. Therefore, just as no one comes to wisdom save through grace, justice, and knowledge, so no one comes to contemplation save by clear-sighted meditation, by a holy life and devout prayer. As grace is the foundation of an upright will, and of a clear-sighted enlightened reason, so we must first pray, then live holily, and, thirdly, we must look long and attentively at the manifestations of truth; and so attending, we must rise, step by step, until we reach the high mountain where God of Gods is seen in Sion.

Since it is imperative first to make the ascent of Jacob's Ladder before we can hope to descend, let us place the first step of the ascent at the bottom, holding up this whole sensible world before us as a mirror, through which we may rise to God, the supreme Craftsman. In that way we shall be true Israelites passing forth from the land of Egypt to the land of promise, and also true Christians going forth from this world to the Father, and lovers of Wisdom who answer the Call which says: "Come unto me all ye that desire me, and be ye filled with mine offspring." "For from the greatness and beauty of created things, their Creator may be seen and known."

The supreme wisdom, power, and benevolence of the Creator are reflected in all created things. This is intimated in a threefold manner by the adjustment of external and internal senses in man. The bodily senses minister to the mind, whether it be engaged in rational investigation, in docile faith, or in intellectual contemplation. In contemplation it considers the actual existence of things; in faith it examines the unfolding of events; and in reasoning it surmises their potential pre-excellence.

The first point of view, which is that of contemplation, considering things in themselves, discerns in them weight, number, and measure: weight which marks the point to which they tend, number whereby they are distinguished, and measure whereby they are limited. Hereby it sees in things mode, species, order, as well as substance, virtue and action, from which the mind may arise, as from footprints, to the knowledge of the power, wisdom and boundless goodness of the Creator.

The second point of view, which is that of faith, when it considers the universe goes on to reflect upon its origin, its course, and its end. For "by faith we understand that the world was framed by the word of God." By faith we know that the three epochs—of nature, of the law, and of grace—have succeeded one another in order. By faith we know that the world will terminate with a final judgment. In the first, we observe God's power; in the second, His providence; and in the third, His justice.

The third point of view, that of reason, when it investigates the universe recognises that some things have only being, others being and life, and others possess not only being and life, but knowledge and discernment. This gives us three levels of reality, ranging from lowest to highest. From this viewpoint, also, it is clear that some things are merely corporeal, and some partly corporeal and partly spiritual, while others, ranking highest in perfection and dignity, are purely spiritual. Likewise some things, it is seen, are mutable and corruptible, such as terrestrial things; others are mutable and incorruptible, such as celestial bodies; whence it may be concluded that some things are both immutable and incorruptible, such as supercelestial things. From these visible things, therefore, the human mind rises up to consider the power and goodness and wisdom of God in whom reside Being and Life and Intelligence, in a purely spiritual, incorruptible, and immutable state. . . .

## The Mirror of the Material World

Speaking of the material world, of sensible things as a mirror wherein God is reflected, we must now proceed to make a distinction. It is possible for the soul to rise to the contemplation of God from a consideration of His footprints in the universe, but it is also possible to see God *in* these footprints, as it were, for God is there by virtue of His essence, His power, and His presence. This new approach leads to a deeper contemplation than that hitherto entertained; it marks a step forward, a second step, in the soul's pursuit of God which brings the soul to contemplate God in all those creatures that appear to it through its outward bodily senses.

We must observe, therefore, that the microcosm of the sensible world enters the microcosm of the soul through the portals of the senses; the soul reacts by apprehension, by fruition, and by judgment. The matter may be looked at in this way. There are in the sensible world some things that are sources in regard to others, there are others which are mere products, and others still which regulate both sources and products. Simple bodies, such as the heavenly bodies and the four elements, must be ranked amongst the first classes since from these elements, by the power of light which neutralises any contrariety in such mixed elements, are generated and produced whatever things are the result of natural operations. Minerals, vegetables, sensible things, and human bodies, being composed of the elements, belong to the class of things generated or produced. Exercising a kind of governance over such sensible realities, there are spiritual substances ranging from the souls of brutes which are altogether immersed in bodies to rational souls which are separable from the body up to spirits that are entirely separate, which are called Intelligences by philosophers but are known as Angels amongst us. The duty of moving the heavenly bodies devolves upon these Intelligences according to the philosophers, and for that reason the administration of the universe is ascribed to them. From the First Cause, God, they receive an influx of His power which they pour out again in their task of administration which regards the natural constitution and consistency of the universe. Theologians also ascribe to them the guiding of the universe according to the command of God, having in view especially the universe of redemption and its works, and in this context the Angels are called "ministering spirits, sent to minister for them who shall receive the inheritance of salvation."

Man, therefore, who is called the microcosm, is endowed with five senses through the gates of which knowledge of all things in the material world enters his soul. Through the sense of sight enter the sublime and luminous bodies together with all other coloured things; through the sense of touch come solid and earthly bodies; through the three intermediate senses, corresponding bodies: through taste, the aqueous, through hearing, the aerial, through smell, the vapourable, which are a mixture of humid and aerial and fiery as is clear from the fumes liberated by the spices. The portals of sense give entrance not only to simple bodies but also to things mixed and compounded of those. Seeing then that by means of the senses we perceive not only their proper sensible objects which are light, sound, smell, taste and the four primary qualities which are known by touch, but also the common sensibles such as number, magnitude, figure, rest and motion; seeing also that everything which is moved, is moved by something else, while certain things move and rest from themselves as do the animals, the senses which reveal to us the motions of the bodies in the universe around us lead us on to a knowledge of spiritual motions as from effects to a knowledge of their causes. . . .

We have now treated of the two first degrees of the soul's ascent to God. In these two steps by which we are led to contemplate God in His footprints, in the manner of two descending wings about His feet, we are taught that all the created things of this material world around us lead the soul of the contemplative and the wise man to the eternal God. The reason to be assigned for this is that sensible things in their totality are simply shadows, echoes, symbols, footprints, images and mirrors, signs divinely given and set before us for the beholding of God, their most powerful, wise and excellent First Principle, the eternal Source and Light and Fountain of all plenitude, of all art Efficient, Exemplary and Intelligent Cause. These things, I say, are so many "exemplata" or samples set before minds uncultured and immersed in the life of sense, so that from things seen they may pass to things invisible. . . .

The visible creatures of the material world point to, and signify, the invisible things of God, partly because God is the Origin, Exemplar and End of all created things (and every effect is a sign of its cause, an example of its exemplar, and an indication of the end to which it leads), partly by its own representative power, partly also from prophetic prefiguring, partly from angelic action, and partly also by virtue of divine institution. By nature every creature is a figure and a symbol of divine Wisdom of which it is a likeness. But this is especially true of such things as are taken up by Holy Scripture or such as are employed by the Holy Spirit for the purpose of constituting them pre-figurations of spiritual things to come; particularly does it apply to those creatures in whose likeness God, through the ministry of His angels, appeared; but most especially is this verified of those things employed by God not only as signs merely but as sacraments as well.

From all this we gather that "the invisible things of God, since the creation of the world, are clearly seen, being perceived through the things that are made," so that those people who will not consider these things and come to behold and bless and love God in all things are inexcusable since they do not wish to pass from darkness to the wondrous light of God. But thanks be to God, through Jesus Christ, who has brought us from the region of darkness into His wondrous light, so that by those lights given to us in the external world we may be prompted and disposed to re-enter the sanctuary of our souls to behold in the mirror of our minds the reflection of God's own Light.

## The Image of God in the Soul's Natural Powers

The two stages of the soul's ascent to God just described, wherein we behold God mirrored in the external world, have guided us to the point where we experience the impulse to enter in within the sanctuary of our souls, there to see God reflected in His image. This third step must now be taken, so that entering in within ourselves we shall leave behind us the outer courts, as it were, to stand in the holy place which surrounds the Holy of Holies itself. There we shall behold the reflection of God as in the light of some candelabrum which reveals the radiance of the Holy Trinity emanating from the surface of our souls. Enter, therefore, into thyself and realise that thy soul loves itself most fervently. This it could not do did it not first know itself, and to know itself it must be present to itself by memory since nothing is assimilated by intellect unless it is remembered. Conclude from this that a trinity of powers adorns thy soul and for this inference depend not on the corporeal eyes of thy body but upon the spiritual eye of thy mind. When you go on to examine the workings and the inclinations of these powers of thy soul, you will be led to see God reflected in yourself, and by means of His image impressed upon the powers of your soul you will come to behold God as "through a glass in a dark manner." . . .

Passing on to the intellectual power of the human soul it is to be remarked that the function of this faculty is to perceive the meaning of terms, proportions and inferences. The meaning of terms it grasps when it knows by means of definition what any particular thing is. Definition, however, is not possible except by reference to some higher and wider notions, and these in turn lead us to some still higher genus, until ultimately we arrive at the very highest and most general ideas without a knowledge of which the more restricted notions contained under them cannot be definitely understood. Unless we know, therefore, what Being as Being is, we are not in a position fully to understand the definition of any particular substance. Nor can Being as Being be known unless it is envisaged in its most general conditions which are unity, truth, and goodness. Being may be considered in many ways: as complete and incomplete, perfect and imperfect, actual and potential, simple and conditioned, as a whole or in part, as static and dynamic, as from itself and as caused, as pure Being and as composite, as absolute and conditioned, as prior and posterior, as immutable and mutable, as simple and composite. But it is a general principle that the imperfect and that which is privative or negative may be understood only in terms of something positive. So the human reason cannot reach a full and final explanation of created things unless it is aided by an understanding of the most pure, actual, complete and absolute Being, in other words, unless it reaches out to the utterly simple and eternal Being of God in whose mind are to be found the ultimate ground and reason of all things. How indeed could the human mind surmise that the particular things with which it comes in contact are defective and incomplete did it not possess some knowledge of a Being who is utterly devoid of imperfection?

. . .

## God's Image Reconstituted by Grace in the Soul

The human soul may be not only a means whereby we come to behold God, the First Principle of all things, but it may lodge within itself this Principle so that we may come to the contemplation of God within ourselves. This is a form of vision, besides, which surpasses the previous one and constitutes the fourth degree of contemplation. When it is said that God is so near and intimate to us it will seem strange that so few people find Him. But the explanation is not far to seek. The soul does not succeed in entering in within itself when its memory is full of cares that distract its attention from itself. It is prevented also by the fact that its intelligence is crowded with phantasms which cloud its insight. Further, the attraction exercised upon it by things of sense draws it away and does not allow it to return to itself in a desire for inward delectation and spiritual joy. In a word, man is so deeply plunged in the life of sense that he cannot possibly discover within himself the Image of God.

Where a man falls, there must he lie, unless someone intervenes to raise him up. In the same way man must have lain, chained by the life of the senses and unable to come to the contemplation of his soul and of eternal truth within it, were it not for the intervention of Truth Itself. Taking unto Itself a human form in Jesus Christ, becoming, as it were, a ladder between earth and heaven, Truth repaired God's original ladder smashed in Adam. No matter how enlightened a man may be either by nature or by acquired knowledge, he cannot come to the contemplation of his inmost self or experience delight in the Lord except it be through the mediation of Jesus Christ, who says: "I am the door; by me if any man enter in he shall be saved and shall go in and out and shall find pastures." But the approach to this door is conditioned by our faith in Him, our hope in Him, and our love: by faith, hope, and charity. If, therefore, we are to re-enter in within ourselves, as into a long-lost paradise, and come to a fruition of the truth, we must enter by the door of faith, hope, and charity, virtues that are based on the mediation between God and man of His Son, Christ Jesus, who is, as it were, the Tree of Life in the garden of Paradise.

God's Image in the soul of man, then, must be re-constituted by means of the three theological virtues, faith, hope, and charity. These virtues purify, enlighten and perfect the soul, thus repairing God's broken Image, fitting out the soul for the heavenly Jerusalem and constituting it a unit of the Church militant which is the offspring of the heavenly Jerusalem as is suggested by the Apostle: "That Jerusalem which is above is free, which is our mother."

. . .

## The Name of God and Mirror of the Divine Unity: Being

God may be sought in the universe around us or in the inner world of our own soul. In the visible world we behold His footprints; in our souls we discern His image. It is also possible to seek Him in contemplation by raising the eyes of our mind to the light that descends upon us from on high, the light of eternal truth which illumines the minds of men. Seeking God in the visible world in the first degree of contemplation it is as if we stood in the outer court that leads to the tabernacle. Practising the second degree of contemplation, we have advanced a step nearer to the sanctuary; we stand, as it were, in the holy place itself. But it is to those only who reach the third degree of contemplation that it is given to enter, in company with the High Priest, into the Holy of Holies. There they will behold overshadowing the Seat of Mercy two cherubim with outstretched wings from which they may learn that to the invisible and timeless things of God there are two approaches: the one absolute,

10. Limestone carving of the Six Apostles, south porch. Malmesbury Abbey.

wherein God is considered in His nature and essence; the other relative, which takes account of God's Personal properties.

In the first approach our minds are turned towards God as He exists in His proper essence and we feel that our first designation of Him must be: "He who is." But in the second approach we are led to view Him under the guise of goodness and then it seems that God's first name is simply "The Good." In these approaches our attitude is borne out by the two Testaments. In the Old, stress was laid upon the unity of the Godhead, as may be seen from God's reply to Moses, "I am who am," whereas in the New, the emphasis falls upon the presence of a plurality of Persons in God, as may be deduced from the manner of conferring Baptism "in the name of the Father, and of the Son, and of the Holy Ghost." And the Master, Christ, holding out to the young man, who had observed the Law, the offer of a more perfect life, spoke as if God's principal and exclusive attribute was that of goodness. "No one is good but God alone." Damascene, therefore, following Moses, declared that "He who is" must be looked upon as God's chief designation, whereas Dionysius, following Christ, says that God's proper name and designation is "The Good."

Beginning, therefore, with the contemplation of God's essential unity, it is necessary to direct our attention to the concept of Being. Being so certainly exists that it cannot be conceived as not existing. Only in a perfect flight from nothingness is Being to be found in all its purity, for Being and nothingness are absolutely opposed. . . .

Open the eyes of your mind then to Being in all its purity and be persuaded that it represents something absolutely underived. We must necessarily consider as first what cannot be said to originate in nothingness or in another. For if Being is not, absolutely speaking, first in all things, originating from itself and due to no other thing, then what is? Being presents itself to your mind as altogether free from non-being and therefore is it without beginning, without end, eternal. Nor does it allow of the presence in itself of that which is not itself and is, therefore, without composition and perfectly simple. And since possibility presupposes non-being of some sort, Being excludes it and appears as supremely and completely actual. So you may justly account Being as devoid of imperfection and therefore absolutely perfect, and as indivisible and therefore supremely one. Summing up, it may be said that Being in its entire purity, simple and absolute, is primary, eternal, superlatively simple, actual, perfect, and unity itself.

All these things concerning Being are so certain that the opposite of them cannot be thought by anyone who understands what is implied by Being. Besides, these attributes of Being may be shown to flow from one of them as from their source. For if we take Being as Being absolutely, then it is primordial, that is, it imposes itself as something which is not to be derived from anything else and yet is not to be thought of as the cause of itself, from which it follows that it must be conceived as eternal. Since it is thus primordial and eternal, no composition can mar its perfection and therefore it must be utterly simple. But granted these characters of primacy, eternity and simplicity, Being must also exclude possibility and therefore must be equated with Pure Act. But if Being as Being is primordial, eternal, simple and entirely in act, is it not absolutely perfect? To Being so endowed nothing is lacking and nothing can be superadded. To repeat, Being is primordial, eternal, actual, and perfect. Therefore we reason that it is supereminently one, unique. Of any particular thing we may predicate many things, but of Being only can we say simply "it abounds" or designate it "superabundance" with reference to all other things. Accordingly, if we predicate all we have discerned to characterise Being of God we find He is primordial, eternal, simple, actual, perfect. So perfect indeed is He that we cannot consider Him as not existing or to be anything but God, one unique God. "Hear, therefore, O Israel, the Lord our God is one God." Should you see this in pure simplicity of heart you will be enlightened to some extent with the illumination of eternal light.

(from *The Journey of the Mind to God*)

## *A Way of Seeing*

*Plato had suggested in his myth of the cave that man must "turn around" (be converted) in order to arrive at the Eternals of which things in this world are mere suggestions. Christianity not only personalized this myth, but recognized that the Eternal is present in nature, that it can be seen there and that it grows in being imaged. St. Ambrose suggested that man must use the images of God in creation as he journeys toward God: let the sun remind man of virtue sending forth rays felt by all whom they touch; let the soaring eagle suggest detachment from earth; let the promise of redemption be seen in the movement of the stars through their ordained pattern. The most delightful example of this view of creation as the mirror of God may be found in the spirituality of the Franciscans. Founded by St. Francis of Assisi, who rejected the life of a wealthy merchant to embrace "the lady Poverty," this order of mendicant friars traversed the hills of Italy in brown robes and sandalled feet to bring men to the love of God. They combined ascetical detachment from earth with a keen appreciation of earth's beauty and spiritual value.*

## THE CANTICLE OF BROTHER SUN

### St. Francis of Assisi

Highest omnipotent good Lord
Glory and honor to thy name adored
  And praise and every blessing;
  Of everything thou art the source
No man is worthy to pronounce thy name.

Praised by His creatures all,
Praised be the Lord my God.
  By Messer Sun, my brother above all
  Who by his rays lights us and lights the day
  Radiant is he, with his great splendor,
Thy glory, Lord, confessing.

By Sister Moon and Stars my Lord is praised,
Where clear and fair they in the heavens are raised.
  By Brother Wind, my Lord, thy praise is said,
  By air and clouds and blue sky o'erhead
By which thy creatures all are kept and fed.

By one most humble, useful, precious, chaste
By Sister Water, O my Lord, thou art praised.
  And praised is my Lord
  By Brother Fire—he who lights up the night
Jocund, robust is he and strong and bright.

Praised art thou, my Lord, by Mother Earth—
Thou who sustainest her, and governest,
And to her flowers, fruit, herbs, dost color give and birth.

And praised is my Lord
By those who, for thy love, can pardon give,
  And bear the weakness and the wrongs of men.
  Blessed are those who suffer thus in peace,
By thee, the Highest, to be crowned in heaven.

Praised by our Sister Death, my Lord, art thou,
From whom no living man escapes.
  Who die in mortal sin have mortal woe,
  But blessed they who die doing thy will—
The second death can strike at them no blow.

Praises and thanks and blessings to my Master be;
Serve ye Him all, with great humility.

*This belief in the* imago *revolutionized the world of art. Since man, with his soul fashioned in the image of his Maker, is of inestimable worth, each man is a worthy subject of the artist's attention. Emphasis on the individual marks the transition from classicism. The figures on the south portal of Chartres, for instance, are definite persons with specific occupations, not the huddled masses of late Roman design.*

*All nature becomes the province of the artist. Since, as Thomas Aquinas says, "God enjoys all things, for each accords with His essence," every object is to be cherished by the artist. Every cloud or leaf, bud or flower is a trace of God and merits hours of meticulous activity. The borders of the illuminated manuscripts reflect the appreciation of nature and respect for God's handiwork that is the hallmark of medieval art. This art-expressing-dogma is marked by its organic character and its symbolism. The organic relationships are especially evident in manuscripts where decoration and script are related to each other and to the whole. In the same spirit, paintings were made for spaces on walls, not to hang alone, and through the early years, all sculpture occupied a selected niche. Symbolism is the other mark: the four Evangelists, for example, were depicted together with an angel, a lion, an ox and an eagle, or the symbols alone were shown. Keys indicated St. Peter, the pilgrim's staff St. James, an early missionary to Spain. To a largely illiterate people, these symbols were a means of instruction and inspiration and symbolism carried over into daily life. The very popular game of chess was a morality play: the black and white of good and evil, the freely moving king, the powerful queen, the rooks as peasants with their limited movements, the bishops and the knights—it was a whole world in miniature.*

*The vitality of religious thought underlying medieval art shines out at its highest in the cathedrals. In France alone from 1170 to 1270 eighty cathedrals were built. The entire community participated in their construction, craftsmen at their trades, peasants carrying stones and assisting the builders. The manor lords were proud to carry stones for the glory of God and the pride of the village. Churches were no longer the low, rounded basilicas of Roman times with their emphasis on proportion and completeness; rather, reflecting the spirit of the builders, they aspired to the heavens. Out of stone and craftsmanship the City of God was to be erected.*

## THE DEER'S CRY

### St. Patrick of Armagh

I rise today
  through a mighty strength, the invocation of the Trinity,
  through a belief in the Threeness,
  through confession of the Oneness
  of the Creator of creation.
I rise today
  through the strength of Christ's birth and His baptism,
  through the strength of His crucifixion and His burial,
  through the strength of His resurrection and His ascension,
  through the strength of His descent for the judgment of doom.
I rise today
  through the strength of the love of cherubim,

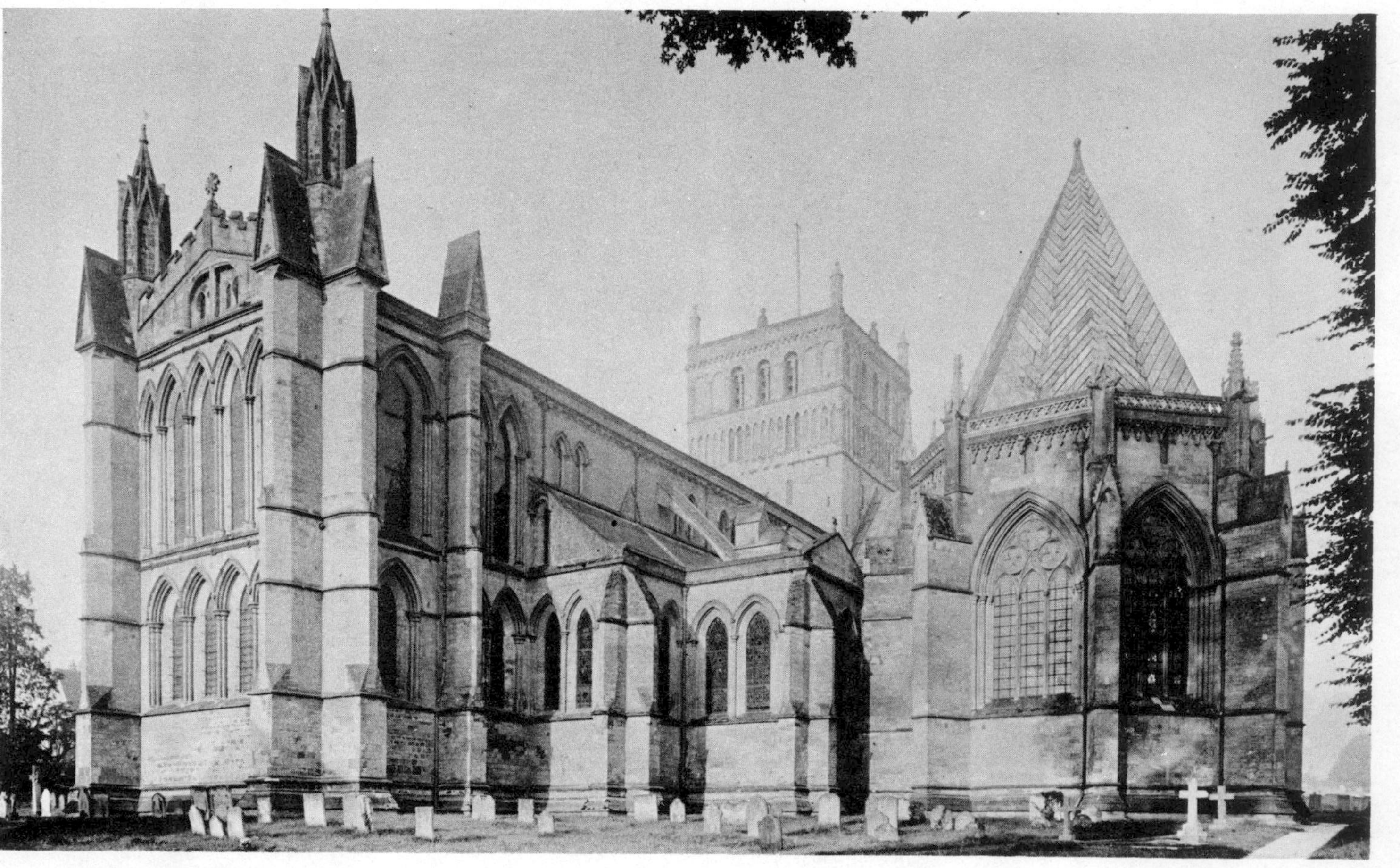

11. Chapter-house, Cathedral Church of St. Mary, Virgin. Southwell, England.

in obedience of angels,
in service of archangels,
in the hope of resurrection to meet with reward,
in prayers of patriarchs,
in predictions of prophets,
in preachings of apostles,
in faiths of confessors,
in innocence of virgins,
in deeds of righteous men.
I rise today
through the strength of heaven;
light of the sun,
radiance of the moon,
splendor of fire,
speed of lightning,
swiftness of the wind,
depth of the sea,
stability of the earth,
firmness of the rock.
I rise today
through God's strength to pilot me;
God's might to uphold me,
God's wisdom to guide me,
God's eye to look before me,
God's ear to hear me,
God's word to speak for me,
God's hand to guard me,
God's way to lie before me,
God's shield to protect me,
God's hosts to save me
from snares of the devil,
from temptations of vices,
from every one who desires me ill,
afar or anear
alone or in a multitude.
I summon today all these powers between me and evil,
against every cruel, merciless power that opposes my body and soul,
against incantations of false prophets,

against black laws of pagandom,
against false laws of heretics,
against the craft of idolatry,
against spells of women and smiths and wizards,
against every knowledge that corrupts man's body and soul.
Christ shield me today
against poison, against burning,
against drowning, against wounding,
so that reward may come to me in abundance.
Christ with me, Christ before me, Christ behind me,
Christ in me, Christ beneath me, Christ above me,
Christ on my right, Christ on my left,
Christ when I lie down, Christ when I sit down,
Christ when I arise,
Christ in the heart of every man who thinks of me,
Christ in the mouth of every man who speaks of me,
Christ in the eye that sees me,
Christ in the ear that hears me.
I rise today
through a mighty strength, the invocation of the Trinity,
through a belief in the Threeness,
through a confession of the Oneness
of the Creator of creation.

## THE WOLF OF GUBBIO

At a time when Saint Francis was living in the city of Gubbio, a huge wolf appeared in the neighborhood. He was terrible and ferocious, and not only devoured beasts but human beings, so that all the townspeople lived in great fear, because he had often approached the city. Everyone went armed when they ventured out of the town, but despite all this no one was able to protect himself if he encountered the beast alone. And for fear of this wolf matters had come to such a pass that no one dared to leave the city.

Saint Francis felt great compassion for the people of the place because of this, and wished to go out and meet the wolf; but all the townspeople begged him not to do so. But he made the sign of the cross and went out into the country with his companions, putting all his trust in God. And when the others were unwilling to go any further, Saint Francis made his way to the place where the wolf had his lair. Now when the wolf saw the crowd of townspeople who had come out to watch this miracle, he rushed at Saint Francis with open jaws. And as he approached, Saint Francis made the sign of the cross over him, and called to him, saying: "Come here, Brother Wolf. In the name of Christ I command you not to attack me or anyone else." And wonderful to tell, immediately Saint Francis made the sign of the cross, the terrible wolf closed his jaws and halted in his charge. And he obeyed Saint Francis' command and came to lie down at his feet as gently as a lamb.

Then Saint Francis said to him, "Brother Wolf, you have done great harm in these parts, and committed many grave crimes, ravaging and slaying God's creatures without His leave. Not only have you killed and eaten beasts, but you have dared to kill and devour men, who are made in the likeness of God. For these things you deserve to hang as a robber and vile murderer; all the people cry out in complaint against you, and the whole district hates you. But I wish to make peace between you and them, and if you will commit no more crimes against them, they will forgive your past crimes and neither men nor hounds will hunt you any more."

At these words, by the movements of his body, tail, and eyes, and by bowing his head, the wolf showed that he accepted Saint Francis' proposal and was willing to accept it. Then Saint Francis said: "Brother Wolf, since you are ready to make this peace and keep it, I undertake that your food shall be regularly provided by the people of this district as long as you shall live, so that you will not suffer hunger any more; for I know well that you did all this evil because of hunger. But since I have obtained this favour for you, Brother Wolf, I want you to promise me that you will never again hurt man or beast. Do you promise this?" And by bowing his head, the wolf gave a clear sign that he promised. Then Saint Francis said: "Brother Wolf, I want you to pledge me your good faith on this promise, for without this I cannot trust you." And when Saint Francis held out his hand to receive the pledge, the wolf raised his paw and placed it gently in Saint Francis' hand, giving proof of his good faith as best he could.

Then Saint Francis said: "Brother Wolf, in the name of Jesus Christ, I command you to come with me. Trust me and we will go and ratify this peace in the name of God." And the wolf obediently went with him, as

12. Tapestry of *Hunt of the Unicorn,* III, detail. French or Flemish, late XV century.

gentle as a lamb. When the townspeople saw this, they were utterly dumbfounded, and the news immediately spread throughout the neighbourhood, so that all the people, great and small, men and women, young and old, hurried to the town square to see the wolf of Saint Francis.

And when all the people were gathered there, Saint Francis rose and preached to them, telling them among other things how it was on account of sin that God allowed such calamities. "The flames of hell, which the damned will have to endure for ever," said Saint Francis, "are far more terrible than the fangs of a wolf, that can do no more than destroy the body. How much more should men fear the jaws of hell, when so many people stand in fear and terror of so small a beast? Therefore return to God, dearest people, and do fitting penance for your sins, and God will deliver you from the wolf in this present life and from the fires of hell in the life to come." And Saint Francis ended his sermon by saying: "Listen, my brothers. Brother Wolf, who stands here before you, has promised and given me his pledge to make peace with you and never offend you in any way if you promise to provide him with the food he needs each day. And I will stand surety for him that he will faithfully observe this pact of peace."

Then with one accord the people promised to feed the wolf every day. And Saint Francis said to the wolf before them all: "And you Brother Wolf, do you promise to keep the pact of peace with them, and never to hurt man nor beast nor any other creature?" And the wolf knelt down and bowed his head, and by gentle movements of his body, tail and ears showed as best he could that he was ready to keep his pact with them. Then Saint Francis said: "Brother Wolf, outside the gates you gave me your pledge to keep this promise; now I want you to give me this pledge in front of all the people, that you will not betray me in the promise I have made for you." And raising his right paw, the wolf placed it in Saint Francis' hand.

While these things were taking place, all the people were filled with such admiration and joy, both out of their devotion to the Saint and because of the unique nature of the miracle and the pact, that they all began to shout to heaven, praising and blessing God who had sent Saint Francis to them, and by his merits delivered them from this cruel beast.

After this the wolf lived two years in Gubbio, and he used to enter the houses in a friendly way, going from door to door without harming anyone or anyone harming him. The people fed him kindly, and as he went about the town, not a single dog barked at him. At length, after two years, Brother Wolf died of old age, and the townspeople were deeply grieved, for whenever they had seen him going so gently about the town, they remembered more vividly the virtue and holiness of Saint Francis.

*(Anonymous, XII century, Italy)*

## DE LUSCINIA

### Alcuin

Whoever stole you from that bush of broom,
I think he envied me my happiness,
O little nightingale, for many a time
You lightened my sad heart from its distress,
And flooded my whole soul with melody.
And I would have the other birds all come
And sing along with me thy threnody.

So brown and dim that little body was,
But none could scorn thy singing. In that throat
That tiny throat, what depth of harmony,
And all night long ringing thy changing note.
What marvel if the cherubim in heaven
Continually do praise Him, when to thee
O small and happy, such a grace was given?

## HIS EPITAPH

### Alcuin

Here halt, I pray you, make a little stay
O wayfarer, to read what I have writ,
And know by my fate what thy fate shall be,
What thou art now, wayfarer, world renowned,
I was; what I am now, so shall thou be.
The world's delight I followed with a heart
Unsatisfied: ashes am I, and dust.

Wherefore bethink thee rather of thy soul
Than of thy flesh;—this dieth, that abides.
Dost thou make wide thy fields? In this small house
Peace holds me now; no greater house for thee.
Wouldst have thy body clothed in royal red?
The worm is hungry for that body's meat.
Even as the flowers die in a cruel wind,
Even so, of flesh, shall perish all thy pride.

Now in thy turn, wayfarer, for this song
That I have made for thee, I pray you, say:
"Lord Christ, have mercy on thy servant here,"
And may no hand disturb this sepulchre,
Until the trumpet rings from heaven's height,
"O thou that liest in the dust, arise,
The Judge of the unnumbered hosts is here!"

Alcuin was my name; learning I loved.
O thou that readest this, pray for my soul.

## THE GOLDEN LEGEND OF ST. CHRISTOPHER

Christopher was of the lineage of the Canaanites and he was of a right great stature and had a terrible and fearful cheer and countenance. And he was 12 cubits of length and as it is read in some histories that when he served and dwelled with the king of Canaan it came in his mind that he would seek the greatest prince in the world and him would he serve and obey. And so far he went that he came to a right great king of whom the renown was generally that he was the greatest of the world. And when the king saw him, he received him into his service and made him to dwell in his court. Upon a time a minstrel sang before him a song in which he named oft the devil and the king, which was a Christian man, made anon the cross on his visage. And when Christopher saw that, he had great marvel what sign it was and wherefore the king made it and he demanded of him. And because the king would not say, he said: If thou tell me not, I shall no longer dwell with thee and then the king told him, saying: Always when I hear the devil named I fear he should have power over me and I garnish me with this sign that he grieve not or annoy me. Then Christopher said to him: Doubtest thou the devil that he hurt thee not? Then is the devil more mighty and greater than thou art. I am then deceived of my hope and purpose, for I had supposed I had found the most mighty and the most greatest Lord of the world. But I commend thee to God for I will go seek him for to be my lord and I his servant. And then departed from this king and hasted him for to seek the devil. And as he went by a great desert, he saw a great company of knights of which a knight cruel and horrible came to him and demanded whither he went and Christopher said to him: I go to seek the devil for to be my master. And he said: I am he that thou seekest. And then Christopher was glad and bound him to be his servant perpetual and took him for his master and lord. And as they went together by a common way, they found there a cross, erect and standing. And anon as the devil saw the cross, he was afeard and fled and left the right way and brought Christopher about by a sharp desert. And after, when they were past the cross, he brought him to the highway that they had left. And when Christopher saw that, he marvelled and demanded whereof he doubted and had left the high and fair way and had gone so far by so aspre a desert. And the devil would not tell him in no wise. Then Christopher said to him: If thou wilt not tell me, I shall anon depart from thee and serve thee no more. Wherefore the devil was constrained to tell him and said: There was a man called Christ and which was hanged on the cross and when I see his sign I am sore afraid and flee from it wheresoever I see it. To whom Christopher said: Then he is greater and more mightier than thou, when thou art afraid of his sign and I see well that I have laboured in vain, when I have not founden the greatest lord of the world. And I will serve thee no longer, go thy way then, for I will go seek Christ. And when he had long sought and demanded where he should find Christ, at last he came to a great desert, to an hermit that dwelt there and this hermit preached to him of Jesus Christ and informed him in the faith diligently and said to him: This king whom thou desirest to serve, requireth the service that thou must oft fast. And Christopher said to him: Require of me some other thing and I shall do it for that which thou requirest I may not do. . . . And then the hermit said to him: Knowest thou such a river in which many be perished and lost? To whom Christopher said: I know it well. Then said the Hermit: Because thou art noble and high of stature and strong in thy members, thou shalt be resident by that river and thou shalt bear over all them that pass there which shall be a thing right convenable to our Lord Jesus Christ whom thou desirest to serve and I hope he shall show himself to thee. Then said Christopher: Certes, this service may I well do and I promise to him for to do it. Then went Christopher to the river and there made his habitacle for him and bare a great pole in his hand instead of a staff by which he sustained himself in the water and bore over all manner of men without ceasing. And there he abode, thus doing, many days. And in a time, as he slept in his lodge, he heard the voice of a child which called to him and said: Christopher, come out and bear me over. Then he awoke and went out, but he found no man. And when he was again in the house, he heard the same voice and he ran out and found nobody. The third time he was called and came thither, and found a child beside the rivage of the river, which prayed him goodly to bear him over the water. And then Christopher lifted up the child on his shoulders and took his staff and entered into the river for to pass. And the water of the river arose and swelled more and more; and the child was heavy as lead and always as he went farther the water increased and grew more and the child more and more waxed heavy, insomuch that Christopher had great anguish and was afeard to be drowned. And when he was escaped with great pain and passed the water and set the child aground, he said to the child: Child, thou hast put me in great peril, thou weighest almost as if I had all the world upon me, I might bear no greater burden. And the child answered: Christopher, marvel thee nothing. For thou hast not only borne the world upon thee, but thou hast borne him that created and made all the world upon thy shoulders. I am Jesus Christ the king to whom thou servest in this work. And because thou know what I say to be the truth, set thy staff in the earth by thy house and thou shalt see tomorrow that it shall bear flowers and fruit. And anon he vanished from his eyes. And then Christopher set his staff in the earth and when he arose on the morn, he found his staff like a palmier bearing flowers, leaves and dates.

And then Christopher went into the city of Lycia. . . . He went to the place where they martyred Christian men and comforted them in Our Lord. And then the judges smote him in the face and Christopher said to them: If I were not Christian, I should avenge mine injury. And then Christopher pitched his rod in the earth and prayed to Our Lord that for to convert the people it might bear flowers and fruit and anon it did so. And then he converted 8000 men.

*(Anonymous, VIII century, Syria)*

## HYMN FOR GOOD FRIDAY

### Peter Abelard

Alone to sacrifice Thou goest, Lord,
Giving Thyself to death whom Thou hast slain.
For us Thy wretched folk is any word,
Who know that for our sins this is Thy pain?

For they are ours, O Lord, our deeds, our deeds,
Why must Thou suffer torture for our sin?
Let our hearts suffer for Thy passion, Lord,
That sheer compassion may Thy mercy win.

This is that night of tears, the three days' space,
Sorrow abiding of the eventide,
Until the day break with the risen Christ,
And hearts that sorrowed shall be satisfied.

So may our hearts have pity on Thee, Lord,
That they may sharers of the glory be:
Heavy with weeping may the three days pass,
To win the laughter of Thine Easter Day.

## THE SYMBOLISM OF CHURCHES

### William Durandus

All things as many as pertain to offices and matters ecclesiastical, be full of divine significance and mysteries and overflow with a celestial sweetness; if so be that a man be diligent in his study of them and know how to draw HONEY FROM THE RACK AND OIL FROM THE HARDEST STONE. But who KNOWS THE ORDINANCES OF HEAVEN OR CAN FIX THE REASONS THEREOF ON THE EARTH. . . . Whereof, albeit of the things handed down by our forefathers, capable we are not to explain all, yet if any among them there be any thing which is done without reason, it should forthwith be put away. Wherefore I, William, by the alone tender mercy of God, Bishop of the Holy Church at Mende, will knock diligently at the door, if so be that the KEY OF DAVID will open to me; that the KING MAY BRING ME INTO HIS TREASURY; and show unto me the heavenly pattern which was showed unto Moses in the mount; so that I may learn those things which pertain to Rites Ecclesiastical, whereof they teach and what they signify and that I may be able plainly to reveal and make manifest the reasons of them, by His help WHOSE SPIRIT BLOWETH WHERE IT LISTETH, dividing to each severally as it will to the praise and glory of the Trinity. . . .

Now in Holy Scripture there be divers senses: as historic, allegoric, tropologic and anagogic. Wherefore according to Boethius, all Divine authority ariseth from a sense with historic or allegoric or both. And according to Saint Jerome, we ought to study the Scripture in three ways: firstly, according to the letter; secondly, after the allegory, that is, the spiritual meaning; thirdly, according to the blessedness of the future.

History is *things signified by words;* as when a plain relation is made how certain things took place, as when the children of Israel after their deliverance from Egypt, made a Tabernacle to the Lord.

Allegory is when one thing is said and another meant; as when by one deed another is intended; which other thing, if it be visible, the whole is simply an allegory, if invisible and heavenly, an anagogue. Also an allegory is when one state of things is described by another; as when the Patience of Christ and the Sacraments of the Church is set forth by mystical words or deeds. As in that place: THERE SHALL COME FORTH A ROD OF THE STEM OF JESSE, AND A BRANCH SHALL GROW OUT OF HIS ROOTS: which is, in plain language, the Virgin Mary shall be born of the family of David, who was the son of Jesse. This is an example of mysticism in words; truth is also set forth by mystic deeds; as the Chronicle of Israel's freedom from Egyptian slavery, wrought by the blood of a lamb, signifies that the Church is freed by the Passion of Christ from demoniacal servitude. The word allegory is derived from the Greek *allon* which means foreign and *gore* which is sense; that is, in a foreign sense.

Tropology is an injunction unto morality: or a moral speech, either with a symbolical or an obvious bearing, devised to evince and instruct our behaviour, *Symbolical:* as where he saith: LET THY GARMENTS BE ALWAYS WHITE: AND LET THE OIL OF THY HEAD NEVER FAIL. That is, let all thy works be pure and charity never fail from thy mind. And, again, it is fit that David should slay the Goliath within us; that is, that humbleness may subdue our pride. *Obvious* as in that saying: DEAL THY BREAD TO THE HUNGRY. And in that text: LET US NOT LOVE IN WORD, NEITHER IN TONGUE, BUT IN

DEED AND TRUTH. Now tropology has its name from *tropos,* a turning, and *logos,* which is a discourse.

Anagogue is so called from *ana* which is upwards and *goge,* a leading: as it were, an upward leading. Whence the anagogic sense is that which leadeth from the visible to the invisible, as light, made the first day, signifieth a thing invisible, namely the angelic nature which was made in the beginning. *Anagoge,* therefore, is that sense which leadeth the mind upwards to heavenly things; that is, to the Trinity and Orders of Angels, and speaketh concerning future rewards and the future life which is in the Heaven: and it useth both obvious and mystical expressions: obvious as in that saying, BLESSED ARE THE PURE IN HEART: FOR THEY SHALL SEE GOD; mystical, as that, BLESSED ARE THEY WHO HAVE MADE WHITE THEIR ROBES THAT THEY MAY HAVE RIGHT UNTO THE TREE OF LIFE, AND ENTER IN THROUGH THE GATE INTO THE CITY. Which signifieth, Blessed are they who make pure their thoughts, so that they may have a right to see God, WHO IS THE WAY, THE TRUTH, AND THE LIFE; and after the example of the Fathers, enter into the kingdom of heaven.

In like manner, Jerusalem is understood historically of that city whither pilgrims journey; allegorically of the church militant, tropologically of every faithful soul; anagogically, of the celestial Jerusalem which is our country.

. . .

[Now] let us consider a church and its parts. The word Church hath two meanings; the one, a material building wherein the Divine Offices are celebrated; the other a spiritual fabric which is the collection of the faithful. The church, that is, the people forming it, is assembled by its ministers and collected together into one place by HIM WHO MAKETH MEN TO BE OF ONE MIND IN A HOUSE. For as the material church is constructed from the joining together of various stones, so is the spiritual church by that of various men.

The Greek *ecclesia* is in Latin translated by *convocatio* because it calleth men to itself; the which title doth better befit the spiritual than the material church.

The material typifieth the spiritual church as shall be explained when we treat of its consecration. Again, the church is called Catholic, that is, universal because it hath been set up in, or spread all over the world.

. . .

The Church Militant is also called *Sion* because amidst its wanderings, it expecteth the promise of a heavenly rest; for Sion signifieth *expectation*. But the Church Triumphant, our future home, the land of peace is called *Jerusalem;* for it signifieth *the vision of peace*. . . . Again, the Church is called the *Body of Christ;* sometimes a *Bride,* because Christ hath betrothed her to Himself as saith the Gospel: HE THAT HATH THE BRIDE, IS THE BRIDEGROOM; sometimes a *Mother,* for daily in Baptism she beareth sons to God; sometimes a *Daughter,* according to the saying of the prophet, IN THE DAY OF THY FATHERS THOU SHALT HAVE CHILDREN; sometimes a *Widow,* because SHE SITTETH SOLITARY THROUGH AFFLICTIONS and, like Rachel, WILL NOT BE COMFORTED. Sometimes she is called a *city* because of the communion of her holy citizens, being defended by the munitions of the Scriptures, whereby heretics are kept off.

. . .

The arrangement of a material church resembleth that of the human body: the Chancel, or place where the Altar is, representeth the head; the Transepts, the hands and arms, and the remainder—toward the west, the rest of the body. The sacrifices of the altar denoteth the vows of the heart. Furthermore, according to Richard de Sancto Victore, the arrangement of a church typifieth the three states in the church; of virgins, of the continent, of the married. The Sanctuary is smaller than the Chancel and this than the Nave: because the virgins are fewer in number than the continent and these than the married. And the Sanctuary is more holy than the Chancel; and the Chancel than the Nave, because the order of virgins is more worthy than that of the continent; and the continent more worthy than the married.

Furthermore, the Church consisteth of four walls, that is, is built on the doctrine of the Four Evangelists; and hath length, breadth, and height; the height representeth courage, the length fortitude, which patiently endureth till it attaineth its Heavenly Home; the breadth is charity which, with long suffering, loveth its friends in God, and its foes for God, and again, its height is the hope of future retribution, which despiseth prosperity and adversity, hoping to SEE THE GOODNESS OF THE LORD IN THE LAND OF THE LIVING.

Again, in the Temple of God, the foundation is Faith, which is conversant with unseen things; the roof, Charity, WHICH COVERETH A

MULTITUDE OF SINS. The door, Obedience, of which the Lord saith, IF THOU WILT ENTER INTO LIFE, KEEP THE COMMANDMENTS. The pavement Humility, of which the Psalmist saith, MY SOUL CLEAVETH TO THE PAVEMENT.

The four side walls, the four cardinal virtues, justice, fortitude, temperance, prudence. Hence the Apocalypse saith: THE CITY LIETH FOUR SQUARE. The windows are hospitality with cheerfulness and tenderness with charity. Concerning this house saith the Lord: WE WILL COME UNTO HIM AND MAKE OUR ABODE WITH HIM. But some churches are built in the shape of a cross, to signify that we are crucified to the world and should tread in the steps of the Crucified, according to the saying, LET HIM TAKE UP HIS CROSS AND FOLLOW ME. Some are also built in the form of a circle to signify that the church hath been extended through out the circle of the world, as saith the Psalmist: AND THEIR WORDS UNTO THE END OF THE WORLD. Or because from the circle of this world, we reach forth to that crown of eternity which shall encircle our brows. . . .

The door of the church is Christ; according to that saying in the Gospel, I AM THE DOOR. The Apostles are also called doors.

The piers of the church are Bishops and Doctors who specially sustain the church of God by their doctrine. These from the majesty and clearness of their Divine message are called silver, according to that in the Song of Solomon, HE MADE SILVER COLUMNS. Although the piers are more in number than seven, yet they are called seven, according to that saying WISDOM HATH BUILDED HERSELF A HOUSE: SHE HATH HEWN OUT SEVEN PILLARS, because bishops ought to be filled with the seven-fold influences of the Holy Ghost; and Saints James and John, as the Apostle testifies, SEEMED TO BE PILLARS. The bases of the columns are the Apostolic bishops who support the frame of the whole church.

## ON QUATERNITIES

### Rodulfus Glaber

In creating the universe, God distinguished all things by a variety of appearances and forms, so that man learning with the aid of objects presented to his view, conceived by his reason, would be able to rise almost to the simple knowledge of the Divinity. It is in this seeking to pierce and apprehend the hidden meaning of the figures that the Greek Fathers of the church, no less than superb as philosophers, are distinguished. Among the different subjects on which they discoursed is the system of quaternity, whose study can serve at once the knowledge of this world and of the future, higher world. For these quaternities and their respective influences, once determined with precision, can dispose the spirit of those who meditate on them.

There are four Gospels which constitute in our mind the higher world; and the lower is composed of four elements. There are, as well, four virtues which dominate all the others and we form from their union the remaining virtues. As a further parallel we see our body composed of four senses, with touch less subtle than the others and destined only to serve them. That which the element of fire is in the sensible world, prudence is in the intellectual sphere because it raises itself and aspires to reach God. As the air to the corporal body, so fortitude is to the intellectual, as it supports all living beings and fortifies all who need assistance in any activity. In the same way water is represented by temperance. Is it not in effect the nourishment of humanity, the mother of a crowd of virtues, the conserver of the faith in the hearts which burn with divine love? The earth in its turn represents in this world the justice of the intellectual world, that is, the fixed and unchanging rule of impartial distribution. One can easily convince himself that the four Gospels are comprised of stories entirely analogous. The Gospel of Matthew holds the mystic figure of earth and of justice since he stresses more than the others the bodily substance of Christ Incarnate. That of Mark is the symbol of temperance which corresponds to water; because by the baptism of John he shows us faults washed away by penance. That of Luke is analogous to air and to fortitude because he occupies space and is filled with a multitude of accounts. The other, finally, according to John, in insinuating in our mind the simple knowledge of God and faith in our hearts, is it not an exact representation of ether, or fire, of prudence and that which raises by its sublimity above all? The man himself is in harmony with the mysterious enchantment of accord in the elements, the virtues and the Gospels, which have been created for him; the philosophers indeed define his substance as a microcosm, that is, a little world.

Indeed the sight and hearing, which serve as instruments of intelligence, correspond to the ether of fire, because it is the element most subtle whose elevation above the others assures it a rank most honorable and brilliant. Next comes smell; it belongs to the same category as air and fortitude. As to taste, it represents closely water and temperance. And then to touch, the grossest as well as most solid of the senses, it corresponds naturally to earth and justice. This harmony of legends seems by its admirable clarity to be a mute concert to the praise of God; because, in the midst of this invariable variety in which they follow the law, in calling one another by turn, they do not cease to proclaim the First Source from which they proceed and toward which they yearn to return to find repose.

In the spirit of the same system one may consider with no less attention the river which takes its course in the eastern Eden and then divides into four famous streams. The first among them, the Murat, which is interpreted as the opening of the mouth, signifies prudence which gives always with abundance its salutary counsels. Indeed, since it is by negligence that man lost Paradise, he must take prudence as his guide to reenter. The second, the Ceyhan, where is the deep abyss of the earth, signifies temperance, the virtue which nourishes chastity and prunes with a mighty stroke the pernicious foliage of vice. The third is the Tigris which passes through Assyria, a name which we translate as the guide; it represents fortitude because it turns aside all the vices of prevarication to lead man with the help of God to eternal bliss. The fourth is the Euphrates meaning abundance, designating justice which nourishes and revives all souls sincerely desiring it. These rivers in their mystical image represent the four virtues of which we have spoken as well as the four Gospels. Again these virtues are typified in the division of the history of the world into four epochs. From the beginning of the world to the vengeance of God in the deluge, there were men who practiced the laws of nature, knowing the Creator only by His bounty; that was the reign of prudence, including Abel, for instance, and Enoch, Noe and all the others who were enlightened by reason and understood well true values. From the time of Abraham and the other patriarchs who were led by signs and visions, as Isaiah, Jacob, Joseph and others, temperance ruled in its turn and we see them all, in good or bad fortune, loving their Maker above all things. When Moses and the other prophets, all men of great vigor, founded their institutions and their laws, that was fortitude which upheld them while they gave laborious attention to the precepts of the law. Finally, from the Incarnation to the present time, it is justice which fills and directs all our age, according to the word of truth of John the Baptist: It is necessary that we be filled with all justice.

# VEXILLA REGIS

## Fortunatus

Vexilla regis prodeunt;
Fulget crucis mysterium,
Qua vita mortem pertulit,
Et morte vitam protulit.

Forth comes the Standard of the King,
All hail, thou Mystery adored!
Hail, Cross! on which the Life himself
Died, and by death our life restored.

Quae vulnerata lanceae
Mucrone diro, criminum
Ut nos lavaret sordibus,
Manavit unda et sanguine.

On which our Saviour's holy side,
Rent open with a cruel spear
Of blood and water poured a stream,
To wash us from defilement clear.

Impleta sunt quae concinit
David fideli carmine,
Dicendo nationibus;
Regnavit a ligno Deus.

O sacred wood! in Thee fulfilled
Was David's holy truthful lay!
Which told the world, that from a tree
The Lord should all the nations sway.

Arbor decora et fulgida,
Ornata Regis purpura,
Electa digno stipite,
Tam sancta membra tangere.

Most royally empurpled o'er,
How beauteously thy stem doth shine!
How glorious was its lot to touch
Those limbs so holy and divine.

Beata, cujus brachiis
Pretium pependit saeculi;
Statera facta corporis,
Tulitque praedam tartari.

Thrice blest, upon whose arms outstretched,
The Saviour of the world reclined;
Balance sublime! upon whose beam
Was weighed the ransom of mankind.

O crux, ave, spes unica,
Hoc Passionis tempore
Piis adauge gratiam,
Reisque dele crimina.

Hail Cross! thou only hope of man,
Hail on this holy Passionday!
To saints increase the grace they have
From sinners purge the guilt away.

Te, fons salutis, Trinitas,
Collaudet omnis spiritus;
Quibus Crucis victoriam
Largiris, adde praemium.
Amen.

Salvation's spring, blest Trinity,
Be praise to Thee through earth and skies;
Thou through the Cross the victory
Didst give; oh, also give the prize.
Amen.

# *The Universal Church*

*The cathedrals were evidence of medieval man's attitude toward his church, which was for him the visible organ of the Eternal City. As religious belief was influential in every area of experience, the Church as the embodiment of this belief and its authority was central to medieval culture, and its influence filtered into every aspect of behavior.*

*Worship and the sacramental system met the human and spiritual needs of man at every point. His physical birth into the world was followed by his birth "of water and the Holy Spirit" in baptism. At the age when he might seek knighthood in the service of a lord or be apprenticed in his trade, he was confirmed by the Church to make him a strong and perfect Christian and soldier of Christ. Since he was human and prone to err, he could seek penance for the forgiveness of his sins. In the sacrament of the Eucharist, he received the body of His Lord to nourish his soul. Matrimony spiritualized the contract of marriage, making it a union of two persons in Christ and promising grace for the burdens of family life. Those who were called to the priesthood were ordained in the sacrament that conferred on them the powers vested in the Apostles to say Mass and administer the sacraments to the faithful. And as death came, the sacrament of extreme unction was designed to prepare the soul for its departure from the world it had passed through under the aegis of mother Church.*

## PAGEANT FOR CORPUS CHRISTI

Order of the Pageant of the Play of Corpus Christi in the mayoralty of William Alne, compiled by Roger Burton, town clerk.

1. Tanners

God the Almighty Father, creating and forming the heavens, angels, archangels, Lucifer and the angels who fell with him to hell.

2. Plasterers

God the Father in his own substance, creating the earth and all which is therein, in the space of five days.

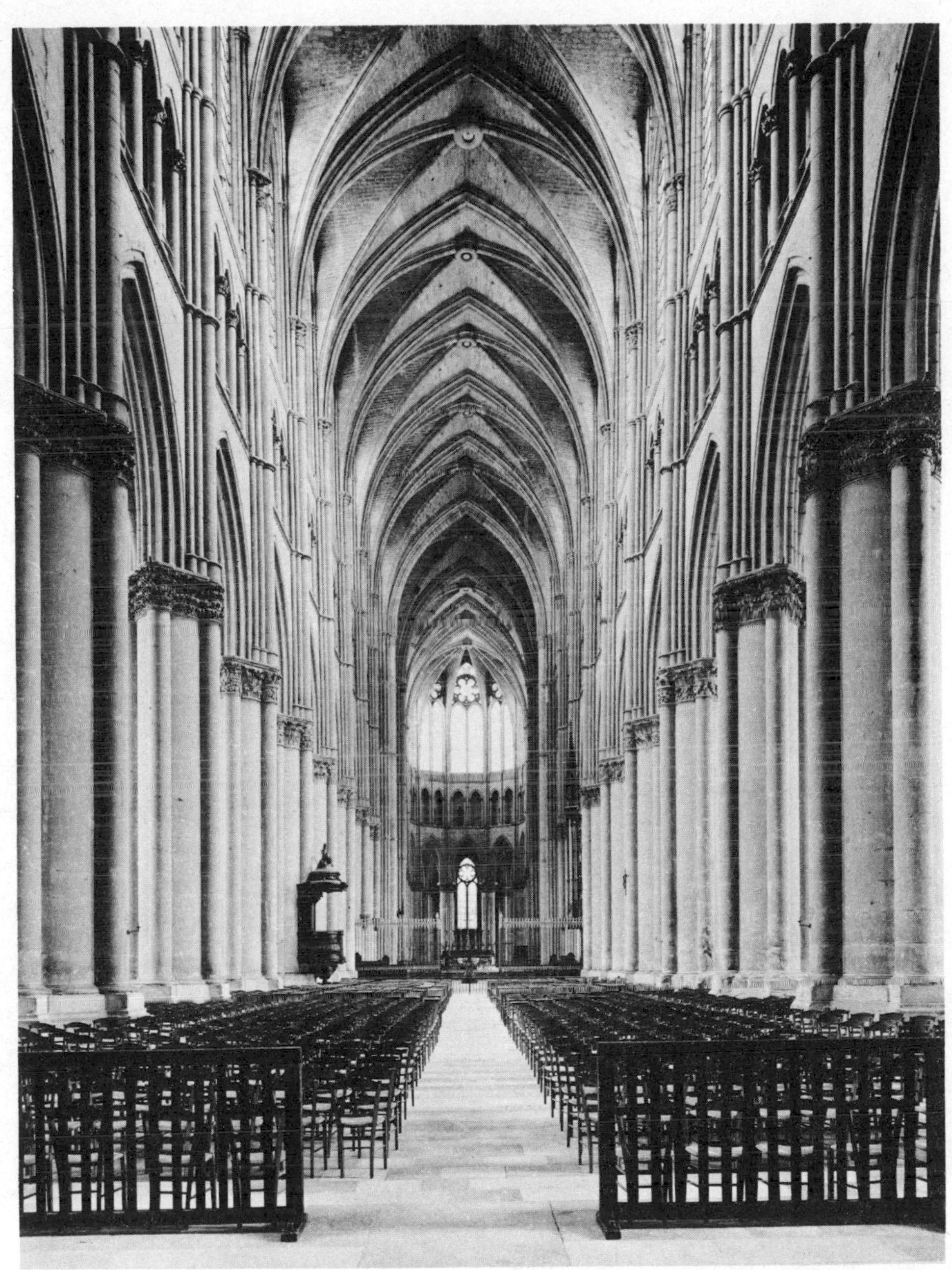

13. Nave, Reims Cathedral.

3. Cardmakers

God the Father creating Adam of the clay of the earth and making Eve of Adam's rib, and inspiring him with the breath of life.

4. Fullers

God forbidding Adam and Eve to eat of the tree of life.

5. Coopers

Adam and Eve and a tree betwixt them; the serpent deceiving them with apples; God speaking to them and cursing the serpent and with a sword driving them out of Paradise.

6. Armourers

Adam and Eve, an angel with a spade and distaff assigning them work.

7. Gaunters

Abel and Cain offering their victims in sacrifice.

8. Shipwrights

God warning Noah to make an ark of floatable wood.

9. Pessoners and Mariners

Noah in the Ark with his wife; the three sons of Noah with their wives; with diverse animals.

10. Parchment makers; Bookbinders

Abraham sacrificing his son, Isaac, on an altar; a boy with wood and an angel.

11. Hosiers

Moses lifting up the serpent in the wilderness; King Pharaoh; eight Jews wandering and expecting.

12. Spicers

A doctor declaring the saying of the prophets of the future birth of Christ; Mary; an angel saluting her; Mary greeting Elizabeth.

13. Pewterers and Founders

Mary, Joseph wishing to put her away; an angel speaking to them that they go to Bethlehem.

14. Tylers

Mary, Joseph, a midwife; the Child born, lying in a manger betwixt an ox and an ass, and an angel speaking to the shepherds, and to the players in the next pageant.

15. Chandlers

The shepherds talking together, the star in the East; an angel giving the shepherds the good tidings of the Child's birth.

16. Orfevers [goldsmiths] and Goldbeaters; Moneymakers

The three kings coming from the East; Herod asking them about the Child; the son of Herod, two counsellors, and a messenger; Mary with the Child, a star above, and the three kings offering gifts.

(*Anonymous, XII century, England*)

*The Church set standards and defined goals for all human activities and was closely involved in the mundane concerns of daily life. A religious ceremony accompanied the dubbing of a knight, the planting of crops, the commencement of a merchant venture. Each guild of craftsmen was under the patronage of a particular saint for whose feast day a festival program was prepared. Many of these programs had developed from the Church service. In the Mass it was possible at several points to add a trope, an insertion of words with music into the liturgy, to be sung by the choir. The* Quem Quacritis *trope of Easter, for example, enacted the coming of the three women to the empty tomb where they were questioned by the angel. With passing years more scenes were added and when the foot race of Peter and John to the tomb was introduced, the whole action was moved to the village green. There it expanded into mystery plays and the later morality plays in which virtues and vices were personified. Thus drama, buried since classical time, was reborn in the representation of the liturgy.*

## THE SECOND SHEPHERD'S PLAY

Characters

| | |
|---|---|
| FIRST SHEPHERD | MAK'S WIFE |
| SECOND SHEPHERD | MARY |
| THIRD SHEPHERD | The CHILD CHRIST |
| MAK, *the Sheep-stealer* | AN ANGEL |

. . .

*Mak comes upon three shepherds; he pretends to lie down with them, but while they sleep, he steals a sheep and goes home.*

MAK [*at his own door*]. How, Gill, art thou in? Get us some light.

HIS WIFE. Who makes such din this time of the night?
I am set for to spin: I hope not I might

Rise a penny to win: I shrew them on height.
So fares
A housewife that has been
To be raced thus between:
There may no jobs be seen
For such small chores.

MAK. Good wife, open the door. See'st thou not what I bring?

WIFE. I may let thee draw the latch. Ah! come in, my sweeting.

MAK. Yea, thou dost not reck of my long standing.

WIFE. By thy naked neck, thou art like for to hang.

MAK. Go away:
I am worthy my meat,
For in a strait can I get
More than they that swink and sweat
All the long day.
Thus it fell to my lot, Gill, I had such grace.

WIFE. It were a foul blot to be hanged for the case.

MAK. I have scaped, Gillot, oft as hard a blow.

WIFE. But so long goes the pot to the water, men says,
At last comes it home broken.

MAK. Well know I the token,
But let it never be spoken;
But come and help fast.
I would he were slain; I list well eat:
This twelvemonth was I not so fain of one sheep-meat.

WIFE. Come they ere he be slain, and hear the sheep bleat!

MAK. Then might I be ta'en: that were a cold sweat.
Go bar
The gate door.

WIFE. Yes, Mak,
For and they come at thy back.

MAK. Then might I pay for all the pack:
The devil of them give warning!

WIFE. A good trick have I spied, since thou can none:
Here shall we him hide, till they be gone;
In my cradle abide. Let me alone,

And I shall lie beside in childbed and groan.

MAK. Thou advise well.
And I shall say thou wast delivered
Of a knave child this night.

WIFE. Now well is me! Day bright,
That ever I was bred!
This is a good guise and a far cast;
Yet a woman's advice helps at the last.
I care never who spies: again go thou fast.

MAK. But I come ere they rise; else blows a cold blast.
I will go sleep. [Mak *goes back to the field.*]
Yet sleep all this company.
And I shall go stalk privily,
As it had never been I that carried their sheep.

FIRST SHEPHERD. *Resurrex a mortruis:* have hold my hand.
*Judas carnas dominus!* I may not well stand:
My foot sleeps, by Jesus, and I water fasting!
I thought that we laid us full near England.

SECOND SHEPHERD. Ah ya!
Lord, I have slept well!
As fresh as an eel,
As light I me feel
As leaf on a tree.

THIRD SHEPHERD. *Benedicite!* be herein! So my body quakes,
My heart is out of skin, what-so it makes.
Who makes all this din? So my brow aches,
To the door will I win. Hark fellows, wake!
We were four.
See ye anywhere Mak now?

FIRST SHEPHERD. We were up ere thou.

SECOND SHEPHERD. Man, I give God a vow,
Yet went he nowhere.

THIRD SHEPHERD. Methought he was wrapped in a wolf-skin.

FIRST SHEPHERD. So are many happed now, namely within.

SECOND SHEPHERD. When we had long napped; methought with a gin
A fat sheep he trapped, but he made no din.

THIRD SHEPHERD. Be still:
Thy dream makes thee mad.
It is but phantom, by the rood.

FIRST SHEPHERD. Now God turn all to good,
If it be his will.

SECOND SHEPHERD. Rise, Mak, for shame! thou liest right long.

MAK. Now Christ's holy name be us among,
What is this? For Saint James!—I may not well go.
I trow I be the same. Ah! my neck has lain wrong
Enough
Mickle thank, since yester-even.
Now, by Saint Stephen!
I was frightened by a dream;
My heart jumped out of my breast
I thought Gill began to croak, and travail full sad,
Well nigh at the first cock,—of a young lad,
For to mend our flock: then be I never glad.
To have two to provide for,—more than ever I had.
Ah, my head!
A house full of young mouths,
The devil knock out their brains!
Woe is he has many bairns,
And thereto little bread.
I must go home, by your leave, to Gill, as I thought.
I pray you look my sleeve, that I steal nought:
I am loth you to grieve, or from you take aught.

THIRD SHEPHERD. Go forth, ill might thou thrive, now would I we sought,
This morn,
That we had all our store.

FIRST SHEPHERD. But I will go before,
Let us meet.

SECOND SHEPHERD. Where?

THIRD SHEPHERD. At the crooked thorn.

MAK [*at his own door again*]. Undo this door! Who is here?
How long shall I stand?

WIFE. Who makes such a stir? Now walk in the waning of the moon.

MAK. Ah, Gill, what cheer? It is I, Mak, your husband.

HIS WIFE. Then may we see here the devil in a band,
Sir Guile.
Lo, he comes with noise,
As he were holden in the throat.
I may not sit at my work
a hand-long while.

MAK. Will ye hear what fare she makes—to get her an excuse?
And do naught but plays—and claws her toes.

WIFE. Why, who wanders, who wakes, who comes, who goes?
Who brews, who bakes? Who makes for me this hose?
And then
It is pity to behold
Now in hot, now in cold,
Full woful is the household
That wants a woman.
But what end hast thou made with the shepherds, Mak?

MAK. The last word that they said, when I turned my back,
They would look that they had their sheep, all the pack.
I hope they will not be well paid, when they their sheep lack.
Pardie!
But howso the game goes,
To me they will suspect,
And make a foul noise,
And cry out upon me.
But thou must do as thou promised.

WIFE. I accord me thereto.
I shall swaddle him right in my cradle.
If it were a greater sleight, yet could I help our ends.
I will lie down straight. Come wrap me up.

MAK. I will

WIFE. Behind!
Come Coll and his mate,
They will nip us full narrow.

MAK. But I may cry out "Harrow!"
The sheep if they find.

WIFE. Hearken aye when they call: they will come anon.

Come and make ready all, and sing by thine own,
Sing "Lullay!" thou shall, for I must groan,
And cry out by the wall on Mary and John,
Full sore.
Sing "Lullay" full fast
When thou hears at the last;
And but I play a false cast
Trust me no more.

[*Reënter the* Three Shepherds.]

Third Shepherd. Ah, Coll! good morn: why sleep'st thou not?

First Shepherd. Alas, that ever was I born! We have a foul blot.
A fat wether have we lorn.

Third Shepherd. Marry, Gods forbid!

Second Shepherd. Who should do us that scorn? That were a foul spot.

First Shepherd. Some knave.
I have sought with my dogs,
All Horbury thickets,
And of fifteen hogs
Found I but one ewe.

Third Shepherd. Now trust me if you will, by Saint Thomas of Kent!
Either Mak or Gill—was at that assent.

First Shepherd. Peace, man, be still; I saw when he went.
Thou slander'st him ill; thou ought to repent.
Good speed.

Second Shepherd. Now as ever might I thrive,
If I should even here die,
I would say it were he,
That did that same deed.

Third Shepherd. Go we thither I advise, and run on our feet.
May I never eat bread, the truth till I wit.

First Shepherd. Nor drink in my head, with him till I meet.

Second Shepherd. I will rest in no stead, till that I him greet,
My brother.
One thing I will promise:
Till I see him in sight
Shall I never sleep one night
Where I do another.

THIRD SHEPHERD. Will ye hear how they sing! Our Sire! list, how they croon!

FIRST SHEPHERD. Heard I never none crack so clear out of tune.
Call on him.

SECOND SHEPHERD. Mak! Undo your door soon.

MAK. Who is it that spoke as it were noon?
Loudly?
Who is that I say?

THIRD SHEPHERD. Good fellows! were it day?

MAK. As far as ye may,
Good, speak soft!
Over a sick woman's head,—that is at malease,
I had liefer be dead, or she had any disease.

WIFE. Go to another stead; I may not well breath;
Each foot that ye tread, goes near make me sneeze
So he!

FIRST SHEPHERD. Tell us, Mak, if ye may,
How fare ye, I say?

MAK. But are ye in this town today?
Now how fare ye?
Ye have run in the mire, and are yet wet.
I shall make you a fire, if ye will sit.
A horse would I hire; think ye of it.
Well quit is my hire, my dream, this is it:
A season.
I have bairns if ye knew,
Well more than enough,
But we must drink as we brew,
And that is but reason.
I would ye dined e'er ye went: methink that ye sweat.

SECOND SHEPHERD. Nay, neither mends our mode, drink nor meat.

MAK. Why, sir, ails you aught but good?

THIRD SHEPHERD. Yes, our sheep that we gat,
Are stolen as they went. Our loss is great.

MAK. Sirs, drink!
Had I been there,
Some should have bought it full dear.

FIRST SHEPHERD. Marry, some men trow that ye were,
And that makes us repent.

SECOND SHEPHERD. Mak, some men trow that it should be ye.

THIRD SHEPHERD. Either ye or your spouse; so say we.

MAK. Now if ye have suspicion to Gill or to me,
Come and rip our house, and then may ye see
Who had her.
If I any sheep got,
Either cow or stot,
And Gill, my wife rose not
Here since she laid her.
As I am both true and leal, to God here I pray,
That this be the first meal, I shall eat this day.

FIRST SHEPHERD. Mak, as I have weal, arise thee, I say!
"He learned timely to steal, that could not say nay."

WIFE. I swelter.
Out, thieves, from my house!
Ye come to rob us for the nonce.

MAK. Hear ye not how she groans?
Your heart should melt.

WIFE. Out thieves, from my bairn! Nigh him not there.

MAK. Knew ye how she had fared, your hearts would be sore.
Ye do wrong, I you warn, that thus comes before
To a woman that has fared, but I say no more.

WIFE. Ah, my middle!
I pray to God so mild,
If ever I you beguiled,
That I eat this child,
That lies in this cradle.

MAK. Peace, woman, for God's pain, and cry not so:
Thou spill'st thy brain, and mak'st me full woe.

SECOND SHEPHERD. I know our sheep be slain, what find ye two?

THIRD SHEPHERD. All work we in vain: as well may we go.
But, hatters!
I can find no flesh,
Hard nor soft,
Salt nor fresh,
But two bare platters:

Live cattle but this, tame nor wild,
None, as have I bliss; as loud as he smiled.

WIFE. No, so God me bless, and give me joy of my child.

FIRST SHEPHERD. We have marked amiss: I hold us beguiled.

SECOND SHEPHERD. Sir, done!
Sir, our lady him save,
Is your child a boy?

MAK. Any lord might him have
This child to his son.
When he wakens he snatches, that joy is to see.

THIRD SHEPHERD. In good time, be his steps, and happy be they!
But who were his good parents, tell now to me!

MAK. So fair fall their lips!

FIRST SHEPHERD. Hark now, a lie!

MAK. So God them thank,
Parkin, and Gibbon Waller, I say,
And gentle John Horne, in good faith,
He made all the noise,
With the great shank.

SECOND SHEPHERD. Mak, friends will we be, for we are all one.

MAK. Why! now I hold for me, for help get I none.
Farewell all three: all glad were ye gone.

THIRD SHEPHERD. Fair words may there be, but love there is none.

FIRST SHEPHERD. Gave ye the child anything?

SECOND SHEPHERD. I trust not one farthing.

THIRD SHEPHERD. Fast again will I fling,
Abide ye me there. [*He returns to* Mak's *cot.*]
Mak, take it to no grief, if I come to thy bairn.

MAK. Nay, thou dost me great reprieve, and foul hast thou fared.

THIRD SHEPHERD. The child will it not grieve, that little day-star.
Mak, with your leave, let me give your bairn
But sixpence.

MAK. Nay, go 'way: he sleeps.

THIRD SHEPHERD. Methinks he peeps.

MAK. When he wakens he weeps.
I pray you go hence.

THIRD SHEPHERD. Give me leave him to kiss, and lift up the clout.
What the devil is this? He has a long snout.

FIRST SHEPHERD. He is marked amiss. We wait ill about.

SECOND SHEPHERD. Ill-spun weft, I-wis, aye cometh foul out;
Aye so!
He is like to our sheep.

THIRD SHEPHERD. How, Gib, may I peep?

FIRST SHEPHERD. I trow, nature will creep,
Where it may not go.

SECOND SHEPHERD. This was a quaint trick, and a far cast;
It was a high fraud.

THIRD SHEPHERD. Yea, sirs, was't.
Let burn this bawd and bind her fast.
A false scold hangs at the last;
So shall thou.
Will ye see how they swaddle
His four feet in the middle?
Saw I never in a cradle
A hornèd lad ere now.

MAK. Peace, bid I! What! let be your fare;
I am he that him gat, and yon woman him bare.

FIRST SHEPHERD. What devil shall he be called? Lo, God, Mak's heir.

SECOND SHEPHERD. Let be all that. Now God give him care! I say.

WIFE. A pretty child is he,
As sits on a woman's knee;
A dilly-down, perdie!
To make a man laugh.

THIRD SHEPHERD. I know him by the earmark—that is a good token.

MAK. I tell you, sirs, hark: his nose was broken.
Since then, told me a clerk, that he was bewitched.

FIRST SHEPHERD. This is a false work.—I would fain be avenged.
Get a weapon!

WIFE. He was taken by an elf;
I saw it myself.
When the clock struck twelve,
Was he mis-shapen.

SECOND SHEPHERD. Ye two are right deft,—same in a stead.

THIRD SHEPHERD. Since they maintain their theft,—let's do them to dead.

MAK. If I trespass eft, gird off my head.
With you will I be left.

FIRST SHEPHERD. Sirs, do my advice
For this trespass,
We will neither curse nor flout,
Fight, nor chide,
But seize him tight,
And cast him in canvas. [*They toss* Mak *in a sheet.*]

. . .

FIRST SHEPHERD [*as the three return to the fold*]. Lord, how I am sore, in point for to burst.
In faith I may no more, therefore will I rest.

SECOND SHEPHERD. As a sheep of seven score, he weighed in my fist.
For to sleep anywhere, methink that I list.

THIRD SHEPHERD. Now I pray you,
Lie down on this green.

FIRST SHEPHERD. On these thefts yet I consider.

THIRD SHEPHERD. Whereto should ye worry?
Do as I say you.

[*Enter an* Angel *above, who sings "Gloria in Excelsis," then says:*]

ANGEL. Rise, herd-men, gracious, for now is he born
That shall take from the fiend, what Adam had lorn:
That fiend to overthrow, this night is he born.
God is made your friend: now at this morn,
He behests;
To Bedlem go see,
There lies that Divine One,
In a crib full poorly,
Betwixt two beasts.

FIRST SHEPHERD. This was a quaint voice that ever yet I heard.
It is a marvel to relate thus to be scared.

SECOND SHEPHERD. Of God's son of heaven, he spoke up word.
All the wood like the lightning, methought that he made
Appear.

THIRD SHEPHERD. He spake of a bairn
In Bedlem, I you warn.

FIRST SHEPHERD. That betokens yonder star.
Let us seek him there.

SECOND SHEPHERD. Say, what was his song? Heard ye not how he cracked it?
Three breves to a long.

THIRD SHEPHERD. Yea, marry, he shouted it.
Was no crochet wrong, nor no thing that lacked it.

FIRST SHEPHERD. For to sing us among, right as he trilled it,
I can.

SECOND SHEPHERD. Let us see how ye croon
Can ye bark at the moon?

THIRD SHEPHERD. Hold your tongues, have done.

FIRST SHEPHERD. Hark after, then.

SECOND SHEPHERD. To Bedlem he bade that we should go.
I am full feared that we tarry too long.

THIRD SHEPHERD. Be merry and not sad: of mirth is our song,
Everlasting glad, our road may we take,
Without noise.

FIRST SHEPHERD. Hie we thither quickly;
If we be wet and weary,
To that child and that lady
We have it not to delay.

SECOND SHEPHERD. We find by the prophecy—let be your din—
Of David and Isaiah, and more than I can mind,
They prophesied by clergy, that on a virgin
Should he light and lie, to pardon our sin
And slake it,
Our kind from woe;
For Isaiah said so,
*Cite virgo*
*Concipiet a child that is naked.*

THIRD SHEPHERD. Full glad may we be, and abide that day
That lovely to see, that shall have all power.
Lord, well for me for once and for aye,

Might I kneel on my knee some word for to say
To that child.
But the angel said
In a crib was he laid;
He was poorly arrayed,
Both meek and mild.

FIRST SHEPHERD. Patriarchs that have been, and prophets beforn,
They desired to have seen this child that is born.
They are gone full clean, that have they lorn.
We shall see him, I ween, ere it be morn
By token.
When I see him and feel,
Then know I full weel
It is true as steel
That prophets have spoken.
To so poor as we are, that he would appear,
First find, and declare by his messenger.

SECOND SHEPHERD. Go we now, let us fare: the place is us near.

THIRD SHEPHERD. I am ready and eager: go we in fear
To that light!
Lord! if thy wills be,
We are rude all three,
Thou grant us of thy glee,
To comfort thy wight.

. . .

[*The* Shepherds *arrive at Bethlehem.*]

FIRST SHEPHERD. Hail, comely and clean; hail, young child!
Hail, maker, as I mean, of a maiden so mild!
Thou hast banned, I ween, the devil so wild,
The false guiler of woe, now goes he beguiled.
Lo, he merry is!
Lo, he laughs, my sweeting
A welcome meeting!
I have given my greeting
Have a bob of cherries?

SECOND SHEPHERD. Hail, sovereign Savior, for thou hast us sought!
Hail freely, leaf and flow'r, that all thing has wrought!
Hail full of favor, that made all of nought!
Hail! I kneel and I cower. A bird have I brought
To my bairn!
Hail, little tiny darling,
Of our creed thou art crop!
I would drink in thy cup,
Little day-star.

THIRD SHEPHERD. Hail, darling dear, full of godhead!
I pray thee be near, when that I have need.
Hail! sweet is thy cheer: my heart would bleed
To see thee sit here in so poor weed,
With no pennies.
Hail! put forth thy hand.
I bring thee but a ball
Have and play thee with all,
And go to the tennis.

MARY. The Father of Heaven, God omnipotent,
That set all aright, his son has he sent.
My name could he say, and laugh as if he knew.
I conceived him full even, through might, as God meant;
And new is he born.
He keep you from woe:
I shall pray him so;
Tell forth as ye go,
And mind on this morn.

FIRST SHEPHERD. Farewell, lady, so fair to behold,
With thy child on thy knee.

SECOND SHEPHERD. But he lies full cold,
Lord, well is me: now we go forth, behold!

THIRD SHEPHERD. Forsooth, already it seems to be told
Full oft.

FIRST SHEPHERD. What grace we have found.

SECOND SHEPHERD. Come forth, now are we won.

THIRD SHEPHERD. To sing are we bound.
Let us sing it aloud!

(*Anonymous, XIV century, England*)

## *The Church and Society*

*The Church was also the source of medieval justice. The local lord, however capricious and unsound his rulings, was subordinate to the Church as a judicial power. As such, the institution held tremendous and widespread powers. It might excommunicate not only from the sacraments of the Church but also from all communication with the faithful. Its tones were not gentle to the obdurate: "May he be seized with jaundice and smitten with blindness; and may he bring his present life to a miserable ending by a most wretched death and undergo everlasting damnation with the devil, where, bound with red hot chains, may he groan forever and ever, and may the worm that never dies feed on his flesh and the fire that cannot be quenched be his food and his sustenance eternally." A tyrannical ruler opposing the Church might find his kingdom under interdict—cut off from all participation in the life of the Church—until his unhappy people forced him to capitulate. The state upheld the rulings of the Church in order to maintain peace, glad of this support to its stability. In France anyone excommunicated for a year and a day had his property seized; in England only forty days were allowed for submission. Thus, with its efforts bent on establishing a kingdom not of this world, the Church became a more formidable power than any kingdom of its time.*

# THE TWO SWORDS

## Pope Boniface VIII

That there is only one Holy, Catholic and Apostolic Church we are compelled to believe and to hold, our faith urging us and this we do firmly believe and simply confess; and outside of which there is no salvation or remission of sins, as the bridegroom proclaims in Canticles: "My dove, my perfect one is but one; she is the only one of her mother, the chosen of her that bore her." The Church represents one mystical body whose head is Christ; and of Christ God is the head. In it there is "one Lord, one faith, one baptism." At the time of the flood, there was one ark of Noah prefiguring the one Church; it had been finished in one cubit, had one helmsman and commander, Noah. We read that outside of it all things existing on earth were destroyed. This Church we venerate, and this alone, the Lord saying through the prophet: "Deliver, O God, my soul from the sword and my darling from the hand of the dog." He prayed for the soul, that is for Himself, for the head, and at the same time for the body which He called the one and only Church on account of the promised unity of faith, sacraments, and love of the Church. That is the "seamless garment" of the Lord which was not rent but fell by lot. Therefore, in this one and only Church there is one body and one head, not two heads as if it were a monster; namely, Christ and the vicar of Christ, Peter, with his successors; because the Lord said to Peter: "Feed my sheep." He said, "My sheep," using a general term and not designating these or those sheep, so that it must be understood that He committed to his care all His sheep. If, then, the Greeks and others say that they were not committed to Peter and his successors, they necessarily admit that they are not of the sheep of Christ, for the Lord says, in John, "There shall be one fold and one shepherd."

In this Church and in its power there are two swords, a spiritual and a temporal. This we are taught in the Gospel for when the Apostles said, "Behold, here are two swords"—that means in the Church, since the Apostles were speaking—the Lord did not reply that it was too many, but enough. Thus he who denies that the temporal sword is under the power of Peter, has wrongly interpreted the word of the Lord when He said, "Put up again thy sword into its scabbard." Both swords, the spiritual and the material, are in the power of the Church, the one to be used for the Church, the other by the Church; the one by the priest, the other by kings and knights but at the will and sufferance of the priest. It is fitting that one sword be under the other and the temporal authority be subject to the spiritual power. For when the Apostle says, "There is no power but that of God and the powers that are of God are ordained," they would not be ordained unless one sword were under the other and one, as inferior, were led by the other to great deeds. Because according to St. Dionysius it is the law of Divinity that the lowest are to be led through the intermediate to the superior. It is becoming, therefore, to confess that the spiritual power excells in dignity and nobility every form of earthly power as spiritual interests exceed temporal ones. This is also made clear in the giving of tithes, and the benediction and sanctification; from the recognition of this power and from the

14. Ivory plaque from a book cover. Christ enthroned with symbols of the Evangelists. Germany, X-XI century.

exercise of government over those same things. For, the truth bearing witness, the spiritual power has to establish the earthly power, and to judge if it be not good. Thus, in the case of the Church and the ecclesiastical power, is verified the prophecy of Jeremiah: "Lo, I have set thee over the nations and kingdoms this day."

Therefore, if the earthly power err, it shall be judged by the spiritual power; if the lesser spiritual power err, it shall be judged by the higher. But if the greatest spiritual power err, it can be judged only by God, not by man, as the Apostle testifies: "The spiritual man judgeth all things; and he himself is judged by no man." This authority, moreover, although it is given to man and exercised by him, is not human but divine, being given to Peter from the mouth of God and founded for him and his successors on a rock through Christ Himself when He said to Peter: "Whatsoever thou shalt bind," etc. Therefore, whoever resists this power so ordained by God, resists the ordination of God, unless he pretends, like the Manicheans, that there are two beginnings. But this we judge to be false and heretical since, as Moses testifies, not in the beginnings but "in the beginning," God created the heavens and the earth. Indeed we declare, announce and define, that it is altogether necessary to salvation for every human creature to be subject to the Roman Pontiff.

(*The Encyclical "Unam Sanctam"*)

## ON MONARCHY

### Dante Alighieri

. . .

The first question, then, is whether Temporal Monarchy is necessary for the welfare of the world; and that it is necessary can, I think, be shown by the strongest and most manifest arguments; for nothing, either of reason or of authority, opposes me. Let us take first the authority of the Philosopher in his *Politics*. There, on his venerable authority, it is said that where a number of things are arranged to attain an end, it behooves one of them to regulate or govern the others, and the others to submit. And it is not only the authority of his illustrious name, which makes this worthy of belief, but also reason, instancing particulars.

Further, the whole human race is a whole with reference to certain parts, and with reference to another whole, it is a part. For it is a whole with reference to particular kingdoms and nations, as we have shown; and it is a part with reference to the whole universe, as is manifest without argument. Therefore, as the lower portions of the whole system of humanity are well adapted to that whole, so that whole is said to be well adapted to the whole which is above it. It is only under the rule of one prince that the parts of humanity are well adapted to their whole, as may easily be collected from what we have said; therefore it is only by being under one Princedom, or the rule of a single Prince, that humanity as a whole is well adapted to the Universe, or its Prince, who is the One God. And it therefore follows that Monarchy is necessary for the welfare of the world.

. . .

And all is well and at its best which exists according to the will of the first agent, who is God. This is self-evident, except to those who deny that the divine goodness attains to absolute perfection. Now, it is the intention of God that all created things should represent the likeness of God, so far as their proper nature will admit. Therefore was it said: "Let us make man in our image, after our likeness." And though it could not be said that the lower part of creation was made in the image of God, yet all things may be said to be after His likeness, for what is the whole universe but the footprint of the divine goodness? The human race, therefore, is well, nay at its best state, when, so far as can be, it is made like unto God. But the human race is then most made like unto God when most it is one; for the true principle of oneness is in Him alone. Wherefore it is written: "Hear, O Israel; the Lord thy God is one God." But the race of man is most one when it is united wholly in one body, and it is evident that this cannot be, except when it is subject to one prince. Therefore in this subjection mankind is most made like unto God, and, in consequence, such a subjection is in accordance with the divine intention, and it is indeed well and best for man when this is so, as we showed at the beginning of this chapter.

Again, things are well and at their best with every son when he follows, so far as by his proper nature he can, the footsteps of a perfect father. Mankind is the son of heaven, which is most perfect in all its works; for it is "man and the sun which produce man," according to the second book on Natural Learning. The human race, therefore, is at its best when it imitates the movements of heaven, so far as human nature allows. And since the whole heaven is regulated with one motion, to wit, that of the *primum mobile,* and by one mover, who is God, in all its parts, movements, and movers (and this human reason readily seizes from science); therefore, if our argument be correct, the human race is at its best state when, both in its movements, and in regard to those who move it, it is regulated by a single Prince, as by the single movement of heaven, and by one law, as by the single motion. Therefore it is evidently necessary for the welfare of the world for there to be a Monarchy, or single Princedom, which men call the Empire. And this thought did Boethius breathe when he said: "Oh happy race of men, if your hearts are ruled by the love which rules the heaven."

Wherever there is controversy, there ought to be judgment, otherwise there would be imperfection without its proper remedy, which is impossible; for God and Nature, in things necessary, do not fail in their provisions. But it is manifest that there may be controversy between any two princes, where the one is not subject to the other, either from the fault of themselves, or even of their subjects. Therefore between them there should be means of judgment. And since, when one is not subject to the other, he cannot be judged by the other (for there is no rule of equals over equals), there must be a third prince of wider jurisdiction, within the circle of whose laws both may come. Either he will or he will not be a Monarch. If he is, we have what we sought; if not, then this one again will have an equal, who is not subject to his jurisdiction, and then again we have need of a third. And so we must either go on to infinity, which is impossible, or we must come to that judge who is first and highest; by whose judgment all controversies shall be either directly or indirectly decided; and he will be Monarch or Emperor.

. . .

It is therefore clear that the authority of temporal Monarchy comes down, with no intermediate will, from the fountain of universal authority; and this fountain, one in its unity, flows through many channels out of the abundance of the goodness of God.

And now, methinks, I have reached the goal which I set before me. I have unravelled the truth of the questions which I asked: whether the office of Monarchy was necessary to the welfare of the world; whether it was by right that the Roman people assumed to themselves the office of Monarchy; and, further, that last question, whether the authority of the Monarch springs immediately from God, or from some other. Yet the truth of this latter question must not be received so narrowly as to deny that in certain matters the Roman Prince is subject to the Roman Pontiff. For that happiness, which is subject to mortality, in a sense is ordered with a view to the happiness which shall not taste of death. Let, therefore, Caesar be reverent to Peter, as the first-born son should be reverent to his father, that he may be illuminated with the light of his father's grace, and so may be stronger to lighten the world over which he has been placed by Him alone, who is the ruler of all things spiritual as well as temporal.

*The sense of God-centredness was most apparent in the monasteries. Indeed, it is difficult to overestimate the debt of the medieval period to the monks, for they played an essential role in the transition from barbarian to citizen. Actually, however, cultural gains were but a by-product of the real purposes of monasticism. The first obligation of the monk was the* Opus Dei, *the chanting of the praises of God at stated times of the day, requiring several hours. Next came labor, often in the scriptorium copying books. In the early twelfth century, for example, the monastery at Chartres had 570 volumes in its library. Since many of the monks came from the upper classes, a group of men who would otherwise have been lost to cultural development copied classics, illuminated manuscripts and taught newcomers. The monastery thus gave organization to the artistic development of its time, as well as providing opportunity for research in new methods.*

*The monasteries were the great agencies of service, their reforming energy, as at Cluny and Citeaux, giving example to other clergy. (Their records are often the only history of the time and their chronicles have become the source books of medieval history.) At the same time, the monastery took on political leadership in the existing vacuum. It became a large landowner, and presently a wealthy one. Although monastic authority was generally a boon to the area, its dual role as power of both church and state often distracted from its primary goal.*

# THE MONASTIC LIFE

## John Cassian

### Of the Monk's Robe

Let the robe of the monk be such as may merely cover the body and prevent the disgrace of nudity, and keep off harm from cold, not such as may foster the seeds of vanity and pride: for the same Apostle tells us: "Having food and covering, with these let us be content." "Covering," he says, not "raiment" as is wrongly found in some Latin copies; that is, what may merely cover the body, not what may please the fancy by the splendour of the attire; commonplace, so that it may not be thought remarkable for novelty of colour or fashion among other men of the same profession; and quite free from anxious carefulness, yet not discoloured by stains acquired through neglect. Lastly, let them be so far removed from this world's fashions as to remain altogether common property for the use of the servants of God. For whatever is claimed by one or a few among the servants of God and is not the common property alike of the whole body of the brethern is either superfluous or vain, and for that reason to be considered harmful, and affording an appearance of vanity rather than virtue. And, therefore, whatever models we see were not taught either by the saints of old who laid the foundations of the monastic life, or by the fathers of our own time who in their turn keep up at the present day their customs, these we also should reject as superfluous and useless; wherefore they utterly disapproved of a robe of sackcloth as being visible to all and conspicuous, and what from this very fact will not only confer no benefit on the soul but rather minister to vanity and pride, and as being inconvenient and unsuitable for the performance of necessary work for which a monk ought always to go ready and unimpeded.

. . .

### Of the Tunics of the Egyptians

They also wear linen tunics, which scarcely reach to the elbows, and for the rest leave their hands bare, that the cutting off of the sleeves may suggest that they have cut off all the deeds and works of this world, and the garment of linen teach that they are dead to all earthly conversation, and that thereby they may hear the Apostle saying day by day to them: "Mortify your members that are upon the earth;" their very dress also declaring this: "For ye are dead and your life is hid with Christ in God;" and again: "And I live, yet now not I but Christ liveth in me. To me indeed the world is crucified, and I to the world."

## Of Their Cords

They also wear double scarves woven of woolen yarn which the Greeks call succinctoria but which we should name girdles or strings or more properly cords. These falling down over the top of the neck and divided on either side of the throat go round the folds (of the robe) at the armpits and gather them up on either side, so that they can draw up and tuck in close to the body the wide folds of the dress, and so with their arms girt, they are made active and ready for all kinds of work, endeavoring with all their might to fulfil the Apostle's charge: "For these hands have ministered not only to me but to those also who are with me," "Neither have we eaten any man's bread for nought, but with labour and toil working night and day that we should not be burdensome to any of you." And: "If any will not work, neither let him eat."

## Of Their Capes

Next they cover their necks and shoulders with a narrow cape, aiming at modesty of dress as well as cheapness and economy; and this is called in our language as well as their *mafors;* and so they avoid both the expense and the display of cloaks and great coats.

## Of the Sheepskin and the Goatskin

The last article of their dress is the goatskin, which is called *melotes,* and a staff, which they carry in imitation of those who foreshadowed the lines of the monastic life in the Old Testament, of whom the Apostle says: "They wandered about in sheepskins and goatskins, being in want, distressed, afflicted; of whom the world was not worthy; wandering in deserts, and in mountains, and in dens, and in caves of the earth." And this garment of goatskin signifies that having destroyed all wantonness of carnal passions they ought to continue in the utmost sobriety of virtue, and that nothing of the wantonness or heat of youth, or of their old lightmindedness, should remain in their bodies.

15. Wood statue of St. James the Less (?), detail. Germany, 1265-1280.

## Of the Staff of the Egyptians

For Elisha, himself one of them, teaches that the same men used to carry a staff; as he says to Gehazi, his servant, when sending him to raise the woman's son to life: "Take my staff and run and go and place it on the lad's face that he may live." And the prophet would certainly not have given it to him to take unless he had been in the habit of constantly carrying it about in his hand. And the carrying of the staff spiritually teaches that they ought never to walk unarmed among so many barking dogs of faults and invisible beasts of spiritual wickedness (from which the blessed David, in his longing to be free, says: "Deliver not, O Lord, to the beasts the soul that trusteth in Thee"), but when they attack them they ought to beat them off with the sign of the cross and drive them far away; and when they rage furiously against them they should annihilate them by the constant recollection of the Lord's passion and by following the example of His mortified life.

. . .

## Of the Modification in the Observances Which May Be Permitted in Accordance with the Character of the Climate of the Custom of the District

So much may be said, that we may not appear to have left out any article of the dress of the Egyptians. But we need only keep to those which the situation of the place and the customs of the district permit. For the severity of the winter does not allow us to be satisfied with slippers or tunics or a single frock; and the covering of tiny hoods or the wearing of a sheepskin would afford a subject for derision instead of edifying the spectators. Wherefore we hold that we ought to introduce only those things which we have described above and which are adapted to the humble character of our profession and the nature of the climate, that the chief thing about our dress may be not the novelty of the garb, which might give some offence to men of the world, but its honourable simplicity.

. . .

## Of the Ordeal by Which One Who Is to Be Received in the Monastery Is Tested

One, then, who seeks to be admitted to the discipline of the monastery is never received before he gives, by lying outside the doors for ten days or even longer, an evidence of his perseverance and desire, as well as of humility and patience. And when, prostrate at the feet of all the brethern that pass by, and of set purpose repelled and scorned by them, as if he was wanting to enter the monastery not for the sake of religion but because he was obliged; and when, too, covered with insults and affronts, he has given a practical proof of his steadfastness and has shown what he will be like in temptations by the way he has borne the disgrace; and when, with the ardour of his soul thus ascertained, he is admitted, then they enquire with the utmost care whether he is contaminated by a single coin from his former possessions clinging to him. For they know that he cannot stay long under the discipline of the monastery, nor ever learn the virtue of humility and obedience, nor be content with the poverty and difficult life of the monastery, if he knows that ever so small a sum of money has been kept hid; but, as soon as ever a disturbance arises on some occasion or other, he will at once dart off from the monastery like a stone from a sling, impelled to this by trusting in that sum of money.

## The Reason Why Those Who Are Received in the Monastery Are Not Allowed to Bring Anything with Them

And for these reasons they do not agree to take from him money to be used even for the good of the monastery. First, in case he may be puffed up with arrogance, owing to this offering, and so not deign to put himself on a level with the poorer brethern; and next, lest he fail through this pride of his to stoop to the humility of Christ, and so, when he cannot hold out under the discipline of the monastery, leave it, and afterwards, when he has cooled down, want in a bad spirit to receive and get back—not without loss to the monastery—what he had contributed in the early days of his renunciation when he was aglow with spiritual fervour. And that this rule should always be kept they have been taught in many instances. . . .

## The Reason Why Those Who Give Up the World, When They Are Received in the Monasteries, Must Lay Aside Their Own Clothes and Be Clothed in Others by the Abbot

Wherefore each one on his admission is stripped of all his former possessions, so that he is not allowed any longer to keep even the clothes which he has on his back; but in the council of his brethern he is brought forward into the midst and stripped of his own clothes, and clad by the Abbot's hands in the dress of the monastery, so that by this he may know not only that he has been despoiled of all his old things, but also that he has laid aside all worldly pride, and come down to the want and poverty of Christ, and that he is now to be supported not by wealth sought for by the world's arts, nor by anything reserved from his former state, but that he is to receive out of the holy and sacred funds of the monastery his rations for his service; and that, as he knows that he is thence to be clothed and fed and that he has nothing of his own, he may learn, nevertheless, not to be anxious about the morrow, according to the saying of the Gospel, and may not be ashamed to be on a level with the poor, that is with the body of the brethern, with whom Christ was not ashamed to be numbered, and to call himself their brother, but rather that he may glory that he has been made to share the lot of his own servants.

## The Reason Why Those Who Are Admitted to a Monastery Are Not Permitted to Mix at Once with the Congregation of the Brethern But Are First Committed to the Guest House

When, then, anyone has been received and proved by that persistence of which we have spoken, and laying aside his own garments, has been clad in those of the monastery, he is not allowed to mix at once with the congregation of the brethern, but is given into the charge of an Elder, who lodges apart not far from the entrance of the monastery, and is entrusted with the care of strangers and guests, and bestows all his diligence in receiving them kindly. And when he has served there for a whole year without any complaint, and has given evidence of service towards strangers, being thus initiated in the first rudiments of humility and patience, and by long practice in it acknowledged, when he is to be admitted from this into the congregation of the brethern he is handed over to another Elder, who is placed over ten of the juniors who are entrusted to him by the Abbot, and whom he both teaches and governs in accordance with the arrangement which we read of in Exodus as made by Moses.

## Of the Practices in Which the Juniors Are First Exercised That They May Become Proficient in Overcoming All Their Desires

And his anxiety and the chief part of his instruction—through which the juniors brought to him may be able in due course to mount to the greatest heights of perfection—will be to teach him first to conquer his own wishes; and, anxiously and diligently practising him in this, he will of set purpose contrive to give him such orders as he knows to be contrary to his liking; for, taught by many examples, they say that a monk, and especially the younger ones, cannot bridle the desire of his concupiscence unless he has first learnt by obedience to mortify his wishes. And so they lay it down that the man who has not first learnt to overcome his desires cannot possibly stamp out anger or sulkiness, or the spirit of fornication; nor can he preserve true humility of heart, or lasting unity with the brethern, or a stable and continuous concord; nor remain for any length of time in the monastery.

## The Reason Why the Juniors Are Enjoined Not to Keep Back Any of Their Thoughts from the Senior

By these practices, then, they hasten to impress and instruct those whom they are training with the alphabet, as it were, and first syllables in the direction of perfection, as they can clearly see by these whether they are grounded in a false and imaginary or in a true humility. And, that they may easily arrive at this, they are next taught not to conceal by a false shame any disturbing thoughts in their hearts, but, as soon as ever such arrive, to lay them bare to the senior, and, in forming a judgment about them, not to trust anything to their own discretion, but to take it on trust that that is good or bad which is considered and pronounced so by the examination of the senior. Thus it results that our cunning adversary cannot in any way circumvent a young and inexperienced monk, or get the better of his ignorance, or by any craft deceive one whom he sees to be protected not by his own discretion but by that of his senior, and who cannot be persuaded to hide from his senior those suggestions of his which like fiery darts he has shot into his heart; since the devil, subtle as he is, cannot ruin or destroy a junior unless he has enticed him either through pride or shame to conceal his thoughts. For they lay it down as an universal and clear proof that a thought is from the devil if we are ashamed to disclose it to the senior.

## How Thorough Is the Obedience of the Juniors Even in Those Things Which Are Matters of Common Necessity

Next, the rule is kept with such strict obedience that, without the knowledge and permission of their superior, the juniors not only do not dare to leave their cell but on their own authority do not venture to satisfy their common needs. And so they are quick to fulfil without any discussion all those things that are ordered by him, as if they were commanded by God from heaven; so that sometimes, when impossibilities are commanded them, they undertake them with such faith and devotion as to strive with all their powers and without the slightest hesitation to fulfil them and carry them out; and out of reverence for their senior they do not even consider whether a command is an impossibility. But of their obedience I omit to speak more particularly at present. . . .

## How They Leave off Every Kind of Work at the Sound of Some One Knocking at the Door, in Their Eagerness to Answer at Once

And so, sitting in their cells and devoting their energy equally to work and to meditation, when they hear the sound of some one knocking at the door, and striking on the cells of each, summoning them to prayer or some work, every one eagerly dashes out from his cell, so that one who is practising the writer's art, although he may have just begun to form a letter, does not venture to finish it, but runs out with the utmost speed, at the very moment when the sound of the knocking reaches his ears, without even waiting to finish the letter he has begun; but, leaving the lines of the letter incomplete, he aims not at abridging and saving his labour, but rather hastens with the utmost earnestness and zeal to attain the virtue of obedience, which they put not merely before manual labour and reading and silence and quietness in the cell, but even before all other virtues, so that they consider that everything should be postponed to it, and are content to undergo any amount of inconvenience if only it may be seen that they have in no way neglected this virtue.

. . .

## How, Even if a Large Sum of Money Is Amassed by the Labour of Each, Still No One May Venture to Exceed the Moderate Limit of What Is Appointed as Adequate

And although each one of them may bring in daily by his work and labour so great a return to the monastery that he could out of it not only satisfy his own moderate demands but could also supply the wants of many, yet he is no way puffed up, nor does he flatter himself on account of his toil and this large gain from his labour, but, except for two biscuits, which are sold for scarcely threepence, no one thinks that he has a right to anything further. . . . And though he believes that the whole granary of the monastery forms his substance, and, as lord of all, devotes his whole care and energy to it, yet nevertheless, in order to maintain that excellent state of want and poverty which he has secured and which he strives to preserve unbroken to the very last, he regards himself as a foreigner and an alien to them all, so that he conducts himself as a stranger and a sojourner in this world, and considers himself a pupil of the monastery and a servant instead of imagining that he is lord and master of anything.

(from *The Institutes*)

*Religious belief was thus an ubiquitous factor in medieval culture, and when combined with the lack of general education, it inevitably promoted superstition. While a surprising degree of credulity existed even among the educated, in the lower classes there was no limit to the possibilities of belief. Relics of all sorts were venerated: hay from the manger of Bethlehem, at least two known heads of John the Baptist, twigs from the burning bush of Moses, threads from the mantle of Mary. Magical powers were attributed to the four elements, legends of a Wonder Child abounded, stories of strange powers in nature given to men were circulated. In the dark tradition of fear of the world, the flesh and the devil, men took comfort in tales of the subordination of nature to God and in the nearness of holy relics.*

*"Theology," wrote Thomas Aquinas, "transcends the other sciences." It is not surprising, then, that the medievals aspired to and achieved a high degree of unity of religious belief and that this underlay most of the intellectual activity of the period. With every man believing in the historical drama of salvation and in his own will as a factor in that drama, value judgments and standards for behavior tended to be uniform throughout the Christian world. Two factors, however, mitigated the unity of doctrine that generally prevailed. One was open heresy, a challenge by individual or group against the teaching of the Church. From earliest times the Church had been under siege by various groups stemming back to the pre-Christian teaching of Zoroaster, and emerging from time to time as Gnostics, Manichees or Albigensians. Unable to reconcile the evil in the world of matter with the pure goodness of God, they resolved the difficulty by postulating dual principles, one of light, one of darkness. Some of the medieval troubadours were couriers, their songs carrying a coded message to members of brotherhoods kept secret under pain of death. At a time when the political, social and religious institutions were so intimately related, religious heresy was destructive of political and social order and from the standpoint of the Church, had to be removed lest it corrupt the innocent. Hence, the Inquisition, a court following the legal procedures and punishments of Roman law. Heretics condemned by the Church were punished by the state to preserve the body politic from disorder. That wholly political motives entered in frequently can be seen in the frightful crusade against the Albigensians which was of enormous benefit to the French king, ridding him of recalcitrant vassals.*

*The other source of diversity and disunity in belief and practice was less revolutionary. When a ruler like King Clovis of the Franks was given victory in battle after calling on the*

*God of the Christians, he was converted and baptized with three thousand of his men. The degree of faith of these soldiers was questionable and their knowledge of their new-found faith extremely slight. Insofar as possible the Church tried to absorb the religious customs of the converts and transform them into Christian rituals: the harvest festival and spring planting rites became Ember Days; Midsummer Night was celebrated as the feast of St. John the Baptist rather than the licentious night of the fairy revels. Still many new Christians continued their pagan rites and, short of blood sacrifices, the Church tended to look the other way. Great leeway, too, was allowed to clergy working in the outposts of Christianity. Nearer home, Chaucer could mock the clergy in his stories and Dante could see Popes in Hell without fear of condemnation—a remarkable degree of freedom was permitted, as long as one did not threaten to upset the civil order. This was an age of faith, but not of submission.*

## THE HERESY TRIAL

### John of Salisbury

Master Gilbert, bishop of Poitiers, the most learned man of our day, was summoned to the court to answer the abbot of Clairvaux—a man of the greatest eloquence and highest repute—on certain matters which had been brought up the year before at Paris, but postponed until then. For certain statements had been found in the bishop's commentary on the *De Trinitate* of Boethius and the writings of his pupils which seemed reprehensible to the learned, either because they were inconsistent with accepted beliefs or because, through novelty of expression, they seemed inconsistent. Many attacked him, but the fiercest assailants were Suger, abbot of St. Denis, a learned and eloquent man, and two canons of Poitiers, Calo who later became bishop of the same church and master Arnold, nicknamed "straightface;" the masters of the schools, also, Peter Lombard, later bishop of Paris, and Robert of Melun, afterward bishop of Hereford, led an embittered attack on him. I cannot say whether they acted out of zeal for the faith or jealousy of his fame and merit, or a desire to propitiate the abbot whose influence was then at its height, and whose counsel was most weighty in the affairs of church and state alike. . . .

But most of all the doctors of the church he was most conversant with the works of blessed Hilary and Augustine and often used words from their writings which are uncommon in modern works. One thing is certain: that now several terms are hackneyed in the schools which, when he introduced them seemed to be "impious novelties."

Before the abbot of Clairvaux met Gilbert publicly in court, he sent asking all the leading churchmen, those who were distinguished by their learning or sanctity of office to meet him in his lodging. I speak and write what I myself have seen, knowing that I would imperil my immortal soul and my worldly reputation if I should either relate or write anything untrue in such a matter as this. There will be some, too, ready to refute me if I do not speak the truth; for several men of high repute and weighty judgment are yet living who were present at the meeting. Those present included the late Theobald, archbishop of Canterbury and Geoffrey of Bordeaux and Henry of York and the Abbots Suger of St. Denis and Baldwin of Chatillon-sur-Seine; and of those now living, the archbishop of Canterbury and Roger of York and many others whom it would be tedious to enumerate. The abbot, the most pious and learned among them, then delivered a short and eloquent discourse, concluding that it was their duty to remove all scandals from the church of God and beseeching them to correct him if they thought he was mistaken in the case he had brought against Master Gilbert. If he had pressed his argument foolishly, it was because he had been carried away by charity and zeal for the faith. But if he was not mistaken, he asked them to do their duty and preserve the purity of the faith. For cases such as this were the business not of monks and hermits, but of the prelates of the church who were bound to lay down their lives for their sheep. And he asked them to help in judging whether he was right or wrong, he asked them to listen to the articles in which he differed from the bishop and then approve or reject them. On their agreeing, he said he believed that "God is deity and the converse." As he made this statement Geoffrey of Auxerre, one of his monks, wrote it down word for word and then read it out with the question, "Do you accept this?" after the fashion when decretals of laws were promulgated. And they replied, "We do." Proceeding, the abbot said he believed that "three Persons are one God and the converse." This too was recorded, put to the vote and accepted as before. The more thoughtful men did not approve of this method but they feared offending the abbot and his followers if they did not fall in with his wishes. Then the abbot went on "I believe that the essence or substance of God was incarnate." This was treated in the same way. Fourthly he propounded that "since God is simple and whatever is in God is God, the properties of the persons are the persons themselves and so is the Father paternity, the Son filiality, the Spirit proceeding and the converse."

When this, like the other propositions had been written down and put to the vote, a certain archdeacon of Chalons, master Robert de Brusso, rose holding up his hand and calling for silence and besought them not to give a hasty answer. He had heard, he said, that this had been propounded in the schools of the renowned doctors, brothers Anselm and Ralph of Laon, but rejected by them because they were unwilling to go beyond the definitions of the Fathers. In the same reason, neither Gilbert the Universal who later became bishop of London nor Alberic of Rheims afterward raised to the archbishopric of Bourges had been prepared to accept it. He knew this because he had heard them lecture and had questioned them on the subject. Again Gilbert of Westminster near London whom he considered even more learned than the others, had never been willing to admit this. Consequently his advice was that they should not make a hasty judgment on so weighty a matter, especially as such men had expressly declined to make this definition; the pope and cardinals should be present and the most distinguished men in the western world meet to discuss it. His advice was followed. . . .

# THE VISION OF WILLIAM CONCERNING PIERS THE PLOWMAN

## William Langland

. . .

The king and his knights to the church went
To hear matins and mass, and to the meat after.
Then waked I from my winking, I was woful withal
That I had not heavier slept and seen more.
Ere I a furlong had fared, a faintness me seized,
That further might I not a-foot, for default of sleep.

I sat softly adown, and said my creed,
And so I babbled on my beads that it brought me asleep.
Then saw I much more than I before told,
For I saw the field full of folk that I before showed,
And Conscience with a cross came to preach.
He prayed the people to have pity on themselves,
And proved that these pestilences were for pure sin,
And this southwestern wind on a Saturday at even
Was clearly for pride, and for no cause else,
Peartrees and plumtrees were dashed to the ground,
In ensample to men that we should do the better.
Beeches and broad oaks were blown to the earth,
And turned the tail upward in token of dread
That deadly sin ere Doomsday should destroy them all.
On this matter I might mumble full long,
But I say as I saw, so help me God!
How Conscience with a cross commenced to preach.
He bade wasters go work at what they best could,
And win what they wasted with some sort of craft.
He prayed Peronelle her fur-trimming to leave,
And keep it in her coffer for capital at need.
Thomas he taught to take two staves,
And fetch home Felice from the ducking-stool.
He warned Wat his wife was to blame,
That her head-dress was worth a mark and his hood
worth a groat.
He charged merchant to chasten their children,
Let them lack no respect, while they are young.
He prayed priests and prelates together,
What they preached to the people to prove it in themselves—
"And live as ye teach us, we will love you the better."
And then he advised the orders their rule to obey—
"Lest the king and his council abridge your supplies,
And be steward in your stead, till ye be better ordered.
And ye that seek St. James, and saints at Rome,
Seek me Saint Truth, for He can save you all;
*Qui cum patre et filio,* fare you well!"
Then ran Repentance and rehearsed this theme,
And made William to weep water with his eyes.

## Pride

Pernel Proud-heart flung herself on the ground,
And lay long ere she looked up, and to Our Lady cried,
And promised to Him who all of us made
She would unsew her smock, and wear instead a hair shirt
To tame her flesh with, that frail was to sin:
"Shall never light heart seize me, but I shall hold me down
And endure to be slandered as I never did before.
And now I can put on meekness, and mercy beseech
Of all of whom I have had envy in my heart."

## Lust

Lecher said "Alas!" and to Our Lady cried
To win for him mercy for his misdeeds,
Between God himself and his poor soul
Provided that he should on Saturday, for seven years,
Drink but with duck and dine but once.

## Envy

Envy with heavy heart asketh after shift,
And greatly his guiltiness beginneth to show,
Pale as a pellet, in a palsy he seemed,
Clothed in a coarse cloth, I could him not describe;
A kirtle and a short cloak, a knife by his side;
Of a friar's frock were the fronts of his sleeves.
As a leek that had lain long in the sun
So looked he with lean cheeks; foully he frowned;
His body was swollen; for wrath he bit his lips.
Wrathfully he clenched his fist, he thought to avenge himself
With works or with words, when he saw his time.
"Venom, or varnish, or vinegar, I trow,
Boils in my belly, or grows there, I ween.
Many a day could I not do as a man ought,
Such wind in my belly welleth ere I dine.
I have a neighbor nigh me, I have annoyed him oft,
Blamed him behind his back, to bring him in disgrace,
Injured him by my power, punished him full oft,

Belied him to lords, to make him lose silver,
Turned his friends to foes, with my false tongue;
His grace and his good luck grieve me full sore.
Between him and his household I have made wrath;
Both his life and his limb were lost through my tongue.
When I met in the market him I most hate,
I hailed him as courteously as if I were his friend.
He is doughtier than I, I dare do him no harm.
But had I mastery and might, I had murdered him for ever!
When I come to the church, and kneel before the rood,
And should pray for the people, as the priest teacheth us,
Then I cry upon my knees that Christ gave them sorrow
That have borne away my bowl and my broad sheet.
From the altar I turn mine eye and behold
How Henry hath a new coat and his wife another;
Then I wish it were mine, and all the web with it.
At his losing I laugh, in my heart I like it;
But at his winning I weep, and bewail the occasion.
    I deem that men do ill, yet I do much worse,
For I would that every wight in this world were my servant
And whoso hath more than I, maketh my heart angry.
    Thus I live loveless, like an ill-tempered dog,
That all my breast swelleth with the bitterness of my gall;
No sugar is sweet enough to assuage it at all,
Nor no remedy drive it from my heart;
If shrift then should sweep it out, a great wonder it were."
"Yes, surely," quoth Repentance, and advised him to good.
"Sorrow for their sins saveth full many."
"I am sorry," quoth Envy, "I am seldom other,
And that maketh me so mad, for I may not avenge me."

## Covetousness

Then came Covetousness, I could not describe him,
So hungry and so hollow Sir Harvey looked.
He was beetle-browed with two bleared eyes,
And like a leathern purse flapped his cheeks.
In a torn tabard of twelve winters' age;
Unless a louse could leap, I can not believe

That she could wander on that walk, it was so threadbare.
"I have been covetous," quoth this Caitiff, "I admit it here;
For some time I served Sim at "the Oak"
And was his pledged apprentice, his profit to watch.
First I learned to lie, in a lesson or two,
And wickedly to weigh was my second lesson.
To Winchester and to Weyhill I went to the fair
With many kinds of merchandise, as my master bade,
But had not the grace of guile gone among my ware,
It had been unsold these seven year, so help me God!
Then I betook me to the drapers, my grammar to learn,
To draw the list along, to make it seem longer.
Among these rich striped cloths learned I a lesson,
Pierced them with a pack-needle, and pleated them together,
Put them in a press, and fastened them therein
Till ten yards or twelve were drawn out to thirteen,
And my wife at Westminster, that woolen cloth made,
Spake to the spinners to spin it soft.
The pound that she weighed by, weighed a quarter more
Than my balance did, when I weighed true.
I bought her barley, she brewed it to sell;
Penny-ale and white perry, she poured it together,
For laborers and low folk, that work for their living.
The best in bed-chamber lay by the wall,
Whoso tasted thereof bought it ever after,
A gallon for a groat, God wot, no less
When it came in cups. Such tricks I used.
Rose the retailer is her right name;
She hath been a huckster these eleven winters.
But I swear now soothly that sin will I quit,
And never wickedly weigh, nor false trade practise,
But went to Walsingham, and my wife also,
And pray the Rood of Bronholm to bring me out of debt."

## Gluttony

Now beginneth the Glutton to go to the shrift,
And wanders churchwards, his shrift to tell,
Then Bet the brewster bade him good morrow,

And then she asked him whither he would go.
"To holy church," quoth he, "to hear mass,
Since I shall be shriven, and sin no more."
"I have good ale, gossip," quoth she; "Glutton, what say you?"
"Hast aught in thy purse," quoth he, "any hot spices?"
"Yea, Glutton, gossip," quoth she, "God wot, full good;
I have pepper and peony-seeds, and a pound of garlick,
A farthing worth of fennel-seed, for these fasting days."
Then goeth Glutton in, and great oaths after;
Cis the shoemaker's wife sat on the bench,
Wat the ward of the warren, and his wife both,
Tomkin the tinker and twain of his servants;
Hick the hackney-man, and Hogg the needle seller,
Clarice of Cock's lane, and the clerk of the church,
Sir Piers of Prie-Dieu, and Pernel of Flanders,
Dawe the ditcher and a dozen others.
A fiddler, a rat-catcher, a scavenger of Cheapside,
A rope-maker, a riding-boy, and Rose the dish-maker,
Godfrey of Garlickshire, and Griffin the Welshman,
And of tradesmen a band, early in the morning,
Stand Glutton, with good-will, a treat in good ale.
Then Clement the cobbler cast off his cloak,
And at the 'new fair' made offer to barter it;
And Hick the ostler flung his hood after,
And bade Bett the butcher act on his behalf.
Then were chapmen chosen, the articles to value;
Whoso had the hood should have something to boot.
They rose up rapidly, and whispered together,
And appraised the pennyworths, and parted them by themselves;
There were oaths a-plenty, whoso might hear them.
They could not, in conscience, accord together,
Till Robin, the rope-maker was chosen to arise,
And named for an umpire, to avoid all debate,
For he should appraise the pennyworths, as seemed good to him;
Then Hick the ostler had the cloak,
On condition that Clement should have his cup filled.
And have Hick the ostler's hood, and hold him well served,

And he that first repented should straight arise,
And greet Sir Glutton with a gallon of ale.
  There was laughing and cheating and "Let go the cup!"
Bargains and beverages began to rise,
And they sat so till evensong, and sang some while,
Till Glutton had gulped down a gallon and a gill.

. . .

So that, with all the woe in the world, his wife and his wench
Bore him home to his bed, and brought him therein.
And after all this surfeit, a sickness he had,
That he slept Saturday and Sunday, till sun went to rest.
  Then he waked from his winking, and wiped his eyes;
The first word that he spake was, "Where is the cup?"
His wife warned him then, of wickedness and sin.
Then he was ashamed, that wretch, and scratched his ears,
And 'gan to cry grievously, and great dole to make
For his wicked life, that he had lived.
"For hunger or for thirst, I make my vow,
Shall never fish on Friday digest in my maw,
Till Abstinence, my aunt, have given me leave;
And yet I have hated her all my life-time."

## Sloth

Sloth for sorrow fell down swooning,
Till *Vigilate,* the watcher, fetched water to his eyes,
Let it flow on his face, and fast to him cried,
And said, "Beware of despair, that will thee betray,
'I am sorry for my sins,' say to thyself,
And beat thyself on the breast, and pray God for grace,
For there is no guilt so great that His mercy is not more."
  Then Sloth sat up and sighed sore,
And made a vow before God, for his foul sloth,
"There shall be no Sunday this seven year (save sickness it cause)
That I shall not bring myself ere day to the dear church,
And hear matins and mass, as I a monk were,

No ale after meat shall withhold me thence,
Till I have heard evensong, I promise by the rood.
And yet I shall yield again—if I have so much—
All that I wickedly won, since I had wit.
And though I lack a livelihood I will not stop
Till each man have his own, ere I hence wend;
And with the residue and remnant, by the rood of Chester,
I shall seek Saint Truth, ere I see Rome!"
    Robert the robber, on *Reddite* [repentance] he looked
And because there was not wherewith, he wept full sore.
But yet the sinful wretch said to himself:
"Christ, that upon Calvary on the cross died'st,
Though Dismas my brother besought grace of thee,
And thou hadst mercy on that man for *memento* sake,
Thy will be done upon me, as I have well deserved
To have hell forever if no hope there were.
So rue on me, Robert, that no counsel have,
Nor ever ween to win by any craft that I know,
But, for thy much mercy, mitigation I beseech;
Damn me not on Doomsday because I did so ill."
But what befell this felon, I cannot well show,
But well I know he wept hard, water with his eyes,
And acknowledged his guilt to Christ again thereafter,
That the pikestaff of Penitence he should polish anew,
And leap with it o'er the land, all his lifetime,
For he hath lain by *Latro* [thief], Lucifer's brother.
A thousand of men then throng together,
Weeping and wailing for their wicked deeds,
Crying up to Christ, and to His clean Mother
To give grace to seek Saint Truth, God grant they so might!

## CHARM FOR UNFRUITFUL LAND

Erce, Erce, Erce,    Mother of Earth,
May the All-Wielder,    Lord Eternal,
Give flourishing acres    of sprouting shoots,
Acres bountiful    bringing to harvest
Tall stalks    and shining growth,

Acres of broad harvest of barley,
Acres of white harvest of wheat,
And all the harvests of earth!
May Eternal God and His saints in heaven
Defend earth's growth from every foe
That it may be shielded from every evil,
And every sorcery sowed through the land.
Now I pray the All-Wielder who shaped the world
That there may be no woman so wagging of tongue,
Nor any man so cunning of craft,
That may ever pervert the words thus spoken!

*(Then take the plow and turn the first furrow and say:)*

Be healed, O Earth, O Mother of men,
Be hale and growing by grace of God:
Be filled with food for the use of men!

*(Then take meal of every kind and bake a loaf as broad as the inside of the hand, and knead it with milk and with holy water and lay it under the first furrow. Then say:)*

Acre grow full with food for men
Brightly blowing. Be thou blessed
In the name of the Holy One, Maker of heaven,
And Maker of the earth whereon we live.
May God, who made ground, grant sprouting gifts
That each kind of grain may grow for men.

*(Anonymous, X century, Ireland)*

## THE MILK-WHITE DOE

It was a mother and a maid
That walked the woods among;
And still the maid went slow and sad,
And still the mother sung.

"What ails you, daughter Margaret?
Why go you pale and wan,

16. *The Synagogue*. Strasbourg Cathedral.

Is it for a cast of bitter love,
Or for a false leman?"

"It is not for a false lover
That I go sad to see,
But it is for a weary life
Beneath the greenwood tree.
For ever in the good daylight
A maiden may I go,
But always on the ninth midnight
I change to a milk-white doe.

They hunt me through the forest green
With hounds and hunting men;
And ever it is my fair brother
That is so fierce and keen."

. . .

"Good morrow, mother." "Good morrow, son;
Why do they blow so loud?"
"Oh, they are hunting a white doe
Within the glad greenwood.

And three times have they hunted her
And thrice she's won away,
The fourth time that they follow her
That white doe they shall slay."

. . .

Then out and spoke the forester
As he came from the wood,
"Now never saw I maid's gold hair
Among the wild deer's blood.
And I have hunted the wild deer
In east lands and in west;
And never saw I white doe yet
That had a maiden's breast."

Then up and spoke her fair brother,
Between the wine and bread,

## THE IMAGE

"Behold, I had but one sister
And I have seen her dead.

But ye must bury my sweet sister
With a stone at her foot and her head,
And ye must cover her fair body
With the white roses and red.

And I must out to the greenwood;
The rood shall never shelter me;
And I shall lie for seven long years
On the grass below the hawthorn tree."

(*Anonymous, XIII century, England*)

# PART II
# Service

*The medieval universe was a hierarchical scale of created beings governed by law. Each creature by conforming to the law of its nature would obey its Creator and fulfill its proper role in the universal scheme. From lowest to highest, there corresponded to the ascending degrees of perfection a scale of obligations.*

## *The Structure of Service*

*This legal-moral structure of the universe applied as well to human society where the degrees of obligation image those in the universal scale of being. A man's responsibility is to fulfill his given role at the level and in the social group where he finds himself. This ultimate obligation in its purest sense is that of service. Beyond servile obedience one is called to the ideal of service in love—loyalty. And if king and church represent the ultimate arms of God in this world, the ultimate service is loyalty to king and church.*

*But service implies mutual obligation. The king and the church, while they had the right to expect service from those beneath them, had in their keeping the well-being of those who served them. So, too, in every social, political, or economic group of which a man was a member, mutual service implied mutual concern. The agricultural base of society made mutual aid necessary, the manor lord giving protection in return for service. The exact extent of obligation was recorded in charters and Domesday rolls, but the relationship was seldom purely legal. Care was given to the ill and aging peasants; gifts were made on the occasions of birth and marriage; and on the great festivals such as Twelfth Night, when the Yule logs roared in the fireplaces and the steaming bowl of wassail was presented in ceremony, the entire manor celebrated with a holiday allowance of food and wine.*

*In the towns self-protecting alliances of tradesmen developed into the guilds or craft unions. Every industry was unionized under strict rules for membership, training of apprentices, qualifications of masters, aid to indigent members and the fixing of just prices. Price was based not on the value of the work produced, but on the amount needed to maintain the worker and his family—to provide for all necessities, some comforts and an occasional luxury—so that he might retain his self-respect. God, after all, in fashioning the world, had assumed the title of Supreme Craftsman. So, too, St. Benedict required manual labor of his followers. As a Christian, then, the menial laborer had his claim to dignity.*

*There were established relations between the lord and his vassals. The weakest political relationship, however, was that between the lords themselves so that prior to strong central government, private wars were incessant. In the tenth century the Church announced the Pax Dei, outlawing attacks on Church property and tenants, and gradually She extended its scope. The Truce of God forbade fighting on Sundays and major saints' days—some forty of these. Still later the Crusades tended to drain off surplus energy in battling a common enemy.*

*The medievals were a political people with an emphasis on legality. The old Ripuarian law of the Franks had ruled that each man be judged by his own law wherever he went, thus maintaining some continuity of Roman law; but where two laws collided, the issue had to be settled by ordeal—fire, water, or combat. As authority become more territorial, the court of the lord took the place of the ordeal, with trial by jury of one's peers becoming the accepted practice.*

*The ideal of justice was never higher. Although the standard was human perfection in theory, in actual practice it allowed for the frailty of human nature. The idealism of the age carried it far in establishing lasting institutions. Charters of rights were the rule rather than the exception (the Assizes of Jerusa-*

*lem was a near-perfect constitution). Although the Magna Carta is best known, it is only one in a series of royal charters. In 1265, for example, the summons to the English Parliament called for two knights from each shire and two burgesses from each town, extending participation in government to all freemen.*

*Since money-making was always a subordinate activity in the City of God, there developed a controlled economy, rooted in suspicion of the profit-making individual, who seemed to have lost sight of his ultimate purpose in life. The taking of money on non-productive loans was banned as usury; thus it fell to the Jews who did not come under its prohibition. However, if money was loaned for speculation, voyages or merchant ventures, where there was either danger of loss or chance for gain, interest was permitted.*

# ON LAW

## St. Thomas Aquinas

### Whether There Is an Eternal Law

*We proceed thus to the First Article:*

*Objection* 1. It would seem that there is no eternal law. For every law is imposed on someone. But there was not someone from eternity on whom a law could be imposed, since God alone was from eternity. Therefore no law is eternal.

*Objection* 2. Further, promulgation is essential to law. But promulgation could not be from eternity, because there was no one to whom it could be promulgated from eternity. Therefore no law can be eternal.

*Objection* 3. Further, law implies order to an end. But nothing ordained to an end is eternal, for the last end alone is eternal. Therefore no law is eternal.

*On the contrary,* Augustine says: *That Law which is the Supreme Reason cannot be understood to be otherwise than unchangeable and eternal.*

*I answer that,* As we have stated above, law is nothing else but a dic-

17. *The Merode Altarpiece*, the Master of Flémalle (Robert Campin). Flemish, active by 1406, died 1444.

tate of practical reason emanating from the ruler who governs a perfect community. Now it is evident, granted that the world is ruled by divine providence, as was stated, that the whole community of the universe is governed by the divine reason. Therefore the very notion of the government of things in God, the ruler of the universe, has the nature of a law. And since the divine reason's conception of things is not subject to time, but is eternal, according to *Prov.* viii. 23, therefore it is that this kind of law must be called eternal.

*Reply to Objection* 1. Those things that do not exist in us exist in God, inasmuch as they are known and preordained by Him, according to *Rom.* iv. 17: *Who calls those things that are not, as those that are not.* Accordingly, the eternal concept of the divine law bears the character of an eternal law in so far as it is ordained by God to the government of things foreknown by Him.

*Reply to Objection* 2. Promulgation is made by word of mouth or in writing, and in both ways the eternal law is promulgated, because both the divine Word and the writings of the Book of Life are eternal. But the promulgation cannot be from eternity on the part of the creature that hears or reads.

*Reply to Objection* 3. Law implies order to the end actively, namely, in so far as it directs certain things to the end; but not passively,—that is to say, the law itself is not ordained to the end, except accidentally, in a governor whose end is extrinsic to him, and to which end his law must need be ordained. But the end of the divine government is God Himself, and His law is not something other than Himself. Therefore the eternal law is not ordained to another end.

## Whether There Is in Us a Natural Law

*We proceed thus to the Second Article:*

*Objection* 1. It would seem that there is no natural law in us. For man is governed sufficiently by the eternal law, since Augustine says that *the eternal law is that by which it is right that all things should be most orderly.* But nature does not abound in superfluities as neither does she fail in necessaries. Therefore man has no natural law.

*Objection* 2. Further, by the law man is directed, in his acts, to the end, as was stated above. But the directing of human acts to their end is not a function of nature, as is the case in irrational creatures, which act for an end solely by their natural appetite; whereas man acts for an end by his reason and will. Therefore man has no natural law.

*Objection* 3. Further, the more a man is free, the less is he under the law. But man is freer than all the animals because of his free choice, with which he is endowed with distinction from all the other animals. Since, therefore, other animals are not subject to a natural law, neither is man subject to a natural law.

*On the contrary,* The *Gloss* on *Rom.* ii.1: (*When the Gentiles, who have not the law, do by nature those things that are of the law*) comments as follows: *Although they have no written law, yet they have the natural law, whereby each one knows, and is concious of, what is good and what is evil.*

*I answer that,* As we have stated above, law, being a rule and measure, can be in a person in two ways: in one way, as in him that rules and measures; in another way, as in that which is ruled and measured, since a thing is ruled and measured in so far as it partakes of the rule or measure. Therefore, since all things subject to the divine providence are ruled and measured by the eternal law, as we have stated above, it is evident that all things partake in some way in the eternal law, in so far as, namely, from its being imprinted on them, they derive their respective inclinations to their proper acts and ends. Now among all others, the rational creature is subject to divine providence in a more excellent way, in so far as it itself partakes of a share of providence, by being provident both for itself and for others. Therefore it has a share of the eternal reason, whereby it has a natural inclination to its proper act and end; and this participation of the eternal law in the rational creature is called the natural law. Hence the Psalmist, after saying (Ps. iv. 6): *Offer up the sacrifice of justice,* as though someone asked what the works of justice are, adds: *Many say, Who showeth us the good things?* in answer to which question he says: *The light of Thy countenence, O Lord, is signed upon us.* He thus implies that the light of natural reason, whereby we discern what is good and what is evil, which is the function of the natural law, is nothing else than an imprint on us of the divine light. It is therefore evident that the natural law is nothing else than the rational creatures participation of the eternal law.

*Reply to Objection* 1. This argument would hold if the natural law were something different from the eternal law; whereas it is nothing but a participation thereof, as we have stated above.

*Reply to Objection* 2. Every act of reason and will in us is based on that which is according to nature, as was stated above. For every act of reasoning is based on principles that are known naturally, and every act of appetite in respect of the means is derived from the natural appetite in respect of the last end. Accordingly, the first direction of our acts to their end must needs be through the natural law.

*Reply to Objection* 3. Even irrational animals partake in their own way of the eternal reason, just as the rational creature does. But because the rational creature partakes thereof in an intellectual and rational manner, therefore the participation of the eternal law in the rational creature is properly called a law, since a law is something pertaining to reason, as was stated above. Irrational creatures, however, do not partake thereof in a rational manner, and therefore there is no participation of the eternal law in them, except by way of likeness.

## Whether the Eternal Law Is a Supreme Exemplar Existing in God

*We proceed thus to the First Article:*

*Objection* 1. It would seem that the eternal law is not a supreme exemplar existing in God. For there is only one eternal law. But there are many exemplars of things in the divine mind, for Augustine says that God *made each thing according to its exemplar.* Therefore the eternal law does not seem to be the same as an exemplar existing in the divine mind.

*Objection* 2. Further, it is of the nature of a law that it be promulgated by word, as was stated above. But *Word* is a Personal name in God, as was stated in the First Part, whereas *exemplar* refers to the essence. Therefore the eternal law is not the same as a divine exemplar.

*Objection* 3. Further, as Augustine says: *We see a law above our minds, which is called truth.* But the law which is above our minds is the eternal law. Therefore truth is the eternal law. But the notion of truth is not the same as the notion of an exemplar. Therefore the eternal law is not the same as the supreme exemplar.

*On the contrary,* Augustine says that *the eternal law is the supreme exemplar, to which we must always conform.*

*I answer that,* Just as in every artificer there pre-exists an exemplar of the things that are made by his art, so too in every governor there must pre-exist the exemplar of the order of those things that are to be done by those who are subject to his government. And just as the exemplar of the things yet to be made by an art is called the art or model of the products of that art, so, too, the exemplar in him who governs the acts of his subjects bears the character of a law, provided the other conditions be present which we have mentioned above as belonging to the nature of law. Now God, by His wisdom, is the Creator of all things, in relation to which He stands as the artificer to the products of His art, as was stated in the First Part. Moreover, He governs all the acts and movements that are to be found in each single creature, as was also stated in the First Part. Therefore, just as the exemplar of the divine wisdom, inasmuch as all things are created by it, has the character of an art, a model or an idea, so the exemplar of divine wisdom, as moving all things to their due end, bears the character of law. Accordingly, the eternal law is nothing else than the exemplar of divine wisdom, as directing all actions and movements.

*Reply to Objection* 1. Augustine is speaking in that passage of ideal exemplars which refer to the proper nature of each single thing; and consequently in them there is a certain distinction and plurality, according to their different relations to things, as we stated in the First Part. But law is said to direct human acts by ordaining them to the common good, as we have stated above. Now things which are in themselves diverse may be considered as one, according as they are ordained to something common. Therefore the eternal law is one since it is the exemplar of this order.

*Reply to Objection* 2. With regard to any sort of word, two points may be considered: viz., the word itself, and that which is expressed by the word. For the spoken word is something uttered by the mouth of man, and expresses that which is signified by the human word. The same applies to the human mental word, which is nothing else than something conceived by the mind, by which man expresses mentally the things of which he is thinking. So, too, in God, therefore, the word conceived by the intellect of the Father is the name of a Person; but all the things that are in the Father's knowledge, whether they refer to the essence or to the Persons, or to the works of God, are expressed by this Word, as Augustine declares. But among other things expressed by this Word, the eternal law itself is expressed thereby. Nor does it follow that the eternal law is a Personal name in God. Nevertheless, it is appropriated to the Son, because of the suitability of *exemplar* to *word.*

*Reply to Objection* 3. The exemplars of the divine intellect do not stand in the same relation to things as do the exemplars of the human intellect. For the human intellect is measured by things, so that a human concept is not by reason of itself, but by reason of its consonant with things, since *an opinion is true or false according as things are or are not.* But the divine intellect is the measure of things, since each thing has truth in it in so far as it is like the divine intellect, as we have stated in the First Part. Consequently the divine intellect is true in itself, and its exemplar is truth itself.

## ROLL OF A MANOR IN SUSSEX

Extent of the manor of Bernehorne, made on Wednesday following the feast of St. Gregory the Pope in the thirty-fifth year of the reign of King Edward, in the presence of Brother Thomas, keeper of Marley, John de la More, and Adam de Thurhlegh, clerks, on the oath of Godecoumbe, Walter le Perker, Richard le Knyst, Richard the son of the latter, Andrew of Estone, Stephen Morsprich, Thomas Bremble, William of Swynham, John Pollard, Roger le Glede, John Syward, and John de Lillingewist, who say that there are all the following holdings:

. . .

John Pollard holds a half acre in Aldeithewisse and owes 18d. at the four terms and owes for it relief and heriot.

John Suthinton holds a house and 40 acres of land and owes 3s.6d. at Easter and Michaelmas.

William of Swynham holds one acre of meadow in the thicket of Swynham and owes 1d. at the feast of Michaelmas.

Ralph of Leybourne holds a cottage and 1 acre of land in Pinden and owes 3s. at Easter and Michaelmas and attendance in the court in the manor every three weeks, also relief and heriot. . . .

Alexander Hamound holds a little piece of land near Alde wisse and owes 1 goose of the value of 2d.

The sum of the whole rent of the free tenants, with the value of the goose, is 18s.9d.

They say, moreover, that John of Cayworth holds a house and 30 acres of land, and owes yearly at Easter and Michaelmas 2s.; and he

18. Calendar of September from *The Book of Hours of Jean, Duke of Berry,* Limbourg Brothers. French manuscript, XV century.

owes a cock and two hens at Christmastime of the value of 4d.

And he ought to harrow for 2 days at the Lenten sowing with one man and his own horse and his own harrow, the value of the work being 4d.; and he is to receive from the lord on each day 3 meals, of the value of 5d. and then the lord will be at a loss of 1d. Thus his harrowing is of no value to the service of the lord.

And he ought to carry the manure of the lord for 2 days with 1 cart, with his own 2 oxen, the value of the work being 8d.; and he is to receive from the lord each day three meals as above. And thus the service is worth 3d. clear.

And he shall find one man for 2 days for mowing the meadow of the lord, who can mow, by estimation, 1 acre and a half, the value of the mowing of an acre being 6d.; and the sum is therefore 9d. And he is to receive each day 3 meals of the value given above. And thus that mowing is worth 4d. clear.

And he ought to gather and carry that same hay which he has cut, the price of the work being 3d.

And he shall have from the lord 2 meals for 1 man, of the value of 1½d. Thus the work will be worth 1½d. clear.

And he ought to carry the hay of the lord for 1 day with a cart and 3 animals of his own, the price of the work being 6d. And he shall have from the lord 3 meals of the value of 2½d. And thus the work is worth 3½d. clear.

And he ought to carry in autumn beans or oats for 2 days with a cart and 3 animals of his own, the value of the work being 12d. And he shall receive from the lord each day 3 meals of the value given above. And thus the value of the work is worth 7d. clear.

And he ought to carry wood from the woods of the lord as far as the manor, for two days in summer, with a cart and 3 animals of his own, the value of the work being 9d. And he shall receive from the lord each day 3 meals of the price given above. And thus the work is worth 4d. clear.

And he ought to find 1 man for 2 days to cut heath, the value of the work being 4d., and he shall have 2 meals each day of the value given above; and thus the lord will lose, if he receives his services, 3d. Thus that mowing is worth nothing to the service of the lord.

And he ought to carry the heath which he has cut, the value of the work being 5d. And he shall receive from the lord 3 meals at the price of 2½d. And thus the work will be worth 2½d. clear.

And he ought to carry to Battle, twice in the summer season each time half a load of grain, the value of the work being 4d. And he shall receive in the manor each time 1 meal of the value of 2d. And thus the work is worth 2d. clear.

The total of the rents, with the value of the hens, is 2s.4d. The total of the value of the works is 2s.3½d., owed from the said John yearly.

. . .

And it is to be noted that none of the above-named villeins can give their daughters in marriage, nor cause their sons to be tonsured, nor can they cut down timber growing on the lands they hold, without license of the bailiff or sergeant of the land, and then for building purposes and not otherwise. And after the death of any one of the aforesaid villeins, the lord shall have as a heriot his best animal, if he had any; if, however, he have no living beast, the lord shall have no heriot, as they say. The sons and daughters of the aforesaid villeins shall give, for entrance into the holding after the death of their predecessors, as much as they give of rent a year.

(*Anonymous, XII century, England*)

## CORONATION CHARTER OF HENRY I

In the year of the incarnation of the Lord 1101, Henry, son of King William, after the death of his brother William, by the grace of God, king of the English, to all faithful, greeting.

1. Know that by the mercy of God, and by the common counsel of the barons of the whole kingdom of England, I have been crowned king of the same kingdom; and because the kingdom has been oppressed by unjust exactions, I, from regard to God, and from the love which I have toward you, in the first place, make the holy church of God free, so that I will neither sell nor place at rent, nor, when archbishop, or bishop, or abbot is dead, will I take anything from the domain of the church, or from its men, until a successor is installed into it. And all the evil customs by which the realm of England was unjustly oppressed will I take away, which evil customs I partly set down here.

2. If any of my barons or earls or others who hold from me shall have died, his heir shall not redeem his land as he did in the time of my

brother, but shall relieve it by a just and legitimate relief. Similarly also the men of my barons shall relieve their lands from their lords by a just and legitimate relief.

3. And if any of the barons or other men of mine wishes to give his daughter in marriage, or his sister or niece or relation, he must speak with me about it, but I will neither take anything from him for this permission, nor forbid him to give her in marriage, unless he should wish to join her to my enemy. And if when a baron or other man of mine is dead, a daughter remains as heir, I will give her in marriage according to the judgment of my barons, along with her lands. And if when a man is dead his wife remains and is without children, she shall have her dowry and right of marriage, and I will not give her to a husband except according to her will.

4. And if a wife has survived with children, she shall have her dowry and right of marriage, so long as she shall have kept her body legitimately, and I will not give her in marriage, except it be according to her will. And the guardian of the land and children shall be either the wife or another one of the relatives, as shall seem to be most just. And I require that my barons should deal similarly with the sons and daughters and wives of their men. . . .

7. And if any of my barons or men shall become feeble, however he himself shall give or arrange to give his money, I grant that it shall be so given. Moreover, if he himself, prevented by arms or weakness, shall not have bestowed his money, or arranged to bestow it, his wife or his children or his parents, and his legitimate men shall divide it for his soul, as to them shall seem best.

8. If any of my barons or men shall have committed an offense, he shall not give security to the extent of forfeiture of his money, as he did in the time of my father, or of my brother, but according to the measure of the offense so shall he pay, as he would have paid from the time of my father backward, in the time of my other predecessors; so that if he shall have been convicted, of treachery or of crime, he shall pay as is just.

9. All murders, moreover, before that day in which I was crowned king, I pardon; and those which shall be done, henceforth shall be punished justly according to the law of King Edward.

10. The forests, by the common agreement of my barons, I have retained in my own hand, as my father had them.

11. To those knights who hold their land by the cuirass, I yield of my own gift the lands of their demesne, plows, free from all payments and

from all labor, so that as they have thus been favored by such a great alleviation, so they may readily provide themselves with horses and arms for my service and for the defense of the kingdom.

12. A firm peace in my whole kingdom I establish and require to be kept from henceforth.

13. The law of King Edward I give to you again, with those changes with which my father changed it by the counsel of his barons.

14. If any one has taken anything from my possession since the death of King William, my brother, or from the possessions of any one, let the whole be immediately returned without alteration; and if any one shall have retained anything thence, he upon whom it is found shall pay it heavily to me. Witnesses Maurice, bishop of London, and Gundulf, bishop, and William, bishop-elect, and Henry, earl, and Simon, earl, and Walter Giffard, and Robert de Montfort, and Roger Bigod, and Henry de Port, at London, when I was crowned.

(*Anonymous, c. A.D. 1100, England*)

## RULES OF THE GUILD OF WHITE TAWYERS

In honour of God, of our Lady, and of All Saints, and for the nurture of tranquillity and peace among the good folk, the Megucers, called white tawyers, the folk of the same trade have, by assent of Richard Lacer, mayor, and of the Aldermen, ordained the points underwritten.

In the first place, they have ordained that they will furnish a wax candle, to burn before our Lady, in the church of All-Hallows, near London wall.

Also, that each person of the said trade shall put in the box such sum as he shall think fit, in aid of maintaining said candle.

Also, if by chance any of the said trade shall fall into poverty whether through old age or because he cannot labor or work, and shall have nothing with which to keep himself, he shall have every week from the said box seven pence for his support, if he be a man of good repute. And after his decease, if he have a wife, a woman of good repute, she shall have weekly for her support seven pence from the said box, so long as she shall behave herself well and remain single.

And that no stranger shall work in the said trade, or keep a house for the same in the city, if he be not an apprentice, or a man admitted to the franchise of the said city.

And that no one shall take the serving man of another to work with him, during his term, unless it be with the permission of his master.

And if anyone of the said trade shall have work in his house that he cannot complete, or if for want of assistance such work shall be in danger of being lost, those of the said trade shall aid him. so that the said work shall be not lost.

And if anyone of the said trade shall depart this life and have not wherewithal to be buried, he shall be buried at the expense of the common box. And when any one of the said trade shall die, all those of the said trade shall go to the vigil and make offering on the morrow.

*(Anonymous, XIII century, England)*

## ON LABOR

### St. Benedict of Nursia

Idleness is an enemy of the soul. Because this is so the brethren ought to be occupied at specified times in manual labour and at other fixed hours in holy reading. We therefore think that both these may be arranged for as follows: from Easter to the first of October, on coming out from Prime, let the brethern labour till about the fourth hour. From the fourth till close upon the sixth hour let them employ themselves in reading. On rising from table after the sixth hour let them rest on their beds in strict silence; but if anyone shall wish to read, let him do so in such a way as not to disturb any one else.

Let *None* be said somewhat before the time, about the middle of the eighth hour, and after this all shall work at what they have to do till evening. If, however, the nature of the place or poverty require them to labour at gathering in the harvest, let them not grieve at that, for then are they truly monks when they live by the labour of their hands, as our Fathers and the Apostles did. Let everything, however, be done with moderation for the sake of the faint-hearted.

From the first of October till the beginning of Lent let the brethren be occupied in reading till the end of the second hour. At that time

19. Bronze chandelier. Flemish or German metalwork, XV century.

*Tierce* shall be said, after which they shall labour at the work enjoined them till *None*. At the first signal for the hour of *None* all shall cease to work, so as to be ready when the second signal is given. After their meal they shall be employed in reading or on the psalms.

On the days of Lent, from the morning till the end of the third hour, the brethren are to have time for reading, after which let them work at what is set them to do till the close of the tenth hour. During these Lenten days let each one have some book from the library which he shall read through carefully. These books are to be given out at the beginning of Lent.

It is of much import that one or two seniors be appointed to go about the monastery at such times as the brethren are free to read, in order to see that no one is slothful, given to idleness or foolish talking instead of reading, and so not only makes no profit himself but also distracts others. If any such be found (which God forbid) let him be corrected once or twice, and if he amend not let him be subjected to regular discipline of such a character that the rest may take warning. Moreover one brother shall not associate with another at unsuitable hours.

On Sunday also, all, save those who are assigned to various offices, shall have time for reading. If, however, any one be so negligent and slothful as to be unwilling or unable to read or meditate, he must have some work given him, so as not to be idle. For weak brethren or those of delicate constitutions, some work or craft shall be found to keep them from idleness, and yet not such as to crush them by the heavy labour or to drive them away. The weakness of such brethren must be taken into consideration by the abbot. . . .

Let him (the abbot) make no distinction of persons in the monastery. Let not one be loved more than another, save such as be found to excel in obedience or good works. Let not the free-born be put before the serf-born in religion, unless there be other reasonable cause for it. If upon due consideration the abbot shall see such cause he may place him where he pleases; otherwise let all keep their own places, because *whether bond or free we are all one in Christ,* and bear an equal burden of service under one Lord; for *with God there is no accepting of persons.* For one thing only are we preferred by Him, if we are found better than others in good works and more humble. Let the abbot therefore have equal love for all and let all, according to their deserts, be under the same discipline. . . .

(from *The Rule of St. Benedict*)

# *Chivalry*

*The social outgrowth of the sense of obligation was chivalry. The search of the knights for the Holy Grail, retold in much medieval literature, shows chivalry at its shining best. Chaucer's "true and gentle, perfect knight" had loved chivalry, truth and honor, generosity and courtesy from boyhood. The knight pledged fealty to his lord and, in offering homage, was proud of himself as a man rather than feeling demeaned by his subordination. The lord accepted the responsibilities of leadership, he in turn being the man of a greater lord and ultimately of the king. To his other virtues was added that of loyalty. The medievals found in loyalty their highest virtue: St. Ambrose, for example, wrote of the fall of Adam as a failure in loyalty, and Dante reserved special scorn for those who sinned against this essential claim on their honor.*

## THE SONG OF ROLAND

. . .

In morning time is risen the Emperere,
Mattins and Mass he's heard, and made his prayer;
On the green grass before the tent his chair,
Where Rollant stood and that bold Oliver,
Neimès the Duke, and many others there.
Guenès arrived, the felon perjurer,
Begins to speak, with very cunning air,
Says to the King: "God keep you, Sire, I swear!
Of Sarraguce the keys to you I bear,
Tribute I bring you, very great and rare,
And twenty men; look after them with care.
Proud Marsilies bade me this word declare:
That the alcaliph, his uncle, you must spare.
My own eyes saw four hundred thousand there,
In hauberks dressed, closed helms that gleamed in the air,
And golden hilts upon their swords they bare.
They followed him, right to the sea they'ld fare;

Marsile they left, that would their faith forswear,
For Christendom they've neither wish nor care.
But the fourth league they had not compassed, ere
Brake from the North tempest and storm in the air;
Then were they drowned, they will no more appear.
Were he alive, I should have brought him here.
The pagan king, in truth, Sire, bids you hear,
Ere you have seen one month pass of this year
He'll follow you to France, to your Empire,
He will accept the laws you hold and fear;
Joining his hands, will do you homage there,
Kingdom of Spain will hold as you declare."
Then says the King: "Now God be praised, I swear!
Well have you wrought, and rich reward shall wear."
Bids through the host a thousand trumpets blare.
Franks leave their lines; the sumpter-beasts are yare;
T'wards France the Douce all on their way repair.

Charles the Great that land of Spain had wasted,
Her castles ta'en, her cities violated.
Then said the King, his war was now abated.
Towards Douce France that Emperour has hosted.
Upon a lance Rollant his ensign raisèd,
High on a cliff against the sky 'twas placèd;
The Franks in camp through all that country baited.
Cantered pagans, through those wide valleys racèd,
Hauberks they wore, their sarks were doubly plated,
Swords to their sides were girt, their helms were lacèd,
Lances made sharp, escutcheons newly painted:
There in the mists beyond the peaks remainèd,
The day of doom four hundred thousand waited.
God! what a grief. Franks know not what is fated.

Passes the day, the darkness is grown deep.
That Emperour, rich Charlès, lies asleep;
Dreams that he stands in the great pass of Size,
In his two hands his ashen spear he sees;
Guenès the count that spear from him doth seize,
Brandishes it and twists it with such ease,

That flown into the sky the flinders seem.
Charlès sleeps on nor wakens from his dream.

And after this another vision saw,
In France, at Aix, in his Chapelle once more,
That his right arm an evil bear did gnaw;
Out of Ardennes he saw a leopard stalk,
His body dear did savagely assault;
But then there dashed a harrier from the hall,
Leaping in the air he sped to Charlè's call,
By the right ear that felon bear he caught,
And furiously the leopard next he fought.
Of battle great the Franks then seemed to talk,
Yet which might win they knew not, in his thought.
Charlès sleeps on, nor wakens he for aught.

Passes the night and opens the clear day;
That Emperour canters in brave array,
Looks through the host often and everyway;
"My lords barons," at length doth Charlès say,
Ye see the pass along these valleys strait,
Judge for me now, who shall in rereward wait."
"There's my good-son, Rollanz," then answers Guenes,
"You've no baron whose valour is so great."
When the King hears, he looks upon him straight,
And says to him: "You devil incarnate;
Into your heart is come a mortal hate.
And who shall go before me in the gate?"
"Oger is here, of Denmark;" answers Guenes,
"You've no baron were better in that place."

The count Rollanz hath heard himself decreed;
Speaks then to Guenes by rule of courtesy:
"Good-father, Sir, I ought to hold you dear,
Since the rereward you have for me decreed.
Charlès the King will never lose by me,
As I know well, nor charger nor palfrey,
Jennet nor mule that canter can with speed,
Nor sumpter-horse will lose, nor any steed;
But my sword's point shall first exact their meed."
Answers him Guenes: "I know; 'tis true indeed."

. . .

That Emperour, Rollanz then calleth he:
"Fair nephew mine, know this in verity;
Half of my host I leave you presently;
Retain you them; your safeguard this shall be."
Then says the count: "I will not have them, me!
Confound me God, if I fail in the deed!
Good valiant Franks, a thousand score I'll keep.
Go through the pass in all security,
While I'm alive there's no man you need fear."

The count Rollanz has mounted his charger.
Beside him came his comrade Oliver,
Also Gerins and the proof count Geriers,
And Otès came, and also Berengiers,
Old Ansëis, and Sansun too came there,
Gerart also of Rossillon the fierce,
And there is come the Gascon Engeliers.
"Now by my head I'll go!" the Archbishop swears.
"And I'm with you," says then the Count Gualtiers,
"I'm Rollant's man, I may not leave him there."
A thousand score they choose of chevaliers.

Gualter del Hum he calls, that Count Rollanz;
"A thousand Franks take, out of France our land;
Dispose them so, among ravines and crags,
That the Emperour lose not a single man."
Gualter replies: "I'll do as you command."
A thousand Franks, come out of France their land,
At Gualter's word they scour ravines and crags;
They'll not come down, howe'er the news be bad,
Ere from their sheaths swords seven hundred flash.
King Almaris, Belferne for kingdom had,
On the evil day he met them in combat.

High are the peaks, the valleys shadowful,
Swarthy the rocks, the narrows wonderful.
Franks passed that day all very sorrowful,
Fifteen leagues round the rumour of them grew.
When they were come, and Terra Major knew,
Saw Gascony their land and their seigneur's,
Remembering their fiefs and their honours,

Their little maids, their gentle wives and true;
There was not one that shed not tears for rue.
Beyond the rest Charles was of anguish full,
In Spanish Pass he'd left his dear nephew;
Pity him seized; he could but weep for rue.

The dozen peers are left behind in Spain,
Franks in their band a thousand score remain,
No fear have these, death hold they in disdain.
That Emperour goes into France apace;
Under his cloke he fain would hide his face.
Up to his side comes cantering Duke Neimes,
Says to the King: "What grief upon you weighs?"
Charlès answers him: "He's wrong that question makes.
So great my grief I cannot but complain.
France is destroyed, by the device of Guene:
This night I saw, by an angel's vision plain,
Between my hands he brake my spear in twain;
Great fear I have, since Rollant must remain:
I've left him there, upon a border strange.
God! If he's lost, I'll not outlive that shame."

Charlès the great, he cannot but deplore.
And with him Franks an hundred thousand mourn,
Who for Rollanz have marvellous remorse.
The felon Guenes had treacherously wrought;
From pagan king has had his rich reward,
Silver and gold, and veils and silken cloths,
Camels, lions, with many a mule and horse.
Barons from Spain King Marsilies hath called,
Counts and viscounts and dukes and almacours,
And the admirals, and cadets nobly born;
Within three days come hundred thousands four.
In Sarraguce they sound the drums of war;
Mahum they raise upon their highest tow'r,
Pagan is none, that does not him adore.
They canter then with great contention
Through Certeine land, valleys and mountains, on,
Till of the Franks they see the gonfalons,
Being in rereward those dozen companions;
They will not fail battle to do anon.

. . . .

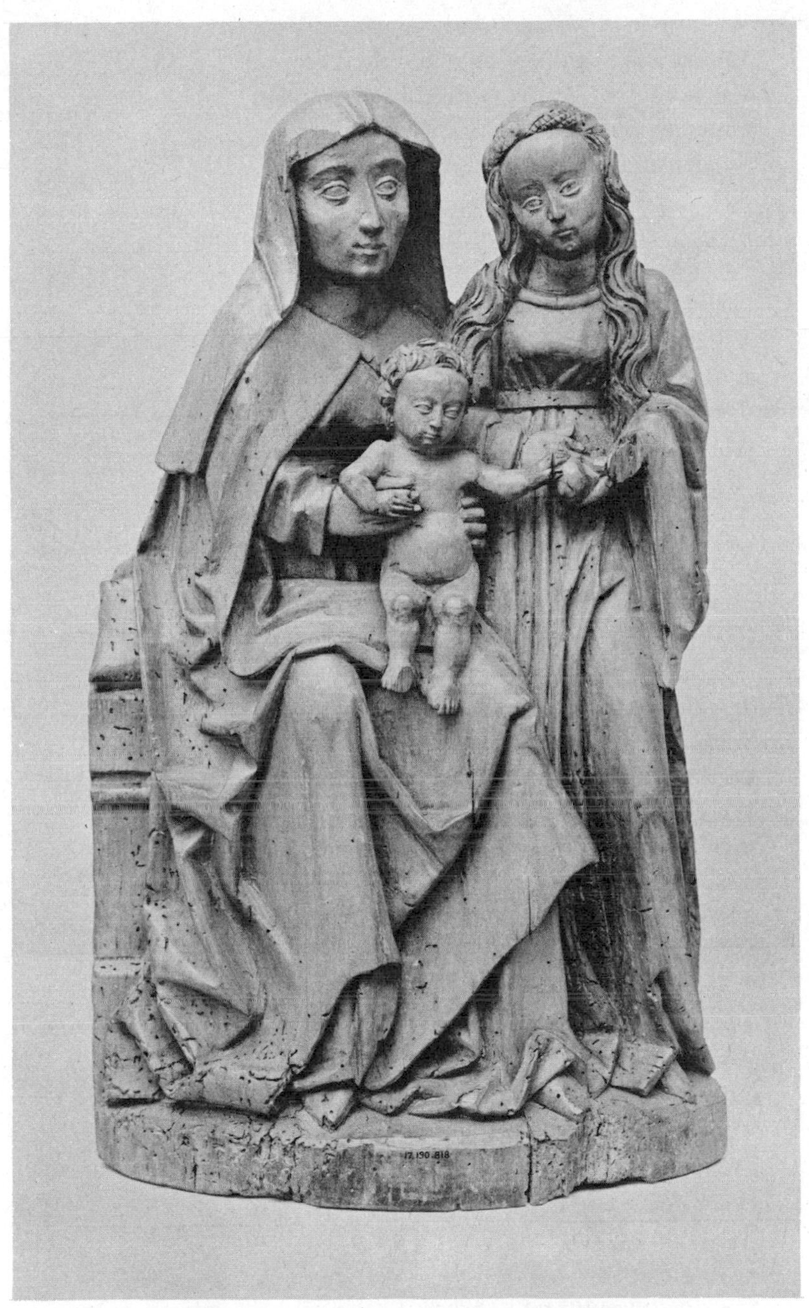

20. Wood relief of St. Anne, Virgin and Child. Germany, XV century.

The battle grows more hard and harder yet,
Franks and pagans, with marvellous onset,
Each other strike and each himself defends.
So many shafts bloodstained and shatterèd,
So many flags and ensigns tatterèd;
So many Franks lose their young lustihead,
Who'll see no more their mothers nor their friends,
Nor hosts of France, that in the pass attend.
Charlès the Great weeps therefor with regret.
What profits that? No succour shall they get.
Evil service, that day, Guenes rendered them,
To Sarraguce going, his own to sell.
After he lost his members and his head,
In court, at Aix, to gallows-tree condemned;
And thirty more with him, of his kindred,
Were hanged, a thing they never did expect.

Now marvellous and weighty the combat,
Right well they strike, Olivier and Rollant,
A thousand blows come from the Archbishop's hand,
The dozen peers are nothing short of that,
With one accord join battle all the Franks.
Pagans are slain by hundred, by thousand,
Who flies not then, from death has no warrant,
Will he or nill, foregoes the allotted span.
The Franks have lost the foremost of their band,
They'll see no more their fathers nor their clans,
Nor Charlemagne, where in the pass he stands.
Torment arose, right marvellous, in France,
Tempest there was, of wind and thunder black,
With rain and hail, so much could not be spanned;
Fell thunderbolts often on every hand,
And verily the earth quaked in answer back
From Saint Michael of Peril unto Sanz,
From Besençun to the harbour of Guitsand;
No house stood there but straight its walls must crack
In full mid-day the darkness was so grand,
Save the sky split, no light was in the land.
Beheld these things with terror every man,
And many said: "We in the Judgement stand;

The end of time is presently at hand."
They spake no truth; they did not understand;
'Twas the great day of mourning for Rollant.

The Franks strike on; their hearts are good and stout.
Pagans are slain, a thousandfold, in crowds,
Left of five score are not two thousands now.
Says the Archbishop: "Our men are very proud,
No man on earth has more nor better found.
In Chronicles of Franks is written down,
What vassalage he had, our Emperour."
Then through the field they go, their friends seek out,
And their eyes weep with grief and pain profound
For kinsmen dear, by hearty friendship bound.
King Marsilies and his great host draw round.

King Marsilies along a valley led
The mighty host that he had gatherèd.
Twenty columns that king had numberèd.
With gleaming gold their helms were jewellèd.
Shone too their shields and sarks embroiderèd.
Sounded the charge seven thousand trumpets,
Great was the noise through all that country went.
Then said Rollanz: "Olivier, brother, friend,
That felon Guenes hath sworn to achieve our death;
For his treason no longer is secret.
Right great vengeance our Emperour will get.
Battle we'll have, both long and keenly set,
Never has man beheld such armies met.
With Durendal my sword I'll strike again,
And, comrade, you shall strike with Halteclere.
These swords in lands so many have we held,
Battles with them so many brought to end,
No evil song shall e'er be sung or said."

When the Franks see so many there, pagans,
On every side covering all the land,
Often they call Olivier and Rollant,
The dozen peers, to be their safe warrant.
And the Archbishop speaks to them, as he can:
"My lords barons, go thinking nothing bad!

For God I pray you fly not hence but stand,
Lest evil songs of our valour men chant!
Far better 't were to perish in the van.
Certain it is, our end is near at hand,
Beyond this day shall no more live one man;
But of one thing I give you good warrant:
Blest Paradise to you now open stands,
By the Innocents your thrones you there shall have."
Upon these words grow bold again the Franks;
There is not one but he "Monjoie" demands.

A Sarrazin was there, of Sarraguce,
Of that city one half was his by use,
'Twas Climborins, a man was nothing proof;
By Guenelun the count an oath he took,
And kissed his mouth in amity and truth,
Gave him his sword and his carbuncle too.
Terra Major, he said, to shame he'ld put,
From the Emperour his crown he would remove.
He sate his horse, which he called Barbamusche,
Never so swift sparrow nor swallow flew,
He spurred him well, and down the reins he threw,
Going to strike Engelier of Gascune;
Nor shield nor sark him any warrant proved,
The pagan spear's point did his body wound,
He pinned him well, and all the steel sent through,
From the hilt flung him dead beneath his foot.
After he said: "Good are they to confuse.
Pagans, strike on, and so this press set loose!"
"God!" say the Franks, "Grief, such a man to lose!"

The count Rollanz called upon Oliver:
"Sir companion, dead now is Engeler;
Than whom we'd no more valiant chevalier."
Answered that count: "God, let me him avenge!"
Spurs of fine gold into his horse drove then,
Held Halteclere, with blood its steel was red,
By virtue great to strike that pagan went,
Brandished his blade, the Sarrazin upset;
The Adversaries of God his soul bare thence.
Next he has slain the duke Alphaïen,

And sliced away Escababi his head,
And has unhorsed some seven Arabs else;
No good for those to go to war again.
Then said Rollanz: "My comrade shews anger,
So in my sight he makes me prize him well;
More dear by Charles for such blows are we held."
Aloud he's cried: "Strike on, the chevaliers!"

From the other part a pagan Valdabron.
Warden he'd been to king Marsilion,
And lord, by sea, of four hundred dromonds;
No sailor was but called his name upon;
Jerusalem he'd taken by treason,
Violated the Temple of Salomon,
The Patriarch had slain before the fonts.
He'd pledged his oath by county Guenelon,
Gave him his sword, a thousand coins thereon.
He sate his horse, which he called Gramimond,
Never so swift flew in the air falcon;
He's pricked him well, with sharp spurs he had on,
Going to strike e'en that rich Duke, Sanson;
His shield has split, his hauberk has undone,
The ensign's folds have through his body gone,
Dead from the hilt out of his seat he's dropt:
"Pagans, strike on, for well we'll overcome!"
"God!" say the Franks, "Grief for a brave baron!"

The count Rollanz, when Sansun dead he saw,
You may believe, great grief he had therefor.
His horse he spurs, gallops with great effort,
Wields Durendal, was worth fine gold and more,
Goes as he may to strike that baron bold
Above the helm, that was embossed with gold,
Slices the head, the sark, and all the corse,
The good saddle, that was embossed with gold,
And cuts deep through the backbone of his horse;
He's slain them both, blame him for that or laud.
The pagans say: " 'Twas hard on us, that blow."
Answers Rollanz: "Nay, love you I can not,
For on your side is arrogance and wrong."

Out of Affrike an Affrican was come,
'Twas Malquiant, the son of king Malcud;
With beaten gold was all his armour done,
Fore all men's else it shone beneath the sun.
He sate his horse, which he called Salt-Perdut,
Never so swift was any beast could run.
And Anséis upon the shield he struck,
The scarlat with the blue he sliced it up,
Of his hauberk he's torn the folds and cut,
The steel and stock has through his body thrust.
Dead is that count, he's no more time to run.
Then say the Franks: "Baron, an evil luck!"

Swift through the field Turpin the Archbishop passed;
Such shaven-crown has never else sung Mass
Who was his limbs such prowess might compass;
To th'pagan said: "God send thee all that's bad!
One thou hast slain for whom my heart is sad."
So his good horse forth at his bidding ran,
He's struck him then on his shield Toledan,
Until he flings him dead on the green grass.

. . .

The count Rollanz, his sword with blood is stained,
Well has he heard what way the Franks complained;
Such grief he has, his heart would split in twain:
To the pagan says: "God send thee every shame!
One hast thou slain whom dearly thou'lt replay."
He spurs his horse, that on with speed doth strain;
Which should forfeit, they both together came.

Grandonie was both proof and valiant,
And virtuous, a vassal combatant.
Upon the way there, he has met Rollant;
He'd never seen, yet knew him at a glance,
By the proud face and those fine limbs he had,
By his regard, and by his contenance;
He could not help but he grew faint thereat,
He would escape, nothing avail he can.
Struck him the count, with so great virtue, that

To the nose-plate he's all the helmet cracked,
Sliced through the nose and mouth and teeth he has,
Hauberk close-mailed, and all the whole carcass,
Saddle of gold, with plates of silver flanked,
And of his horse has deeply scarred the back;
He's slain them both, they'll make no more attack:
The Spanish men in sorrow cry, "Alack!"
Then say the Franks: "He strikes well, our warrant."

Marvellous is the battle in its speed,
The Franks there strike with vigour and with heat,
Cutting through wrists and ribs and chines indeed,
Through garments to the lively flesh beneath;
On the green grass the clear blood runs in streams.
Then pagans say: "No more we'll suffer, we.
Terra Major, Mahummet's curse on thee!
Beyond all men thy people are hardy!"
There was not one but cried then: "Marsilie,
Canter, o king, thy succour now we need!"

Marvellous is the battle now and grand,
The Franks there strike, their good brown spears in hand.
Then had you seen such sorrowing of clans,
So many a slain, shattered and bleeding man!
Biting the earth, or piled there on their backs!
The Sarrazins cannot such loss withstand.
Will they or nill, from off the field draw back;
By lively force chase them away the Franks.

Their martyrdom, his men's, Marsile has seen,
So he bids sound his horns and his buccines;
Then canters forth with all his great army.
Canters before a Sarrazin, Abisme,
More felon none was in that company;
Cankered with guile and every felony,
He fears not God, the Son of Saint Mary;
Black is that man as molten pitch that seethes;
Better he loves murder and treachery
Than to have all the gold of Galicie;
Never has man beheld him sport for glee;
Yet vassalage he's shown, and great folly,

So is he dear to th' felon king Marsile;
Dragon he bears, to which his tribe rally.
That Archbishop could never love him, he;
Seeing him there, to strike he's very keen,
Within himself he says all quietly:
"This Sarrazin great heretick meseems,
Rather I'ld die, than not go slay him clean,
Ne'er did I love coward nor cowardice."

. . .

The count Rollanz great loss of his men sees,
His companion Olivier calls, and speaks:
"Sir and comrade, in God's Name, That you keeps,
Such good vassals you see lie here in heaps;
For France the Douce, fair country, may we weep,
Of such barons long desolate she'll be.
Ah! King and friend, wherefore are you not here?
How, Oliver, brother, can we achieve?
And by what means our news to him repeat?"
Says Oliver: "I know not how to seek;
Rather I'ld die than shame come of this feat."

Then says Rollanz: "I'll wind this olifant,
If Charlès hear, where in the pass he stands,
I pledge you now they will return, the Franks."
Says Oliver: "Great shame would come of that;
And a reproach on every one, your clan,
That shall endure while each lives in the land,
When I implored, you would not do this act;
Doing it now, no praise from me you'll have:
So wind your horn, but not by courage rash,
Seeing that both your arms with blood are splashed."
Answers that count: "Fine blows I've struck them back."

Then says Rollant: "Strong is it now, our battle;
I'll wind my horn, so the King hears it, Charlès."
Says Oliver: "That act were not a vassal's.
When I implored you, comrade, you were wrathful.
Were the King here, we had not borne such damage.
Nor should we blame those with him there, his army."

21. *The Visitation*. Reims Cathedral, c. 1225-1245.

Says Oliver: "Now by my beard, hereafter
If I may see my gentle sister Alde,
She in her arms, I swear, shall never clasp you."

Then says Rollanz: "Wherefore so wroth with me?"
He answers him: "Comrade, it was your deed:
Vassalage comes by sense, and not folly;
Prudence more worth is than stupidity.
Here are Franks dead, all for your trickery;
No service more to Carlun may we yield.
My lord were here now, had you trusted me,
And fought and won this battle then had we,
Taken or slain were the king Marsilie.
In your prowess, Rollanz, no good we've seen!
Charlès the great in vain your aid will seek—
None such as he till God His Judgement speak;—
Here must you die, and France in shame be steeped;
Here perishes our loyal company,
Before this night great severance and grief."

That Archbishop has heard them, how they spoke,
His horse he pricks with his fine spurs of gold,
Coming to them he takes up his reproach:
"Sir Oliver, and you, Sir Rollant, both,
For God I pray, do not each other scold!
No help it were to us, the horn to blow,
But, none the less, it may be better so;
The King will come, with vengeance that he owes;
These Spanish men never away shall go.
Our Franks here, each descending from his horse,
Will find us dead, and limb from body torn;
They'll take us hence, on biers and litters borne;
With pity and with grief for us they'll mourn;
They'll bury each in some old minister-close;
No wolf nor swine nor dog shall gnaw our bones."
Answers Rollant: "Sir, very well you spoke."

Rollant hath set the olifant to his mouth,
He grasps it well, and with great virtue sounds.
High are those peaks, afar it rings and loud,
Thirty great leagues they hear its echoes mount.

So Charlès heard, and all his comrades round;
Then said that King: "Battle they do, our counts."
And Guenelun answered, contrarious:
"That were a lie, in any other mouth."

The Count Rollanz, with sorrow and with pangs,
And with great pain sounded his olifant:
Out of his mouth the clear blood leaped and ran,
About his brain the very temples cracked.
Loud is its voice, that horn he holds in hand;
Charlès hath heard, where in the pass he stands,
And Neimès hears, and listen all the Franks.
Then says the King: "I hear his horn, Rollant's;
He'ld never sound, but he were in combat."
Answers him Guenes: "It is no battle, that.
Now are you old, blossoming white and blanched,
Yet by such words you still appear infant.
You know full well the great pride of Rollant;
Marvel it is, God stays so tolerant.
Noples he took, not waiting your command;
Thence issued forth the Sarrazins, a band
With vassalage had fought against Rollant;
He slew them first, with Durendal his brand,
Then washed their blood with water from the land;
So what he'd done might not be seen of man.
He for a hare goes all day, horn in hand;
Before his peers in foolish jest he brags.
No race neath heav'n in field him dare attack.
So canter on! Nay, wherefore hold we back?
Terra Major is far away, our land."

The count Rollanz, though blood his mouth doth stain,
And burst are both the temples of his brain,
His olifant he sounds with grief and pain;
Charlès hath heard, listen the Franks again.
"That horn," the King says, "hath a mighty strain!"
Answers Duke Niemes: "A baron blows with pain!
Battle is there, indeed I see it plain,
He is betrayed, by one that still doth feign.
Equip you, sir, cry out your old refrain,

That noble band, go succour them amain!
Enough you've heard how Rollant doth complain."

That Emperour hath bid them sound their horns.
The Franks dismount, and dress themselves for war,
Put hauberks on, helmets and golden swords;
Fine shields they have, and spears of length and force
Scarlat and blue and white their ensigns float.
His charger mounts each baron of the host;
They spur with haste as through the pass they go.
Nor was there one but thus to's neighbour spoke:
"Now, ere he die, may we see Rollant, so
Ranged by his side we'll give some goodly blows."
But what avail? They've stayed too long below.

The even-tide is light as was the day;
Their armour shines beneath the sun's clear ray,
Hauberks and helms throw off a dazzling flame,
And blazoned shields, flowered in bright array,
Also their spears, with golden ensigns gay.
That Emperour, he canters on with rage,
And all the Franks with wonder and dismay;
There is not one can bitter tears restrain,
And for Rollant they're very sore afraid.
The King has bid them seize that county Guene,
And charged with him the scullions of his train;
The master-cook he's called, Besgun by name:
"Guard me him well, his felony is plain,
Who in my house vile treachery has made."
He holds him, and a hundred others takes
From the kitchen, both good and evil knaves;
Then Guenè's beard and both his cheeks they shaved,
And four blows each with their closed fists they gave,
They trounced him well with cudgels and with staves,
And on his neck they clasped an iron chain;
So like a bear enchained they held him safe,
On a pack mule they set him in his shame:
Kept him till Charles should call for him again.

High were the peaks and shadowy and grand,
The valleys deep, the rivers swiftly ran.

Trumpets they blew in rear and in the van,
Till all again answered that olifant.
That Emperour canters with fury mad,
And all the Franks dismay and wonder have;
There is not one but weeps and waxes sad
And all pray God that He will guard Rollant
Till in the field together they may stand;
There by his side they'll strike as well they can.
But what avail? No good there is in that;
They're not in time; too long have they held back.

In his great rage on canters Charlemagne;
Over his sark his beard is flowing plain.
Barons of France, in haste they spur and strain;
There is not one that can his wrath contain
That they are not with Rollant the Captain,
Whereas he fights the Sarrazins of Spain.
If he be struck, will not one soul remain.
—God! Sixty men are all now in his train!
Never a king had better Capitains.

Rollant regards the barren mountain-sides;
Dead men of France, he sees so many lie,
And weeps for them as fits a gentle knight:
"Lords and barons, may God to you be kind!
And all your souls redeem for Paradise!
And let you there mid holy flowers lie!
Better vassals than you saw never I.
Ever you've served me, and so long a time,
By you Carlon hath conquered kingdoms wide;
That Emperour reared you for evil plight!
Douce land of France, o very precious clime,
Laid desolate by such a sour exile!
Barons of France, for me I've seen you die,
And no support, no warrant could I find;
God be your aid, Who never yet hath lied!
I must not fail now, brother, by your side;
Save I be slain, for sorrow shall I die.
Sir companion, let us again go strike!"

. . .

But what avail? Though fled be Marsilies,
He's left behind his uncle, the alcaliph
Who holds Alferne, Kartagene, Garmalie,
And Ethiope, a cursèd land indeed;
The blackamoors from there are in his keep,
Broad in the nose they are and flat in the ear,
Fifty thousand and more in company.
These canter forth with arrogance and heat,
Then they cry out the pagans' rallying-cheer;
And Rollant says: "Martyrdom we'll receive;
Not long to live, I know it well, have we;
Felon he's named that sells his body cheap!
Strike on, my lords, with burnished swords and keen;
Contest each inch your life and death between,
That ne'er by us Douce France in shame be steeped.
When Charles my lord shall come into this field,
Such discipline of Sarrazins he'll see,
For one of ours he'll find them dead fifteen;
He will not fail, but bless us all in peace."

When Rollant sees those misbegotten men,
Who are more black than ink is on the pen
With no part white, only their teeth except,
Then says that count: "I know now very well
That here to die we're bound, as I can tell.
Strike on, the Franks! For so I recommend."
Says Oliver: "Who holds back, is condemned!"
Upon those words, the Franks to strike again.

Franks are but few; which, when the pagans know,
Among themselves comfort and pride they shew;
Says each to each: "Wrong was that Emperor."
Their alcaliph upon a sorrel rode,
And pricked it well with both his spurs of gold;
Struck Oliver, behind, on the back-bone,
His hauberk white into his body broke,
Clean through his breast the thrusting spear he drove;
After he said: "You've borne a mighty blow.
Charlès the great should not have left you so;
He's done us wrong, small thanks to him we owe;
I've well avenged all ours on you alone."

Oliver feels that he to die is bound,
Holds Halteclere, whose steel is rough and brown,
Strikes the alcaliph on his helm's golden mount;
Flowers and stones fall clattering to the ground,
Slices his head, to th' small teeth in his mouth;
So brandishes his blade and flings him down;
After he says: "Pagan, accurst be thou!
Thou'lt never say that Charles forsakes me now;
Nor to thy wife, nor any dame thou'st found,
Thou'lt never boast, in lands where thou wast crowned,
One pennyworth from me thou'st taken out,
Nor damage wrought on me nor any around."
After, for aid, "Rollant!" he cries aloud.

Oliver feels that death is drawing nigh;
To avenge himself he hath no longer time;
Through the great press most gallantly he strikes,
He breaks their spears, their buckled shields doth slice,
Their feet, their fists, their shoulders and their sides,
Dismembers them: whoso had seen that sight,
Dead in the field one on another piled,
Remember well a vassal brave he might.
Charlè's ensign he'll not forget it quite;
Aloud and clear "Monjoie" again he cries.
To call Rollanz, his friend and peer, he tries:
"My companion, come hither to my side.
With bitter grief we must us now divide."

. . .

Oliver feels death's anguish on him now;
And in his head his two eyes swimming round;
Nothing he sees; he hears not any sound;
Dismounting then, he kneels upon the ground,
Proclaims his sins both firmly and aloud,
Clasps his two hands, heavenwards holds them out,
Prays God himself in Paradise to allow;
Blessings on Charles, and on Douce France he vows,
And his comrade, Rollanz, to whom he's bound.
Then his heart fails; his helmet nods and bows;

Upon the earth he lays his whole length out:
And he is dead, may stay no more, that count.
Rollanz the brave mourns him with grief profound;
Nowhere on earth so sad a man you'd found.

So Rollant's friend is dead; whom when he sees
Face to the ground, and biting it with's teeth,
Begins to mourn in language very sweet:
"Unlucky, friend, your courage was indeed!
Together we have spent such days and years;
No harmful thing twixt thee and me has been.
Now thou art dead, and all my life a grief."
And with these words again he swoons, that chief,
Upon his horse, which he calls Veillantif;
Stirrups of gold support him underneath;
He cannot fall, whichever way he lean.

Soon as Rollant his senses won and knew,
Recovering and turning from that swoon.
Bitter great loss appeared there in his view:
Dead are the Franks; he'd all of them to lose,
Save the Archbishop, and save Gualter del Hum;
He is come down out of the mountains, who
Gainst Spanish men made there a great ado;
Dead are his men, for those the pagans slew;
Will he or nill, along the vales he flew,
And called Rollant, to bring him succour soon:
"Ah! Gentle count, brave soldier, where are you?
For by thy side no fear I ever knew.
Gualter it is, who conquered Maëlgut,
And nephew was to hoary old Droün;
My vassalage thou ever thoughtest good.
Broken my spear, and split my shield in two;
Gone is the mail that on my hauberk grew;
This body of mine eight lances have gone through;
I'm dying. Yet full price for life I took."
Rollant has heard these words and understood,
Has spurred his horse, and on towards him drew.

Grief gives Rollanz intolerance and pride;
Through the great press he goes again to strike;

22. Statue of King Clothar. Detail of doorway from Abbey of Moutiers-Saint-Jean, Burgundy, France.

To slay a score of Spaniards he contrives,
Gualter has six, the Archbishop other five.
The pagans say: "Men, these, of felon kind!
Lordings, take care they go not hence alive!
Felon he's named that does not break their line,
Recreant, who lets them any safety find!"
And so once more begin the hue and cry,
From every part they come to break the line.

Count Rollant is a noble and brave soldier,
Gualter del Hum's a right good chevalier,
That Archbishop hath shewn good prowess there;
None of them falls behind the other pair;

Through the great press, pagans they strike again.
Come on afoot a thousand Sarrazens,
And on horseback some forty thousand men.
But well I know, to approach they never dare;
Lances and spears they poise to hurl at them,
Arrows, barbs, darts and javelins in the air.
With the first flight they've slain our Gualtïer;
Turpin of Reims has all his shield broken,
And cracked his helm; he's wounded in the head,
From his hauberk the woven mail they tear,
In his body four spear-wounds doth he bear;
Beneath him too his charger's fallen dead.
Great grief it was, when that Archbishop fell.

Turpin of Reims hath felt himself undone,
Since that four spears have through his body come;
Nimble and bold upon his feet he jumps;
Looks for Rollant, and then towards him runs,
Saying this word: "I am not overcome.
While life remains, no good vassal gives up."
He's drawn Almace, whose steel was brown and rough,
Through the great press a thousand blows he's struck:
As Charlès said, quarter he gave to none;
He found him there, four hundred else among,
Wounded the most, speared through the middle some,
Also there were from whom the heads he'd cut:
So tells the tale, he that was there says thus,
The brave Saint Giles, whom God made marvellous,
Who charters wrote for th' Minster at Loüm;
Nothing he's heard that does not know this much.

The count Rollanz has nobly fought and well,
But he is hot, and all his body sweats;
Great pain he has, and trouble in his head,
His temples burst when he the horn sounded;
But he would know if Charles will come to them,
Takes the olifant, and feebly sounds again.
That Emperour stood still and listened then:
"My lords," said he, "Right evilly we fare!
This day Rollanz, my nephew shall be dead:

I hear his horn, with scarcely any breath.
Nimbly canter, whoever would be there!
Your trumpets sound, as many as ye bear!"
Sixty thousand so loud together blare,
The mountains ring, the valleys answer them.
The pagans hear, they think it not a jest;
Says each to each: "Carlum doth us beset."

The pagans say: "That Emperour's at hand,
We hear their sound, the trumpets of the Franks;
If Charlès come, great loss we then shall stand,
And wars renewed, unless we slay Rollant;
All Spain we'll lose, our own clear father-land."
Four hundred men of them in helmets stand;
The best of them that might be in their ranks
Make on Rollanz a grim and fierce attack;
Gainst these the count had well enough in hand.

The count Rollanz, when their approach he sees
Is grown so bold and manifest and fierce
So long as he's alive he will not yield.
He sits his horse, which men call Veillantif,
Pricking him well with golden spurs beneath,
Through the great press he goes, their line to meet,
And by his side is the Archbishop Turpin.
"Now, friend, begone!" say pagans, each to each;
"These Frankish men, their horns we plainly hear;
Charle is at hand, that King in Majesty."

The count Rollanz has never loved cowards,
Nor arrogant, nor men of evil heart,
Nor chevalier that was not good vassal.
That Archbishop, Turpins, he calls apart:
"Sir, you're afoot, and I my charger have;
For love of you, here will I take my stand,
Together we'll endure things good and bad;
I'll leave you not, for no incarnate man:
We'll give again these pagans their attack;
The better blows are those from Durendal."
Says the Archbishop: "Shame on him that holds back!

Charle is at hand, full vengeance he'll exact."

The pagans say: "Unlucky were we born!
An evil day for us did this day dawn!
For we have lost our peers and all our lords.
Charles his great host once more upon us draws,
Of Frankish men we plainly hear the horns,
"Monjoie" they cry, and great is their uproar.
The count Rollant is of such pride and force
He'll never yield to man of woman born;
Let's aim at him, then leave him on the spot!"
And aim they did: with arrows long and short,
Lances and spears and feathered javelots;
Count Rollant's shield they've broken through and bored,
The woven mail have from his hauberk torn,
But not himself, they've never touched his corse;
Veillantif is in thirty places gored,
Beneath the count he's fallen dead, that horse.
Pagans are fled, and leave him on the spot;
The count Rollant stands on his feet once more.

. . .

The count Rollanz, when dead he saw his peers,
And Oliver, he held so very dear,
Grew tender, and began to shed a tear;
Out of his face the colour disappeared;
No longer could he stand, for so much grief,
Will he or nill, he swooned upon the field.
Said the Archbishop: "Unlucky lord, indeed!"

When the Archbishop beheld him swoon, Rollant,
Never before such bitter grief he'd had;
Stretching his hand, he took that olifant.
Through Rencesvals a little river ran;
He would go there, fetch water for Rollant.
Went step by step, to stumble soon began,
So feeble he is, no further fare he can,
For too much blood he's lost, and no strength has;
Ere he has crossed an acre of the land,
His heart grows faint, he falls down forwards and
Death comes to him with very cruel pangs.

The count Rollanz wakes from his swoon once more,
Climbs to his feet; his pains are very sore;
Looks down the vale, looks to the hills above;
On the green grass, beyond his companions,
He sees him lie, that noble old baron;
'Tis the Archbishop, whom in His name wrought God;
There he proclaims his sins, and looks above;
Joins his two hands, to Heaven holds them forth,
And Paradise prays God to him to accord.
Dead is Turpin, the warrior of Charlon.
In battles great and very rare sermons
Against pagans ever a champion.
God grant him now His Benediction!

The count Rollant sees the Archbishop lie dead,
Sees the bowels out of his body shed,
And sees the brains that surge from his forehead;
Between his two arm-pits, upon his breast,
Crossways he folds those hands so white and fair.
Then mourns aloud, as was the custom there:
"Thee, gentle sir, chevalier nobly bred,
To th' Glorious Celestial I commend;
Ne'er shall man be, that will Him serve so well;
Since the Apostles was never such prophet,
To hold the laws and draw the hearts of men.
Now may your soul no pain nor sorrow ken,
Finding the gates of Paradise open!"

Then Rollanz feels that death to him draws near,
For all his brain is issued from his ears;
He prays to God that He will call the peers,
Bids Gabriel, the angel, t'himself appear.
Takes the olifant, that no reproach shall hear,
And Durendal in the other hand he wields;
Further than might a cross-bow's arrow speed
Goes towards Spain into a fallow-field;
Climbs on a cliff; where, under two fair trees,
Four terraces, of marble wrought, he sees.
There he falls down, and lies upon the green;
He swoons again, for death is very near.

. . .

Then Rollanz feels that he has lost his sight,
Climbs to his feet, uses what strength he might;
In all his face the colour is grown white.
In front of him a great brown boulder lies;
Whereon ten blows with grief and rage he strikes;
The steel cries out, but does not break outright;
And the count says: "Saint Mary, be my guide!
Good Durendal, unlucky is your plight!
I've need of you no more; spent is my pride!
We in the field have won so many fights,
Combating through so many regions wide
That Charlès holds, whose beard is hoary white!
Be you not his that turns from any in flight!
A good vassal has held you this long time;
Never shall France the Free behold his like."

Rollant hath struck the sardonyx terrace;
The steel cries out, but broken is no ways.
So when he sees he never can it break,
Within himself begins he to complain:
"Ah! Durendal, white art thou, clear of stain!
Beneath the sun reflecting back his rays!
In Moriane was Charlès, in the vale,
When from heaven God by His angel bade
Him give thee to a count and capitain;
Girt thee on me that noble King and great.
I won for him with thee Anjou, Bretaigne,
And won for him with thee Peitou, the Maine,
And Normandy the free for him I gained,
Also with thee Provence and Equitaigne,
And Lumbardie and all the whole Romaigne,
I won Baivere, all Flanders in the plain,
Also Burguigne and all the whole Puillane,
Costentinnople, that homage to him pays;
In Saisonie all is as he ordains;
With thee I won him Scotland, Ireland, Wales,
England also, where he his chamber makes;
Won I with thee so many countries strange
That Charlès holds, whose beard is white with age!
For this sword's sake sorrow upon me weighs,

Rather I'ld die, than it mid pagans stay.
Lord God Father, never let France be shamed!"

Rollant his stroke on a dark stone repeats,
And more of it breaks off than I can speak.
The sword cries out, yet breaks not in the least,
Back from the blow into the air it leaps.
Destroy it can he not; which when he sees,
Within himself he makes a plaint most sweet:
"Ah! Durendal, most holy, fair indeed!
Relics enough thy golden hilt conceals:
Saint Peter's Tooth, the Blood of Saint Basile,
Some of the Hairs of my Lord, Saint Denise,
Some of the Robe, was worn by Saint Mary.
It is not right that pagans should thee seize,
For Christian men thy use shall ever be.
Nor any man's that worketh cowardice!
Many broad lands with thee have I retrieved
Which Charles holds, who hath the great white beard;
Wherefore that King so proud and rich is he."

But Rollant felt that death had made a way
Down from his head till on his heart it lay;
Beneath a pine running in haste he came,
On the green grass he lay there on his face;
His olifant and sword beneath him placed,
Turning his head towards the pagan race,
Now this he did, in truth, that Charles might say
(As he desired) and all the Franks his race;—
'Ah, gentle count; conquering he was slain!'—
He owned his faults often and every way,
And for his sins his glove to God upraised.

But Rollant feels he's no more time to seek;
Looking to Spain, he lies on a sheer peak,
And with one hand upon his breast he beats:
"*Mea Culpa!* God, by Thy Virtues clean
Me from my sins, the mortal and the mean,
Which from the hour that I was born have been
Until this day, when life is ended here!"
Holds out his glove towards God, as he speaks;
Angels descend from heaven on that scene.

The count Rollanz, beneath a pine he sits;
Turning his eyes towards Spain, he begins
Remembering so many divers things:
So many lands where he went conquering,
And France the Douce, the heroes of his kin,
And Charlemagne, his lord who nourished him.
Nor can he help but weep and sigh at this.
But his own self, he's not forgotten him,
He owns his faults, and God's forgiveness bids:
"Very Father, in Whom no falsehood is,
Saint Lazaron from death Thou didst remit,
And Daniel save from the lions' pit;
My soul in me preserve from all perils
And from the sins I did in life commit!"
His right-hand glove, to God he offers it;
Saint Gabriel from 's hand hath taken it.
Over his arm his head bows down and slips,
He joins his hands: and so is life finish'd.
God sent him down His angel cherubin,
And Saint Michael, we worship in peril;
And by their side Saint Gabriel alit;
So the count's soul they bare to Paradis.

Rollant is dead; his soul to heav'n God bare.
That Emperour to Rencesvals doth fare.
There was no path nor passage anywhere
Nor of waste ground no ell nor foot to spare
Without a Frank or pagan lying there.
Charles cries aloud: "Where are you, nephew fair?
Where's the Archbishop and that count Oliviers?
Where is Gerins and his comrade Gerers?
Orès the Duke, and the count Berengiers
And Ivorie, and Ive, so dear they were?
What is become of Gascon Engelier,
Sansun the Duke and Anséis the fierce?
Where's old Gerard of Russillun; oh, where
The dozen peers I left behind me there?"
But what avail, since none can answer bear?
"God!" says the King, "Now well may I despair,
I was not here the first assault to share!"
Seeming enraged, his beard the King doth tear.

Weep from their eyes barons and chevaliers,
A thousand score, they swoon upon the earth;
Duke Neimes for them was moved with pity rare.

No chevalier nor baron is there, who
Pitifully weeps not for grief and dule;
They mourn their sons, their brothers, their nephews,
And their liege lords, and trusty friends and true;
Upon the ground a many of them swoon.
Thereon Duke Neimes doth act with wisdom proof,
First before all he's said to the Emperour:
"See beforehand, a league from us or two,
From the highways dust rising in our view;
Pagans are there, and many of them, too.
Canter therefore! Vengeance upon them do!"
"Ah, God!" says Charles, "so far are they removed!
Do right by me, my honour still renew!
They've torn from me the flower of France the Douce."
The King commands Gebuin and Otun,
Tedbalt of Reims, also the count Milun:
"Guard me this field, these hills and valleys too,
Let the dead lie, all as they are, unmoved,
Let not approach lion, nor any brute,
Let not approach esquire, nor any groom;
For I forbid that any come thereto,
Until God will that we return anew."
These answer him sweetly, their love to prove:
"Right Emperour, dear Sire, so will we do."
A thousand knights they keep in retinue.

(*Anonymous, c. A.D. 1100, France*)

## THE BOOK OF THE ORDER OF CHIVALRY

### Ramon Lull

The office of a knight is the end and the beginning wherefore began the order of chivalry. Then if a knight use not his office, he is contrary to his order and to the beginning of chivalry aforesaid; by which contrariety he is not a knight although he bear the name. For such a knight is more vile than the smith or the carpenter that do their office as they ought to do and have learned. The office of a knight is to maintain and defend the holy catholic faith, by which God the Father sent his Son into the world to take human flesh in the glorious virgin Our Lady Saint Mary. And to honour and multiply the faith suffered in this world many trials, difficulties and a death of anguish. Then likewise as our Lord God hath chosen the clerks to maintain the holy catholic faith with scripture and reason against the miscreants and non-believers, so likewise the glory of God has chosen knights because by force of arms they vanquish the miscreants who labor daily to destroy holy church. And such knights God holds for his friends honored in this world and in that other when they keep and maintain the faith by which we expect to be saved. . . .

Many there are who have offices which God hath given to them in this world to the end that by them he should be served and honored, but the most noble and the most honorable offices that be, are the offices of clerks and knights. Then thus as clerks be not ordained by their clergy, they are against the order of chivalry. Also knights who do not maintain the order of chivalry are contrary to the clerics who are bound to love and maintain the order of chivalry. The order is not given to a man that he should love his order only but he should love the other orders as well. For to love one order and hate another is in nowise to love order. For God hath given no order that is contrary to any other order. Then the religious that loveth so much his own order that he is an enemy of any other order follows not the rule of order. Thus a knight loveth not the office of a knight that so much loveth and praiseth his own order that he criticizes and hateth other orders. For if a knight loved the order of chivalry and destroyed some other order, it should seem that the order should be contrary to God, which may not be so since He hath established order.

So noble is chivalry that every knight ought to be governor of a great country or land. But there are so many knights that the land may not suffice to signify that one ought to be the lord of all things. The emperor ought to be a knight and lord of a knight but because the emperor may not by himself govern all knights, it behooveth him that he have under him kings that are knights to the end that they may aid and help to maintain the order of chivalry. And the kings ought to have under them dukes, earls, viscounts and other lords. And under the barons ought to be knights, who ought to govern after the ordinances of the barons which are in the high degree of chivalry before-named in order to show the excellent lordship, power and wisdom of our lord God glorious who is one only God in Trinity and can and may govern all things. Thus it is not desirable that one knight by himself should govern all the people of this world. For if one knight alone might do so, the lordship, power and wisdom should not be so well signified. . . .

The office of the knight is to maintain and defend his lord worldly or earthly, for a king or high baron has no power to maintain right in his men without aid and help. Then if any man act against the commandment of his king or prince, it behooveth the knights to aid their lord who is but a man only as another is and therefore the evil knight who sooner helps another man who would put down his lord from the seignory that he ought to hold, he follows not the office by which he is called a knight. By the knights ought to be maintained and kept justice for just as judges have the office to judge, so have the knights the office to keep them from violence in exercising the fate of justice. If it must be that chivalry and clergy assembled themselves together in such a manner as knights should befriend them, so if they were sufficient in learning to be judges, no office should be so suitable to be a judge as chivalry for he that by justice may best be advised is more suitable to be a judge than any other.

Knights ought to take coursers and to go to tourneys, to hold open table, to hunt harts, boars and other wild animals. For in doing these things the knights exercise themselves in arms to maintain the order of knighthood. Thus, as all these things aforesaid pertain to a knight regarding his body, in like manner justice, wisdom, charity, loyalty, truth, humility, strength, hope, swiftness and all other virtues similarly pertain to a knight regarding his soul, and therefore the knight who abuses the things that pertain to the order of chivalry touching his soul is not the friend of the order of knighthood. For if it were thus that he made a separation of the virtues listed, saying that they pertain not to the soul and to the order of chivalry together, it should signify that the body and chivalry were both contrary to the soul and to these virtues and that is false. The office of a knight is to maintain the land for because of the fear the common people have of knights, they labour and cultivate the earth lest they should be destroyed. And by their fear of knights, they respect the kings, princes and lords by whom they have their power. But the wicked knight who does not aid his earthly lord and natural country against another prince is a knight without office. And he is like faith without works. . . .

Likewise it behooveth the order of chivalry to love wisdom through which they may love and honor the order of chivalry against the discord and errors that are in those who seek to follow the order of chivalry in folly and ignorance and without understanding. The office of a knight is to maintain and defend women, widows, and orphans, and men diseased and not powerful or strong. For as custom and reason is that the greatest and most mighty help the feeble and lesser, and that they have recourse to the great, right so is the order of chivalry, because it is great, honorable and mighty to succor and aid those that are under him and less mighty and less honored than he is. Thus it is wrong to harm and to use force to women, widows that have need of aid and orphans who have need of governance and to rob and destroy the feeble who have need of strength; and to take away from them what is given to them; these things may not accord to the order of chivalry for this is wickedness, cruelty and tyranny. . . .

The office of a knight is to have a castle and to keep the ways and to defend those who labour on the lands and the earth and they ought to have towns and cities to hold rightly for the people. And to assemble in one place men of diverse crafts who are necessary to the ordinance of this world to keep and maintain the life of man and woman. . . .

## In What Manner a Squire Ought to Be Received into the Order of Chivalry

At the beginning when a squire enters into the order of chivalry, it behooveth him to confess his faults that he has done against God, and he ought to receive chivalry with the intention that in it he will serve our Lord God who is glorious. And if he be cleansed from sin, he ought to receive his Saviour. For to make and dub a knight, one chooses the day of some great feast as Christmas, Easter, Whitsuntide, or such a solemn day, because by the honor of the feast many people assemble in the place where the squire is to be dubbed knight and God ought to be adored and prayed that He give to him grace to live well according to the order of chivalry. The squire ought to fast the vigil of the feast in honor of the saint for whom the feast is made that day and he ought to go to church to pray God and he ought to watch the night before and be in prayer and he ought to hear the word of God touching the faith of chivalry for if he otherwise hears jongleurs and ribald tales of sin, he should begin to dishonor chivalry. On the morning of the feast in which

23. Chapel and bridge of St. Benezet, Avignon, France.

he is to be dubbed, it behooveth him that he have a mass sung solemnly, and the squire ought to come before the altar and offer to the priest, who holds the place of our lord to whose honor he must oblige and submit himself, to keep the honor of chivalry with all his power. In that same day ought to be made a sermon in which should be recounted and declared the twelve articles in which is founded the holy catholic faith, the ten commandments and the seven sacraments and the other things that pertain to the faith. . . . The squire ought to kneel before the altar and lift up to God his eyes corporal and spiritual and his hands to heaven, and the knight ought to gird him in sign of chastity, justice and of charity, with his sword. The knight ought to kiss the squire and to give him a palm, because he is to remember what he receives and promises, and the great charge in which he is obliged and bound and of the great honor that he receives by the order of chivalry. And after when the knight spiritual, that is, the priest, and the knight earthly have done that which pertains to their office in the making of a new knight, the new knight ought to ride all through the town and show himself to the people, so that all men know and see that he is made a knight, and that he is bound to maintain and defend the high honor of chivalry.

## Of the Significance of the Arms of a Knight

As the vestments of the priest when he singeth the mass have some significance which compareth to his office, and the office of the priesthood and of chivalry have great concordance, therefore the office of chivalry requires that all that which is needful to a knight pertaining to the use of his office have some significance by which is signified the nobleness of chivalry and his order.

Unto a knight a sword is given which is made in semblance of the cross to signify how our lord God vanquished in the cross the death of human lineage, and to which he was sentenced for the sin of our first father Adam. Likewise a knight ought to vanquish and destroy the enemies of the cross by the sword. For chivalry is to maintain justice. Therefore is the sword made cutting on both sides to signify that the knight ought to use the sword to maintain chivalry and justice. To a knight is given a spear to signify truth for truth is a thing right and even. And that truth ought to go before falseness. And the iron head of the spear signifies strength which truth ought to have above falseness. And the pennon signifies that truth shows to all faith and has no dread or fear of falseness or of treachery but virtue in sustaining hope and also of other things which are signified by the spear of the knight to signify shamefastness. For a knight without shamefastness may not be obedient to the order of chivalry. And thus as shamefastness makes a man ashamed and causes him to cast down his eyes against the earth, likewise the hat of iron prevents a man from looking on high and makes him to look toward the ground and is the mean between things high and low. For it covers the head of the man which is the most high and principal member in the body of a man. Also shamefastness prevents the knight who has the most noble office and the highest next to the clergy from inclining himself to villainous faults so that the nobleness of his courage does not abandon him to vice, wickedness, nor to any evil engagement. The hauberk signifies a castle and fortress against vice and all difficulties. For as a castle and fortress are closed all about, likewise a hauberk is firm and closed on all parts to the end that it gives significance to a noble knight that in his courage he ought not to enter into treason or other vice. Chauces of iron (leg harness) are given to a knight to keep and hold surely his feet and legs from peril and to signify that a knight with iron ought to hold himself strong, that is to say, with the sword, spear and mace and other garments of iron to take malefactors and punish them. The spurs are given to a knight to show diligence and swiftness because with these things every knight may maintain his order in the high honor that belongs to it. . . .

# THE BOOK OF THE KNIGHT OF LA TOUR LANDRY

## La Tour Landry

### Of the Honour and Respect That Attends a Good Life

My right dear daughters, if you knew the great honour and the great wealth that it is to be well renowned, to bear a good name, and to be well spoken of, which is one of the greatest graces in the world, you would put your heart in pain to attain thereto; just as a knight who desires worship and valour, which he wins by great pain and labour in heat and cold and puts his body in so many adventures of death, and all for winning worship and good name as by strange voyages, hard assaults, by diverse great battles and by many other great perils in arms. And after he has suffered this much, then he is drawn forward and put in much honor and the prince grants him great lordships and authority, for his nobleness and because he has no equal in his good name. Just so it is of a good woman, who everywhere bears a good name of honour and goodness, as one who has at all times troubled to keep her body undefiled and in cleanliness and refused the delights of youth and foul pleasure whereby she has won a good name and much worship, forevermore to be listed among the number of good ladies and all worthy women, and so has also won the love of God and of her husband and of the world and the salvation of her soul, which is the worthiest and best of all. For the soul is the precious margarite unto God. And so it is an example to all creatures how they ought to praise a good woman; for she is as worthy in the sight of God for her goodness and virtue as the knight for his arms and worthiness in battle. But the right rule faileth sometimes, for honor is not given to him at all times that deserves it, as it may be shown in diverse cases of many good women.

## How Christ Speaks of Good Women

It is contained in the gospel of the virgins, as our Lord preached and taught the people, and he spoke on the matter of women that lived in purity; he likened such a woman to a precious margarite, which is a bright thing, round, white and clean, a stone so clean and fair that there is no spot therein, nor trace of uncleanness; and this is said of a woman that is not wedded, who lives in virginity, purity and chastity; or else of a woman who is wedded and keeps truly and honestly the sacrament of marriage, and also of those who worshipfully and perfectly keep their widowhood, living in chastity and sobriety. These are the three kinds of women whom God praises and likens to the precious margarite, that is all fair without any foul spot or any impurity; for Holy Scripture says there is no thing better than a good woman and such a one is rather more praised before God and the angels than man. And for the reason that woman is of lighter courage than man as much as the woman was drawn out of the man and as much as she is more feeble to withstand the temptations of the flesh, so she is worthy to have more merit and praise than man when she does withstand the temptations of the flesh. And therefore God compared a woman to a precious margarite, and also the Scripture says in another place that it would be a foul thing to take a fair sweet rose and put it in a putrid vessel; just so the purity of a maid or of a good woman is that she should not misuse it with unclean men who desire false fleshly pleasure; but the woman should keep evermore the purity of virginity or of true marriage so that the foul sins of impurity may not deface the precious margarite, the purity of maidenhood, the sacrament of marriage, the faith of God and holy church and the chastity of widowhood. For if these three manner of women misuse the virtues, which we have named, the maid her maidenhood, the wife her marriage, the widow her widowhood, then they become like the roses in a putrid vessel, for they have lost their fairness, their sweetness, and their virtue, for the impurity they live in; and then they are no longer like the precious margarite. Well should a woman be displeased and hate herself in her ungodly falseness when for her folly she is put out of the number and memory of all good women. . . . For the harm that follows the defamation of marriage and its breaking is serious enough, but in addition it is a great displeasure to God for such as break their marriage as man and woman suffer the departing of love, the insult to the sacrament and damnable sin. And the devil has such power over them that they give him great delight in their sin and ribaldry and ardent pleasure which they pursue to their endless damnation. But true marriage is ordained by God and its pleasure is without sin; and therefore the fiend of hell has no power in that holy sacrament, but he strives ever more to draw the man or woman by false delight into sin; as a smith ever blowing the fire, just so serves the enemy in hell that strives ever to kindle and light the flame of deadly sin in the hearts of men and women that he might bring their souls to hell.

# SIR GAWAIN AND THE GREEN KNIGHT

## Fytte the First

After the siege and the assault had ceased at Troy, the city had been destroyed and burned to brands and ashes, the warrior who wrought there the trains of treason was tried for his treachery, the truest on earth. This was Aeneas the noble; he and his high kindred afterwards conquered provinces, and became patrons of well nigh all the wealth in the West Isles. As soon as rich Romulus turns him to Rome, with great pride he at once builds that city, and names it with his name, which it now has; Ticius turns to Tuscany and founds dwellings; Longobard raises homes in Lombardy; and, far over the French flood, Felix Brutus establishes Britain joyfully on many broad banks, where war and waste and wonders by turns have since dwelt, and many a swift interchange of bliss and woe.

And when this Britain was founded by this great hero, bold men loving strife bred therein, and many a time they wrought destruction. More strange things have happened in this land since these days than in any other that I know; but of all the British kings that built here, Arthur was ever the most courteous, as I have heard tell. Therefore, I mean to tell of an adventure in the world, which some count strange and extraordinary even among the wonders of Arthur. If ye will listen to this lay but a little while, I will tell it forthright as I heard it told in town, as it is set down in story that cannot be changed, long written in the land of true words.

This King lay royally at Camelot at Christmastide with many fine lords, the best of men, all the rich brethren of the Round Table, with right rich revel and careless mirth. There full many heroes tourneyed betimes, jousted full gaily; then returned these gentle knights to the court to make carols. For there the feast was held full fifteen days alike with all the meat and the mirth that men could devise. Such a merry tumult, glorious to hear; joyful din by day, dancing at night. All was high joy in halls and chambers with lords and ladies as pleased them best. With all the weal in the world they dwelt there together, the most famous knights save only Christ, the loveliest ladies that ever had life, and he, the comeliest of kings, who holds the court. For all this fair company were in their prime in the hall, the happiest troop under heaven with the proudest of kings. Truly it would be hard to name anywhere so brave a band.

When New Year was fresh and but newly come, the court was served double on the dais. As soon as the king with his knights was come into the hall, the chanting in the chapel came to an end; loud was the cry there of clerks and others. Noel was celebrated anew, shouted full often; and afterwards the great ones ran about to take handsel (gifts); called aloud for New Year's gifts, paid them out briskly, busily discussed the gifts; ladies laughed full loud, though they had lost; and he that won was not wroth, that may ye well trow. All this mirth they made till the meat time. When they had washed, worthily they went to their seats, the best man ever above, as it best behooved. Queen Guinevere full beauteous was set in the midst, placed on the rich dais adorned all about. Fine silk at the sides, a canopy over her of precious cloth of Toulouse, and tapestries of Tars that were embroidered and set with the best gems that money could buy. Truly no man could say that he ever beheld a comelier lady than she, with her dancing gray eyes.

But Arthur would not eat till all were served. He was so merry in his mirth, and somewhat childlike in his manner; his life pleased him well; he loved little either to lie long or to sit long, so busied him his young blood and his wild brain. And another custom moved him also, that he through chivalry had taken up; he would never eat upon such a dear day before he was told an uncouth tale of some adventurous thing, of some great marvel that he could believe, of ancient heroes, of arms, or of other adventures; or unless some person demanded of him a sure knight to join with him in jousting, to incur peril, to risk life against life, trusting each in the other, leaving the victory to fortune. This was the king's custom whenever he held court at each goodly feast among his free company in the hall. And so with undaunted face he strides stoutly to his seat on that New Year, making great mirth with everybody.

Thus the great king stands waiting before the high table, talking of trifles full courteously. The good Gawain was placed there beside Guinevere, and Agravain of the Hard Hand sat on the other side, both of them the king's sister's sons and full sure knights. Bishop Baldwin at the top begins the table, and Ywain, Urien's son, ate by himself. These were placed on a dais and honorably served, and after them many a good man at the side tables. Then the first course came in with blare of trumpets, which were hung with many a bright banner. A new noise of kettledrums with the noble pipes, wild and stirring melodies wakened the echoes; that many a heart heaved full high at their tones. Dainties of precious meats followed, foison of fresh viands, and on so many dishes that it was difficult to find place before the people to set on the cloth the silver that held the several courses. Each man as he himself preferred partook without hesitation. Every two had twelve dishes between them, good beer and bright wine both.

Now will I tell you no more of their service, for everybody must pretty well understand that there was no lack of opportunity for the people to take their food. Another noise full new suddenly drew nigh, for scarcely had the music ceased a moment, and the first course properly served in the court, than there burst in at the hall door an awsome being, in height one of the tallest men in the world; from the neck to the waist so square and so thick was he, and his loins and his limbs so long and so great, that half giant I believed him to have been, or, at any rate, the largest of men, and withal the handsomest in spite of his bulk, that ever rode; for though his back and breast were so vast, yet his belly and waist were properly slim; and all his form according, full fairly shaped. At the hue of his noble face men wondered; he carried himself in hostile fashion and was entirely green.

All green was this man and his clothing; a straight coat sat tight to his sides; a fair mantle above, adorned within; the lining showed, with costly trimming of costly white fur; and such his hood also, that was caught back from his locks and lay on his shoulders, the hem well stretched; hose of the same green, that clung to his calf; and clean spurs under, of bright gold upon silk bands richly barred, and his shoes on his shanks as the hero rides. And all this vesture verily was clean verdure, both the bars of his belt, and the other beauteous stones that were set in fine array about himself and his saddle, worked on silk. It would be too difficult to tell the half of the trifles that were embroidered there, with birds and flies, with gay gauds of green,—the gold ever in the middle; the pendants of the poirtel, the proud crupper, the bits,—and all the metal was enamelled; the stirrups that he stood on were coloured the same, and his saddle bow likewise, and his fine reins that glimmered and glinted all of green stones. The horse that he rode on was of the same colour too, a green horse, great and thick, a steed full stiff to guide, in gay embroidered bridle and one right dear to his master.

This hero was splendidly dressed in green; and the hair of his head matched that of his horse; fair flowing locks enfolded his shoulders; a beard as big as a bush hung over his breast; and it, together with his splendid hair that reached from his head, was trimmed evenly all around above his elbows, so that half his arms were caught thereunder in the manner of a king's hood, that covers his neck. The mane of that great horse was much like it, very burly and combed, with knots full many folded in with gold wire about the fair green,—always one knot of the hair, another of gold. The tail and the forelock were twined in the same way, and both bound with a band of bright green, set with full precious stones the whole length of the dock, and tied up with a thong in a tight knot; where rang many bells full bright of burnished gold. Such a steed in the world, such a hero that rides him, was never beheld in that hall before that time. His glances were like bright lightning, so said all that saw him. It seemed as if no man could endure under his blows.

He had neither helm nor hauberk, nor gorget, armour nor breastplate, nor shaft nor shield to guard or to smite; but in his one hand he had a holly twig, that is greenest when groves are bare, and an axe in his other, a huge and prodigious one, a weapon merciless almost beyond description; the head had the vast length of an ell-yard; the blade all of green steel and of beaten gold; the bit brightly burnished, with a broad edge, as well shaped for cutting as sharp razors. The stern warrior gripped it by the steel of its stout staff, which was wound with iron to the end of the wood and all engraven with green in beauteous work. A lace was lapped about it, that was fastened at the head, and tied up often along the helve, with many precious tassels attached on rich embroidered buttons of the bright green. This hero turns him in and enters the hall, riding straight to the high dais, fearless of mischief. He greeted never a one, but looked loftily about, and the first word that he uttered was: "Where is the governor of this company? Gladly I would see that hero and speak with him."

He cast his eye on the knights and rode fiercely up and down, stopped and gan ponder who was there the most renowned.

All gazed fixedly on the man, for everybody marvelled what it might mean, that a knight and a horse could have such a colour; as green grown as the grass, and greener, it seemed; shining brighter than green enamel on gold. All were amazed who stood there, and stalked nearer to him, with all the wonder in the world what he would do; for many marvels had they seen, but such never before. Therefore for phantom and faery the folk there deemed it; and for that reason many a noble warrior was slow to answer, and all were astonished at his voice and sat stone still in a deep silence through the rich hall. Their voices sank as though they had suddenly fallen asleep. I deem however, that it was not all for fear, but somewhat for courtesy. But now let him to whom all defer undertake the wight.

Then Arthur before the high dais beheld that adventure, and saluted the stranger properly, for never was he afraid, and said, "Sir, welcome indeed to this place. I am called Arthur, the head of this hostel. Light courteously down and tarry, I pray thee; and whatso thy will is we shall wit after."

"Nay, so help me that sits on high," quoth the hero. "To dwell any time in this house was not my errand; but because the fame of this people is lifted up so high, and thy town and thy men are held the best, the stoutest in steel gear on steeds to ride, the wightest and the worthiest of the world's kind, and proved opponents in other proper sports; and here courtesy is known, as I have heard tell,—it is this that has enticed me hither certainly at this time. You may be sure by this branch that I bear here that I pass in peace and seek no quarrel; for if I had set out with a company in fighting fashion, I have a hauberk at home and a helm both, a shield and a sharp spear shining bright, and other weapons to wield, I ween well also; but since I wished no war, my weeds are softer. Now if thou be as bold as all men tell, thou wilt grant me graciously the game that I ask."

Arthur knew how to answer, and said: "Sir courteous knight, if it is battle that thou cravest, thou shalt not fail of a fight here."

"Nay, I demand no fight; in faith I tell thee there are but beardless children about on this bench. If I were hasped in arms on a high steed there is no man here to match me, their might is so weak. Therefore I crave in this court a Christmas game, for it is Yule and New Year, and here are many gallants. If there be a man in this house who holds himself so hardy, is so bold in his blood, so rash in his head, that he dares stiffly strike one stroke for another, I shall give him as my gift this rich gisarm, this axe, that is heavy enough, to handle as he likes; and I shall abide the first blow as bare as I sit. If any warrior be wight enough to try what I propose, let him leap lightly to me and take this weapon—I quitclaim it forever, let him keep it as his own—and I shall stand him a stroke firmly on the floor. At another time, by our Lady, thou wilt grant me the boon of dealing him another blow; I will give him respite of a twelvemonth and a day. Now hie, and let us see quickly if any herein dare say aught."

If he had astonished them at first, stiller were then all the retainers in the hall, the high and the low. The warrior on his steed settled himself in his saddle, and fiercely his red eyes he reeled about; bent his thick brows, shining green; and waved his beard, awaiting whoso would rise. When none would answer him, he coughed aloud, stretching himself haughtily and began to speak; "What! Is this Arthur's house," said the hero then, "that is famous through so many realms? Where is now your pride and your conquests, your fierceness, and your wrath and your great words? Now is the revel and the renown of the Round Table overcome by the word of a single man; for all tremble for dread without a blow shown."

With this he laughed so loud that the lord grieved; the blood shot for shame into his fair face. He waxed as wroth as the wind; and so did all that were there. The king so keen of mood then stood near that proud man.

"Sir," said he, "by heaven thy asking is foolish; and as thou hast demanded folly, it behooves thee to find it. I know no man that is aghast of thy great words. Give me now thy gisarm, for God's sake, and I will grant thy boon that thou hast bidden."

Quickly he leaped to him and caught at his hand; and the other alights fiercely on foot. Now Arthur has his axe, and grips the helve; he whirls it sternly about as if he meant to strike with it. The bold stranger stood upright before him, higher than any in the house by a head and more; with stern cheer he stood there, stroked his beard, and with cool countenance drew down his coat, no more afraid or dismayed for Arthur's great strokes than if some one had brought him a drink of wine upon the bench.

Gawain, that sat by the queen, turned to the king: "I beseech now with all courtesy that this affair might be mine."

"Would ye, worthy lord," quoth Gawain to the king, "bid me step from this table and stand by you there,—that I without rudeness might leave this table and that my liege lady liked it not ill—I would come to your help before your rich court; for methinks it is obviously unseemly that such an asking is made so much of in your hall, even though ye yourself be willing to take it upon you, while so many bold ones sit about you on the bench; than whom, I ween, none under heaven are higher of spirit nor more mighty on the field where strife is reared. I am the weakest, I know, and feeblest of wit; and to tell the truth there would be the least loss in my life. I am only to praise forasmuch as ye are my uncle; no other nobility than your blood know I in my body. And since this adventure is so foolish, it belongs not to you; I have asked it of you first; give it to me. Let this great court decide if I have not spoken well."

The heroes took counsel together and they all gave the same advice,—to free the crowned king and give the game to Gawain.

Then the king commanded Gawain to rise from the table; and he right quickly stood up and made himself ready, kneeled down before the king and took the weapon; and Arthur lovingly left it to him, lifted up his hand and gave him God's blessing, and gladly bade him be hardy both of heart and of hand. "Take care, cousin," quoth the king, "that you give him a cut; and if thou handle him properly, I readily believe that thou shalt endure the blow which he shall give after."

Gawain goes to the man with gisarm in hand; and he boldly awaits him, shrinking never a whit. Then speaks to Sir Gawain the knight in the green: "Rehearse we our agreement before we go further. First I conjure thee, hero, how thou art called, that thou tell me it truly, so that I may believe it."

"In good faith," quoth the knight, "Gawain am I called, who give you this buffet, whatever befalls after; and at this time twelvemonth I am to take from thee another with whatever weapon thou wilt, and from no wight else alive."

The other answers again, "Sir Gawain, so thrive I as I am heartily glad that thou shalt give this blow."

"By Gog," quoth the green knight, "Sir Gawain, it delights me that I am to get at thy fist what I have requested here; and thou hast readily and truly rehearsed the whole of the covenant that I asked of the king, save that thou shalt assure me, sir, by thy troth, that thou wilt seek me thyself wheresoever thou thinkest I may be found upon the earth, and fetch for thyself such wages as thou dealest me today before this rich company."

"Where should I seek thee?" quoth Gawain, "where is thy place? I know never where thou livest, by him that wrought me; nor do I know, knight, thy court, nor thy name. But tell me truly the way and how thou art called, and I will use all my wit to win my way thither,—and that I swear thee, for a sooth, and by my sure troth."

"New Year will suffice for that; no more is needed now," quoth the man in green to Gawain the courteous. "To tell the truth, after I have received thy tap, and thou hast smitten me well, I shall promptly inform thee of my house and my home and mine own name. Then thou mayest inquire about my journey and hold promise; and if I speak no speech, then thou speedest the better, for thou mayest linger at ease in thy land and seek no further. Take now thy grim tool to thee and let us see how thou knockest."

"Gladly, for sooth, sir," quoth Gawain as he strokes his axe.

The green knight on the ground prepared himself properly. With the head a little bowed he disclosed the flesh. His long, lovely locks he laid over his crown, and let the naked nape of his neck show for the blow. Gawain gripped his axe and gathered it on high; the left foot he set before on the ground, and let the axe light smartly down on the naked flesh, so that the sharp edge severed the giant's bones, and shrank through the clear flesh and sheared it in twain, till the edge of the brown steel bit into the ground. The fair head fell from the neck to the earth, and many pushed it with their feet where it rolled forth. The blood burst from the body and glistened on the green. Yet never faltered nor fell the hero for all that; but stoutly he started up with firm steps, and fiercely he rushed forth where the heroes stood, caught his lovely head, and lifted it up straightway. Then he turned to his steed, seized the bridle, stepped into the steel bow and strode aloft, holding the head in his hand by the hair; and as soberly the man sat in his saddle as if no mishap had ailed him, though he was headless on the spot. He turned his trunk about—that ugly body that bled. Many a one of them thought that he had lost his reason.

For he held the head straight up in his hand; turned the face toward the highest on the dais; and it lifted up the eyelids and looked straight out, and spoke thus much with its mouth, as ye may now hear:—"Look, Gawain, that thou be ready to go as thou hast promised, and seek loyally, hero, till thou find me; as thou hast promised in this hall in the hearing of these knights. To the green chapel go thou, I charge thee, to receive such a blow as thou hast dealt. Thou deservest to be promptly paid on New Year's morn. As the knight of the green chapel many men know me; therefore, if thou strivest to find me, thou shalt never fail. And so come, for it behooves thee to be called recalcitrant."

With a wild rush he turned the rein, and flew out at the hall door—his head in his hands—so that the fire of the flint flew from the foal's hoofs. To what country he vanished knew none there; no more than they wist whence he was come. . . . Now take care, Sir Gawain, that thou blench not for the pain to prosecute this adventure that thou hast taken on hand.

## Fytte the Second

. . .

Thus in peril and pain and plights full hard through the country this knight (Gawain) wanders all alone till Christmas Eve. At that tide to Mary he made his moan that she might direct his riding and lead him to some dwelling.

Merrily on the morn he rides by a mount into a forest full deep, that was strangely wild. High hills were on each side, and woods beneath of hoar oaks full huge, a hundred together. The hazel and the hawthorn were twined all together, covered everywhere with rough ragged moss, with many unblithe birds upon bare twigs that piteously piped there for pain of the cold. The knight upon Gringolet rides all alone under the boughs, through many a moss and mire, mourning for his trials, lest he should never survive to see the service of that Sire who on that very night was born of a lady to quell our pain. And therefore sighing he said: "I beseech thee, Lord, and Mary, that is mildest mother so dear, for some harbour where I might properly hear mass and thy matins tomorrow. Meekly I ask it, and thereto earnestly I pray my pater and ave and creed." He rode in his prayer and lamented for his misdeeds. Oft-times he blessed himself and said, "Christ's cross speed me."

The hero had not crossed himself more than thrice ere he was aware in the wood of a dwelling on a hill, above a clearing, on a mount, hidden under the boughs of many a huge tree about the ditches; a castle the comeliest ever knight owned, set on a prairie, a park all about, with its beautiful palace, pinnacled full thick, and surrounded with many a tree for more than two miles. The hero gazed at the castle on that one side as it shimmered and shone through the fair oaks. Then he humbly doffed his helm and devoutly he thanked Jesus and St. Julian—who are both gentle—who courteously had directed him and harkened to his cry. "Now bon hostel," quoth the man, "I beseech you yet!" Then he spurs Gringolet with his gilt heels, and he full fortunately takes the way to the chief road, that soon brought the hero to the bridge-end in haste. The bridge was securely lifted, the gates locked fast; the walls were well arrayed; no wind blast did it fear.

The hero sat on his horse, abode on the bank of the deep double ditch that stretched to the place. The wall sank in the water wondrous deep, and again a full huge height it towered aloft, of hard hewn stone up to the top courses, corbelled under the battlement in the best manner; and above fine watchtowers ranged along, with many good loop-holes that showed full clean. A better barbican that hero never looked upon. And farther within he held the high hall, with towers set full thickly above, and fair and wondrous filioles with carved tops cunningly devised. Chalk-white chimneys enough he saw that gleamed full white on the battlements. So many painted pinnacles were set everywhere, built so thick among the crenellations of the castle, that it verily appeared cut out of paper. Fair enough it seemed to the noble knight on his horse if he could only attain the shelter within, to harbour in the hostel, while the holiday lasted. He called, and soon there appeared on the wall a right pleasant porter who took his message and greeted the knight errant.

"Good sir," quoth Gawain, "would you go my errand to the high lord of this house to crave harbour?"

"Yea, by Peter," quoth the porter; "and truly I trow that ye are welcome, sir, to dwell while you like."

Then the man went again quickly, and a crowd of folk with him, to receive the knight. They let down the great draw and eagerly poured out, and kneeled down on their knees on the cold earth to welcome the hero as it seemed to them proper. They opened up wide the gate for him and he raised them courteously, and rode over the bridge. Several attendants held his saddle while he alighted and afterwards good men enough stabled his steed. Then knights and squires came down to bring this hero joyfully into the hall. When he lifted up his helm people enough hurried to take it at his hand, in order to serve the courteous one; his sword and shield they took, too. Then he greeted full courteously the knights each one; and many a proud man pressed there to honour the prince. All hasped in his high weeds, they led him into the hall, where a fair fire burned fiercely upon the hearth. Then the lord of the people came from his chamber to meet courteously the man on the floor. He said, "Ye are welcome to wield as you like what is here; all is your own to have at your will and commandment." "Gramercy," quoth Gawain, "Christ has rewarded you for it." Like glad heroes either folded the other in his arms.

Gawain looked on the man who greeted him so goodly, and thought it a bold hero that owned the castle, a huge warrior for the nonce and of great age. Broad and bright was his beard and all beaver-hued. Firm-gaited was he on his stalwart limbs; with a face as fierce as fire, and a free speech; and to the hero he seemed well suited indeed to govern a nation of good people.

The lord turned to a chamber and promptly commanded to give Gawain a retinue to serve him in lowly wise. . . .

. . .

Then they questioned and inquired sparingly in skillful queries put to the prince himself, till he courteously acknowledged that he was of the court which noble Arthur holds alone, who is the rich, royal king of the Round Table; and that it was Gawain himself that sits in the house, by chance come for that Christmas. When the lord had learned that he had that hero, he laughed aloud, so dear it seemed to him; and all the men in the castle made much joy at appearing promptly in the presence of him who contains in his own person all worth and prowess and gracious traits, and is ever praised; above all men in the world his renown is the greatest. . . .

Then the lady desired to look on the knight and came from her closet with many fair maidens. But she was fairer than all the others in flesh and face, in skin and form, in complexion and demeanour—more beautiful than Guinevere, it seemed to the hero. He walked through the chancel to greet that gracious one. Another lady led her by the left hand, that was older than she; an ancient lady it seemed, and one highly honoured by the knights about her; but unlike to look on were the ladies, for if the younger was fair, yellow was the other. Rich red bloomed on the one everywhere; rough wrinkled cheeks rolled on the other. The kerchiefs of the one broidered with many clear pearls, openly displayed her breast and her bright throat, which shone clearer than snow that falls on the hills. The other covered her neck with a gorget, that wrapped her black chin in milk-white pleats. Her forehead was completely enveloped in silken folds, adorned and tricked with small ornaments; and naught was bare of that lady but the black brows, the two eyes, the nose, and the naked lips; and those were ugly to behold and oddly bleared. A gracious lady in the land one might call her forsooth! Her body was short and thick, her hips round and broad. More pleasant to look on was the being she led.

When Gawain looked on that beauteous one who gazed graciously he took leave of the lord and went toward them. The elder he saluted, bowing full low, the lovelier he took a little in his arms; he kissed her comely, and knightly he greeted her. They welcomed him, and he quickly asked to be their servant if it pleased them. They took him between them and led him conversing to the fireplace in the parlour; and straightway they called for spices, which men speeded to bring them unsparingly, and the pleasant wine therewith each time. The lord leaped merrily up full often, and saw to it that the mirth never faltered. Gaily he snatched off his hood and hung it on a spear and exhorted them to win it as a prize—he to have it who could make the most mirth that Christmas tide. "And I shall try, by my faith, with the help of my friends to compete with the best, ere I lose my apparel." Thus with laughing mien the lord makes merry in order to glad Sir Gawain with games in the hall that night. When it came time, the king commanded lights; Sir Gawain took his leave and went to his bed.

On the morn when as every man knows God was born to die for us, joy waxes in every dwelling in the world for his sake. So it did there on that day, with many dainties at meats and meals, right quaint dishes, and brave men on the dais dressed in their best. The old ancient wife sits the highest, the courteous lord placed by her, as I trow; Gawain and the gay lady together just in the middle, as the courses properly come; and afterwards the rest throughout the hall, as it seemed best to them, each man in his degree was properly served. There was meat, there was mirth, there was much joy, that it were arduous for me to tell thereof, though to note it I took pains belike. But yet I know that Gawain and the lovely lady took comfort in each other's company, in the choice play of their sharp wits, and the pure courtesy of their modest talk; their disport surpassed indeed that of any royal game. Trumps and drums came playing loudly; each man minded his own business and they two minded theirs.

Much delight was taken there that day, and the second; and the third followed as pleasantly. The joy of St. John's Day was gentle to hear of; and it was the last of the festival, the people considered. There were guests to go upon the grey morn; therefore wondrous late they sat up and drank the wine, danced full gayly with sweet carols. At the last, when it was late, they took their leave, each good man to went on his way. Gawain gave his host good-day; but the good man takes him, and leads him to his own chamber, by the fireplace; and there he draws him aside; and properly thanks him for the great worship that he had granted him in honouring his house on that high tide, in embellishing his castle with his good cheer. "Indeed, sir, while I live I shall be the better that Gawain has been my guest at God's own feast."

"Gramercy, sir," quoth Gawain, "in good faith the merit is yours; all the honour is your own,—the high King reward you; and I am your man to work your behest in high and in low as I am bound by right."

The lord eagerly strives to hold the knight longer; but Gawain answers him that he can in no longer wise.

Then the hero asked of him full fairly what extraordinary deed had driven him at that dear time from the king's court, to go all alone so boldly, ere the holidays were wholly over.

"For sooth, sir," quoth the hero, "ye say but the truth; a high errand and a hasty had me from these dwellings; for I am summoned to such a place as I know not in the world whitherward to wend to find it. I would not for all the land in Logres fail to reach it on New Year's morn—so our Lord help me. Therefore sir, this request I require of you here, that ye tell me truly if ever you heard tale of the green chapel, where in the world it stands, and of the knight green in colour that keeps it. There was established by statute an agreement between us that I should meet that man at that landmark if I could but survive. And of that same New Year there now lacks but little, and by God's son, I would gladlier look on that person—if God would let me—than wield any possession in the world. Therefore, indeed—by your good will—it behooves me to wend; I have now at my disposal barely three days; and I were as fain fall dead as fail of mine errand."

Then laughing quoth the lord, "Now it behooves thee to stay; for I shall direct you to that spot by the time's end;—the green chapel upon the ground. Grieve you no more; for ye shall be in your bed, sir, at thine ease some days yet, and set out on the first of the year and come to that place at midmorn, to do what you like. Stay till New Year's morn; and rise and go then. One shall set you on your way; it is not two miles hence."

Then was Gawain full glad; and merrily he laughed: "Now I thank you especially for this above all other things; now that my quest is achieved, I shall dwell at your will, and do whatever else ye decide."

Then the sire seized him and set him beside him, and let the ladies be fetched to please him the better. Fair entertainment they had quietly among themselves; the lord in his jovial, friendly demeanor behaved as a man out of his wits that knew not what he did. Then he spake to the knight, crying loud, "Ye have agreed to do the deed that I bid. Will ye hold this hest here at once?"

"Yea, sir, forsooth," said the true hero, "while I stay in your castle I shall be obedient to your hest."

"Since ye have travelled from afar," quoth the warrior, "and then have sat late with me, ye are not well nourished, I know, either with sustenance or with sleep. Ye shall linger in your loft and lie at your ease tomorrow till mass time; and go to meat when ye will with my wife, who shall sit with you and comfort you with her company till I return home; and I shall rise early and go hunting."

"Yet further," quoth the hero, "let us make an agreement. Whatsoever I win in the wood, it shall be yours; and whatsoever fortune ye achieve, exchange with me therefor. Sweet sir, swap us so, swear truly, whichever one of us gets the worse or the better."

"By God," quoth Gawain the good, "I consent thereto; and whatever game you like, agreeable it seems to me."

"On this beverage just brought the bargain is made," said the lord of that people; and both laughed.

Then they drank and played and amused themselves, these lords and ladies; and then with polite demeanour and many fair gestures, they stood up and lingered a while, and talked quietly, kissed full comely, and took their leave. With many a gay servant and gleaming torches each hero was brought to his bed full softly at the last. Yet before they went to bed they oft rehearsed the covenants. The old lord of that people knew well how to keep up a jest.

## Fytte the Third

Full early before the day the folk arose; the guests that would go called their grooms, and these hastened to saddle the horses, arrange their gear, and truss their mails. The great ones arrayed themselves to ride, leaped up lightly and caught their bridles, each wight on his way where it well pleased him.

The dear lord of the land was not the last; arrayed for the riding, with retainers full many, he ate a sop hastily after he had heard mass, and took his way quickly with his bugle to the field. By the time that any daylight gleamed upon the earth, he with his heroes were mounted on their high horses. Then these hunters that understood it, coupled their hounds, unclosed the kennel doors and called them thereout, blew blithely on bugles three simple calls. At this the brachets bayed and made a wild noise, and the hunters chastised and turned back those that wandered off —a hundred hunters of best they were, as I have heard tell. To their stations the trackers went; hunters cast off the couples; and then arose for the good blasts great uproar in the forest.

At the first noise of the quest the game quaked; the deer moved down into the dale, dazed for dread; hurried to the height; but quickly they were hindered by the beaters, who cried stoutly. They let the harts with the high heads go their way, the wild bucks also with their broad palms, for the generous lord had forbidden that there should be any man meddle with the male deer in the close season. But the hinds were held back with "Hay" and "Ho" and the does driven wih great din to the deep glades. There might one see as they ran the flight of arrows; at each turn under the boughs out fell a shaft, that savagely bit on the brown hide with full broad heads. How they leaped and bled and died by the banks! And ever the hounds with a rush eagerly followed them; hunters with shrill horn hastened after with such a resounding cry as if the cliffs had cracked. What game escaped the men who shot was all run down and torn at the stands. The deer were pestered at the heights, and worried at the waters; the people were so alert at the low station, and the greyhounds so great, that got them quickly and pulled them down as fast as a man could see. The lord, shouting for joy, shot and alighted full oft, and passed the day thus with joy till the dark night.

So this lord sports by the eaves of the linden wood, and Gawain the good man lies in his gay bed; reposes till the daylight gleams on the walls, under the beautiful coverlets, curtained about. And as he fell into a doze, faintly he heard a little din at the door, then distinctly; and he heaved up his head, caught up a corner of his curtain a little, and watched warily in that direction to see what it might be. It was the lady, loveliest to behold, who drew the door to after her right slyly and quietly, and turned toward the bed. The hero grew bashful and laid himself down cunningly and pretended that he slept. And she stepped quietly and stole to his bed, cast up the curtain, and crept within, and seated herself full softly on the bedside and stayed there surprisingly long, to see when he should awake. The man lay pretending a full great while, bothered in his conscience what this affair might mean or amount to. Marvellous it seemed to him. But yet he said to himself: "More seemly would it be to find out by asking what she would." Then he waked, and stretched, and turned to her; unlocked his eyelids, and made believe he was amazed, and crossed himself with his hand, to be the safer for his prayer. With chin and cheek full sweet, of mingled white and red, right lovely she looked, with her small laughing lips.

"Good-morrow, Sir Gawain!" said that fair lady. "Ye are a careless sleeper when one can enter thus. Now ye are certainly taken; unless we can make a truce I shall bind you in your bed, ye may be sure of that!" All laughing the lady shot those jests.

"Good-morrow, fair one," quoth Gawain the blithe. "I shall be at your disposal, and that pleases me well, for I yield me outright and pray for grace,—and that is the best course, I judge, for I am in straits." And thus he returned the jests with many a blithe laugh. "But would ye, lovely lady, grant me leave, free your prisoner, and bid him rise, I would leave this bed and dress myself better. Then I could talk with you in more comfort."

"Nay, forsooth, fair sir," said that sweet one, "ye shall not rise from your bed; I shall manage you better. I shall tie you up securely, and afterwards talk with my knight that I have caught; for I ween well, ye are indeed Sir Gawain, whom all the world worships whereso ye ride. Your honour, your courtesy, is heartily praised, by lords, by ladies, by all alive; and now ye are here, forsooth, and we all alone. My lord and his people are gone far away; the other men in their beds, and my maidens also; the door shut and closed with a strong hasp; and since I have in this house him whom all like, I shall make good use of my time while it lasts. Ye are welcome to my person, to do whatever you wish; I am perforce, and must remain, your servant."

"In good faith," quoth Gawain, "a great privilege it seems to me—though I be not now he that ye speak of. To reach such reverence as ye rehearse here, I am a man unworthy, I know well. By God, I should be glad—if it seemed good to you—to do what I might in speech or in service to enhance your worship;—it were a pure joy."

"In good faith, Sir Gawain," quoth the lady, "if I should speak ill of the fame and the prowess that pleases all others, or esteem it light, it would but show small discernment. But there are ladies enough who were liefer have this courteous one in their power—as I have thee—to dallydearly with your dainty words, to comfort themselves and dispell their cares,—than much of the treasure and gold that they have. But I praise the Lord who rules the skies that through his grace I have wholly in my hand that which all desire."

Great cheer that was so fair of face made him; the knight with discreet speeches answered her every proposal.

"Madame," quoth the merry man, "Mary reward you, for in good faith I have found your generosity noble. People judge a person's deeds largely from the accounts of others; but the praise that they accord my deserts is but idle. It is simply your own nobility, who know nothing but good."

"By Mary," quoth the gracious one, "methinks it is otherwise for were I worth all the store of women alive, and all the wealth of the world were in my hands, and I should bargain and choose to get me a lord, then for the good traits that I have found in the knight here, of beauty and graciousness and gay seeming, and from what I have heard before and hold in this case to be true, there should no hero in the world be chosen before you."

"Indeed, worthy one," quoth the hero, "ye might have chosen much better; but I am proud of the estimation that ye put upon me; and as your devoted servant I hold you my sovereign, and your knight I become; and Christ pay you for it."

Thus they spoke of various things till past the mid-morn; and all the while the lady behaved as if she loved him much. But the hero fared with caution and made courteous pretences. . . . But the lady blessed him and spake in this wise: "A man as good as Gawain is properly held —and courtesy is closed so entirely in him—could not easily have lingered so long with a lady but he had on some trifling excuse or other courteously craved a kiss."

Then said Gawain, "Indeed, be it as you like; I shall kiss at your commandment as becomes a knight, and fear lest he displease you; so urge that plea no more." She comes nearer at that, and takes him in her arms; stoops graciously down and kisses the man. They courteously entrust each other to Christ. She goes forth at the door without more ado and he prepares to rise, and hurries amain; calls to his chamberlain, chooses his weeds, steps forth blithely to mass when he is ready; and then he goes to his meat, behaving always courteously, and makes merry all day till the bright moon rises. . . .

Then the lord commanded to gather in the hall all the household and both the ladies to come down with their maids. Before all the folk on the floor he bade men fetch his venison before him; and all in merry sport he called Gawain, told him the number of the choice beasts, and showed him the fat meat cut from the ribs: "How like you this play? Have I won the prize? Have I properly earned thanks by my woodcraft?"

"Yes, indeed," quoth the other hero; "here is the fairest store that I saw this seven year in the season of winter."

"And all I give you, Gawain," quoth the host, then; "for by our plighted covenant you can claim it as your own."

"That is true," replied the hero, "and I say to you the same; I too have won this worthy thing within doors; and I am sure that with quite as good will it belongs to you." He throws his arms about his fair neck and kisses him as courteously as he knew how. "Take you there my merchandise; I have won no more; though I should give it up willingly even if it were greater."

"It is good," quoth the good man, "gramercy therefor. Perchance it might be better if you would tell me where you won this same favour by your own wit."

"That was not the agreement," said he; "Ask me no more, for ye have got all that belongs to you, be sure of that."

They laughed and made merry in low tones; then they went quickly to supper with new dainties enough.

And afterwards, as they sat by a fireplace in a chamber, servants poured to them oft the choice wine; and again in their jesting they agreed to make the same bargain on the morning that they made before, —whatsoever chance betide to exchange their winnings at night when they met, whatsoever new they win.

*On the following day the lady came to Gawain's bed and insisted that it became every knight who practiced courtesy to claim a kiss. She kissed him and visited a long time, then kissing him again, went her way. The lord hunted a fine boar which he presented to Gawain that night, while Gawain in turn gave him the two kisses. Again, they made the same covenant for the morrow.*

*In the morning the lord went fox-hunting and the lady came again to Gawain's bed.*

All was bliss and good cheer that passed between them. They exchanged goodly words; much happiness they felt, and great was the peril between them, unless Mary thought of her knight.

For that beauteous princess constrained him so sorely, and the danger pressed him so nigh, that of necessity it behooved him either to accept her love or rudely refuse it. He thought much of his courtesy, lest he should prove a clown; and more on his villainy if he should do sin, and be traitor to the hero who owned the castle. "God shield!" quoth the warrior, "that shall not befall!" With a little love-dalliance he laid aside all the pointed speeches that sprang from her mouth.

Quoth the lady to the hero: "Ye deserve blame if ye love not her who is so near you,—of all creatures in the world most wounded in heart;— unless indeed ye have a sweetheart, a dearer being, that pleases you better, and ye have plighted faith so firmly to that gentle one that ye care not to loosen it. Verily now that is what I believe, and I pray you that you tell me truly; for all the loves in the world deny not the truth with guile."

"By St. John," quoth the knight, and courteously he smiled, "I have none, and none will I have."

"That is the worst of all!" quoth the lady. "I am indeed answered, to my sorrow. Kiss me now comely and I shall go hence. I can only mourn in the world as a maid that loved much."

Sighing she stooped down and kissed him seemly; and then she severed from him and said as she stood, "Now, dear, at this departing do give me some comfort; give me somewhat of thy gift, thy glove if it might be, that I may think on thee, sir, to lessen my mourning."

"Now in truth," quoth that man, "I would I had here for thy love, the dearest thing that I wield; for truly ye have right oft in reason deserved a greater reward than I could reckon. But to exchange with you love-tokens, that would profit but little. It is not for your honour to have at this time a glove of Gawain's gift for a keepsake; and I am here on an errand in lands uncouth, and have no men with mails full of precious things for remembrances at this moment; and that mislikes me, lady. But every man must act according to his circumstance, and none should take it ill or repine."

"Now, courteous and honourable one," quoth that lovesome lady, "though I shall have nothing of yours, yet shall ye have of mine."

She reached him a rich ring of red gold work with a gleaming stone standing aloft, that shed blushing beams like the bright sun; know ye well it was worth wealth full huge. But the man refused it, and readily he said: "I desire no great gifts, my gay one, at this time. I have naught to give you, and naught will I take."

She offered it to him full pressingly, and he refused her offer and swore swiftly on his sooth that he would not take it. And she sorrowed that he refused, and said thereafter, "If ye refuse my ring, since it seems too rich, and ye would not be so highly beholden to me, I shall give you my girdle, that will enrich you less."

She lightly caught a lace that went about her sides, knit upon her kirtle under the bright mantle. It was adorned with green silk and ornamented with gold, broidered all around, decked with fringes; and that she offered to the hero, and gaily besought that, though it were unworthy, he would take it. And he denied that he would in any wise take either gold or present ere God sent him grace to achieve the chance that he had chosen there. "And therefore, I pray you, be not displeased, and give over your attempt; for I intend never to consent. I am dearly beholden to you because of your entertainment; and ever in hot and in cold I will be your true servant."

"Now refuse ye this silk," said the lady then, "because it is simple in itself, as it certainly seems to be? Lo! little it is, and less it is worth; but whoso knew the virtues that are knit therein, he would esteem it at a greater price peradventure; for whatsoever man is girt with this green lace, while he has it fittingly wrapped about him, there is no warrior under heaven that can wound him, for he could not be slain by any device in the world."

Then the knight paused, and it came to his heart that it would be a jewel for the peril that awaited him when he arrived at the chapel to undergo his ordeal. Could he manage to be unslain, that were a noble device. Then he indulged her entreaties and suffered her to speak; and she pressed the belt on him and offered it to him eagerly. And he accepted it, and she gave it him with a good will, and besought him for her sake never to discover it, but to conceal it loyally from her lord. The man agreed that never person should know it indeed but they twain. Full oft he thanked her, right glad in heart and thought. By that she had kissed her stout knight three times.

Then she takes her leave and leaves him there, for more entertainment she could not get from that man. When she was gone, Sir Gawain bestirs himself, rises and dresses in noble array. He lays up the love-lace the lady had given him, hides it full cleverly where he can find it again. Then promptly he takes his way to his chapel; quietly approaches the priest and prays him there that he would elevate his life, and teach him better how his soul may be saved when he should go hence. Then he shrives him cleanly and shows his misdeeds, both the more and the less, beseeches mercy, and begs for absolution. And the priest assoils him thoroughly and set him as clean as if doomsday had been due on the morrow. And afterwards Gawain makes more mirth among the fair ladies that day with comely carols and all kinds of joy than ever he did before, till the dark night. . . .

The lord alighted at last at his dear home, found fire on the floor, and the hero beside it, Sir Gawain the good, that glad was withal among the ladies; in their love he had much joy. He wore a mantle of blue that reached to the earth; his surcoat, that was softly furred, became him well; and his hood of the same hung on his shoulder. Trimmed all about with fine fur were both. He met this good man in the middle of the floor, and all joyfully he greeted him, and goodly he said: "Now I shall fulfill our covenant that we have made, where no drink was spared." Then he embraces the knight and kisses him thrice with as much gusto and as soberly as he could give them.

"By Christ," quoth the other knight, "ye get much bliss in the profits of this business—if ye drive good bargains!"

"Of the bargain, no matter," quoth that other, "so long as the debts that I owed are properly paid."

"Mary!" quoth the other man, "my offering is the worse, for I have hunted all this day, and naught have I got but this foul fox-fell; the fiend have the good ones! And that is full poor to pay for such fine things as ye have given me here, three such rare kisses."

"It is enough," quoth Sir Gawain; "I thank you, by the rood." And as they stood there the lord told him how the fox was slain.

With mirth and minstrelsy, with meats at their will, they made as merry as any men could. With laughing of ladies, with merry jests, Gawain and the good man were both as glad as if the court were mad, or else drunk. Both the man and his retinue made many jokes till the season arrived when they must sever; the men had to go to their beds at last. Then humbly this gentle man takes leave of his host first; and fairly he thanks him. "For such a joyous sojourn as I have had here, for the honor you have shown me at this high feast, the high king reward you! I can only give you myself to be one of your men, if that pleases you. For I must needs, as you know, proceed, tomorrow, if ye will grant me some men to show, as you promised, the way to the green chapel, as God will suffer me to take on New Year's day the doom of my fate."

"In good faith," quoth the good man, "with a good will! All that ever I promised you, I will perform." Therewith he assigns a servant to set him in the way, and conduct him by the downs, that he should without hesitation travel through the forest and fare at the best in the woods. The lord thanked Gawain for the worship he had been willing to show him. Then the knight took his leave of the beautiful ladies.

With care and with kissing he speaks to them and many earnest thanks he presses upon them. And they returned him the same again promptly; they entrusted him to Christ with sighings full sad. Afterwards he graciously departs from the household; each man that he met he thanked him for his service and solace, and the various pains with which they had been busy to serve him. And each man was as sad to sever from him there as if they had ever dwelt worthily with that hero. Then with people and with light he was led to his chamber and blithely brought to bed to be at his rest. Whether he slept soundly I dare not say, for he had much to think of on the morrow if he would. Let him lie there; he was near what he sought. If ye will be still a while, I shall tell you how he fared.

## Fytte the Fourth

Now nighs the New Year, and the night passes. The day drives on to the dark, as God bids; but outside wild storms wakened in the earth;

with discomfort enough to the naked, the snow from the north flew sharply, and nipped the game. The blustering wind blew from the heights, and drove each dale full of great drifts. The man who lay in his bed heard it right well; though he locks his lids, full little he sleeps. By each cock that crew, he knew well the hour. Promptly he leaped up ere the day sprang, for there was the light of a lamp that gleamed in his chamber. He called to his chamberlain, who quickly answered him, and bade him bring his burnie and saddle his horse. The chamberlain gets up and fetches him his weeds, and arrays Sir Gawain in proper fashion. First he dressed him in his clothes to keep out the cold, and then he put on the rest of his harness that had been well kept, both mail and plate, and brightly polished. The rings of his rich burnie had been rocked from the rust, and all was fresh as at first; and Gawain was fain to give thanks for it. The attendant had wiped each piece well and often. Then the noblest man betwixt here and Greece bade his steed be brought.

Meanwhile, he threw upon himself his finest weeds; his surcoat with its cognisance of excellent work, virtuous stones set upon velvet, all wrought about and bound with embroidered seams, and fairly furred within with rare skins. Yet left he not the lace, the lady's gift,—that forgot not Gawain for his own good. When he had belted his brand upon his broad haunches, he dressed his love-token double about him, the knight swathed sweetly about his waist the girdle of green silk, which became him well, upon the royal red cloth that was fair to see. But this hero wore not the girdle for its wealth, for pride of the pendants, though they were polished, and though the glittering gold gleamed on the ends; but to save himself when it behooved him to suffer, to await his doom without resistance, with no brand or knife to defend him. By this the good man is ready and goes out quickly. Full often he thanks the distinguished company.

Gringolet the huge and strong was ready, who had been kept skillfully in the safest manner. The proud horse in his splendid condition longed for spurring. The hero approached him, noticed his coat, and said soberly, and by his sooth swore—"Here, in this castle, is a company that are mindful of courtesy. The man who maintains them, joy may he have; the dear lady, love betide her in this life, since they for charity cherish a guest and uphold honor in their hands. May the Being reward them who holds the heaven on high—and also you all. And if I might live any longer in the world I should give you some reward if

I could." Then he stepped into stirrup and strode aloft. His servant offered him his shield; he put it on his shoulder. He spurred Gringolet with his gilt heels, and the steed jumped on the stone; no longer he stood still, but pranced. Gawain's servant who bore his lance and helm was by then on the horse. "This castle I entrust to Christ; may he give it aye good chance!"

The bridge was let down and the broad gates unbarred and borne open on both sides. The hero crossed himself quickly and passed the boards, praised the porter, who knelt before him, giving good day and praying God that He save Gawain. And so he went on his way with his one man that should teach him how to find that dismal place where he should receive the rueful blow.

. . .

. . . Then the knight called full high: "Who dwells in this place to keep covenant with me? For now the good Gawain is passing right here. If any wight wishes ought, then let him come hither fast, now or never, to fulfill his need!"

"Abide," quoth one on the bank over his head. "Thou shalt have in all haste that which I promised thee once."

Yet he kept on with that noise sharply for a while, turning and whetting, ere he would come down. And then he crossed by a crag and came from a hole, whirling out of a dark place with a fell weapon—a Danish axe new dight, to give the blow with. It had fast to the helve a great head, sharpened on the stone. Four feet long was the weapon—no less, by that lace that gleamed full bright. And the man in green was arrayed as before—both his skin and his limbs, locks and beard; save that on foot he strides fairly on the earth. He set the steel shaft to the stone and stalked beside it. When he came to the water, where he did not wish to wade, he hopped over on his axe, and fiercely advanced, with savage ferocity pacing the broad snow-covered glade. Sir Gawain met the knight and bowed to him, not at all low. The other said, "Now, sweet sir, in a covenant a man can trust thee."

"Gawain," quoth the green warrior, "may God preserve thee. Indeed thou art welcome, hero, to my place; and thou hast timed thy travel as a true man should. And thou knowest the covenants made between us; at this time twelvemonth, thou tookest what fell to thee,—and I at this New Year was to repay you handsomely. And now we are in this valley entirely alone; here are no men to part us, however we may behave. Have thy helm off thy head, and have here thy pay. Make no more debate than I offered thee then, when thou whipped off my head at one blow."

"Nay," quoth Gawain, "by God that lent me life, I shall grudge thee not a whit whatever misfortune falls. But arrange thee for thy one stroke and I shall stand still and hinder thee not the least from doing the work as you like."

He bent the neck and bowed down, showing the flesh all bare; and behaved as if he cared not. For no dread would he flinch.

Then the man in the green got ready quickly, gathered up his grim tool to smite Gawain. With all the might in his body he bare it aloft, and aimed a savage blow as though he wished to kill him. Had it driven down as earnestly as he feinted, the ever doughty one would have been dead of his dint. But Gawain glanced to one side on the gisarm as it came gliding down to slay him there in the glade and shrank a little with the shoulders from the sharp iron. The other warrior with a quick motion withheld the bright weapon, and then he reproved the prince with many proud words. "Thou art not Gawain," said the man, "who is held so good, who never flinched for any army by hill nor by vale; and now thou fleest for fear before thou feelest any harm. Such cowardice I never heard of that knight. I neither winced nor fled, sir, when thou didst strike, nor tried any tricks in King Arthur's house. My head flew to my foot, and yet I never budged; and thou, ere any harm taken, art fearful in heart. Wherefore the better man I ought to be called for it."

"I flinched once," quoth Gawain, "and will do so no more. Yet if my head should fall on the stones, I cannot restore it. But make ready, sir, by thy faith, and bring me to the point. Deal to me my destiny, and do it promptly; for I shall stand thee a stroke, and not start again till thine axe has hit me—having here my troth."

"Have at thee then!" quoth the other, and heaves it aloft, and aims as savagely as if he were mad. He strikes at him mightily, but touches the man not; for he withheld his hand cleverly ere it could hurt. Gawain awaits it properly and flinches with no member, but stands still as a stone, or a stump that is twisted in the rocky ground with a hundred roots.

Then merrily spoke the man in green: "So, now thou hast thy heart whole it behoves me to hit. Now keep back the fine hood that Arthur gave thee, and see if thou canst keep thy neck whole from the stroke."

Said Gawain in great anger: "Why, thrash on, thou wild man! Thou threatenest too long. I guess that thine own heart is timid!"

"Forsooth," quoth the other warrior, "thou speakest so fiercely that I will not delay thine errand a bit longer." Then he takes his stride to strike and knits both brow and lip. No wonder Gawain mislikes it and gives up all thought of escape.

Lightly he lifts his axe and lets the edge come down fairly on the bare neck. Yet though he smote rudely, it hurt him but little; only cut him on one side so that it severed the skin. The sharp bit reached the flesh through the fair fat, so that the bright blood shot over his shoulders to the earth. And when the hero saw the blood glint on the snow, he leaped forth more than a spear's length, eagerly seized his helm, cast it on his head, threw his shoulders under his fair shield, pulled out a bright sword, and fiercely spoke. Never in this world since he was born of his mother was he half so blithe.

"Cease, sir, of thy blow! Offer me no more. I have without strife taken a stroke in this place; and if thou givest me more, I shall promptly repay and yield quickly again, trust thou that. Only one stroke falls to me here. The covenant which we made in Arthur's halls provided just that; and therefore, courteous sir, now hold!"

The warrior turned from him and rested on his axe. He set the shaft on the ground, leaned on the head, and beheld how the doughty hero stood his ground grimly, fully armed and devoid of fear. In his heart it pleased him. Then with a great voice and a huge laugh, he spoke merrily to the hero: "Bold sir, in this place be not so savage. Nobody has here unmannerly mishandled thee, nor done but according to covenant made at the king's court. I promised thee a stroke and thou hast it; hold thee well paid. I release thee of the remnant, of all other rights. If I had been skillful peradventure I could have given you a worse buffet.

First I menaced you merrily with a pure feint, and gave thee no blow; which was but justice, considering the covenant we made on the first night and which thou held with me trustily; for truly all the gain thou gave me as a good man should. The second feint this morning, sir, I proffered thee, because thou didst kiss my wife and didst hand the kisses over to me; for these two occasions I gave thee here but two bare feints without harm. A true man truly restores; such an one need dread no harm. At the third time thou didst fail; and so take thee that tap.

For it is my weed that thou wearest, that same woven girdle. Mine own wife gave it thee, I know well, forsooth. Now know I well thy kisses, and thy virtues also. And as for the wooing of my wife, I managed it myself. I sent her to try thee, and truly it seems to me thou art the most faultless hero that ever went on foot. As a pearl is of greater price than white peas, so is Gawain, in good faith, compared with other gay knights. But in this case, sir, you lacked a little, and loyalty failed you. But that was for no amorous work, nor wooing either, but because ye loved your life—the less I blame you."

That other brave man stood a great while in a study; so stricken was he for grief that he groaned within. All the blood of his breast rushed to his face; and he shrank for shame when the warrior talked. This was the first word that the man spoke—"Cursed be cowardice and covetousness both! In you is villainy and vice, that destroy virtue." Then he caught at the knot and loosed the fastening; fiercely reached the belt to the warrior himself. "Lo! there is deception, foul may it fall! For fear of thy knock cowardice taught me to make a truce with covetousness, to forsake my nature, which is generosity and loyalty, that belong to knights. Now am I faulty and false, and a coward have ever been. From treachery and untruth ever come sorrow and care. Here I confess to you, knight, that my conduct is all faulty. Let me but please you now, and after I shall beware."

Then the other laughed and said courteously: "I hold it quite remedied, the harm that I did. Thou hast made a clean confession, acknowledging all thy misdeeds, and hast received the penance openly from the point of my edge. I hold thee quit of that plight and purified as clean as if thou hadst never forfeited since thou was first born. And I give thee, sir, the girdle that is gold hemmed. Since it is green, as is my gown, Sir Gawain, ye may think upon this same adventure where thou goest among great princes; and this shall be a genuine token among chivalrous knights of the adventure of the green chapel, and thee shall come again this New Year to my dwellings, and we shall revel the remnant of this rich feast full well." The lord pressed the invitation and said: "With my wife, who was your great enemy, I think we shall reconcile you."

"Nay, forsooth," quoth the hero, and seized his helm, he took it off quickly and thanked the warrior. "I have had a good visit, bliss betide you; and may He pay you well who directs all mercies. Commend me to that courteous one, your comely mate; both the one and the other, my honoured ladies, who have thus with their craft quaintly beguiled their knight. But it is no wonder that a fool should rave, and through wiles of women be won to sorrow. For so was Adam beguiled by one, and

Solomon by many, indeed; and Samson also, Delilah dealt him his weird; and David thereafter was deceived by Bathsheba, who suffered much sorrow. Since these men were plagued by their wiles, it were a huge gain to love them well and believe them not—if a person but could; for these men were of old the best, and the most fortunate, excellent above all others under the heavens; and all they were beguiled by women whom they had to do with. If I be now deceived, meseems I might be excused.

"But your girdle," quoth Gawain, "God reward you for it! That will I keep with good will; not for the precious gold, nor the samite nor the silk, nor the wide pendants, for its wealth nor for its beauty nor for its fine work; but in sign of my fault I shall behold it oft; when I ride in renown I shall lament to myself the fault and the deceit of the crabbed flesh, how tender it is to catch stains of filth; and thus when pride shall prick me for prowess of arms, a look on this love-lace shall moderate my heart. But one thing I would pray you—may it displease you not—since you are lord of the land yonder where I have stayed worshipfully with you—may the Being who upholds the heavens and sits on high repay you for it!—how name ye your right name? and then no more."

"That shall I tell thee truly," quoth the other then. "Bercilak de Hautdesert I am called in this land through the might of Morgan la Fay, who dwells in my house. She has acquired deep learning, hard won skill, many of the masteries of Merlin;—for she at times has dealt in rare magic with that renowned clerk who knows all your knights at home. Morgan the Goddess is therefore her name; no person is so haughty but she can tame him.

"She sent me in this wise to your rich hall to assay its pride and try if it were true that circulates about the great renown of the Round Table. She prepared for me this wonder to take away your wits, to have grieved Guinevere and caused her to die through fright of that same man, that ghostly speaker with his head in his hand before the high table. That is she, the ancient lady at home. She is even thine aunt, Arthur's half-sister, the daughter of that Duchess of Tintagel upon whom dear Uther afterwards begot Arthur, that is now king. Therefore, I beg you, sir, to come to thine aunt; make merry in my house; my people love thee, and I like thee as well, sir, by my faith as I do any man under God for thy great truth."

But he answered him nay, he would in no wise. They embraced and kissed each other, each entrusted other to the Prince of Paradise, and they parted right there in the cold. Gawain on horse full fair rides boldly to the king's court, and the knight all in green whithersoever he would.

Wild ways in the world Gawain now rides on Gringolet, he who had got the boon of his life. Oft he harboured in houses, and oft without; and many an adventure in vale he had, and won oft; but that I care not at this time to mention in my tale. . . .

(*Anonymous, XIV century, England*)

## *The Service of Woman*

*Closely related to chivalry was the concept of courtly love, the loyal service to the chosen lady. Although the origins of this custom are obscure and debated by scholars, it certainly originated in Provence, which was the center of the Cathar heresy (sometimes called the Church of Love). With its demand of perfect chastity for the Perfecti, its elect members, and its condemnation of the flesh, Catharism was well fitted for a cult of Eros, of passionate, unfulfilled love, for the Cathars held love, though sensual and erotic, to be the source of all good. Then, too, the old Celtic view of woman as prophet, the Eternal Feminine, had survived in many a heretical rite, ready to be adopted as a cult. When all through Europe marriages were made on a landownership basis and romantic love had little part and the requirements of sacramental marriage seemed hard to many a Christianized pagan, the religion of courtly love and of romantic Eros, as an alternative to marriage, opened an avenue of rebellion. The poetry of Provence sung by the troubadours carried the theme of unsatisfied love over the land and gradually it became a highly ritualized part of chivalry with its intricately prescribed conventions.*

*This wooing of woman was a novel idea which introduced an extreme dichotomy in the role of medieval women. She was, on the one hand, a chattel, owned by her father, then by her husband, often fated to a life of hard work and early death from childbearing. Among the nobility her life was easier, but her position was no less subordinate. The tendency of many monks to see her as daughter-of-Eve, source of all evil, did not strengthen her status. But now in song men sought her favor; no request she made to her knight could be denied. The religion of courtly love placed her on a pedestal, an enjoyable, if somewhat unreal, eminence.*

*With the destruction of the Cathars, the theme of passionate love declined. Meanwhile, the actual position of woman had been improving as she functioned as mistress of the manor when her husband was absent in battle or at the court of his lord. Great queens—Blanche of Castile, Eleanor of Aquitaine—typified this new role. But above all, woman triumphed in the cult of the Virgin Mary. Chosen to be the mother of God, hallowed above all other mortals, her veneration became a civilizing factor in subduing the passions of the early Middle Ages. Poets sang her praises, her feasts were numerous, pilgrims thronged to her shrines. The mystical number "four" was assigned to the Trinity to allow place for Mary whose womanly compassion made her more approachable than the Divinity and a kindly intercessor in the scheme of salvation. She became the sublimated object of knightly, chivalrous service, the true Lady.*

## THOUGH OUR SONGS

Though our songs
Cannot banish ancient wrongs,
Though they follow where the rose
    Goes,

And this sound,
Swooning over hollow ground
Fade, and leave the enchanted air
    Bare

Yet the wise
Say that not unblest he dies
Who has known a single May
    Day;

If we have laughed,
Loved and laboured in our craft,
We may pass with a resigned
    Mind.

(*Anonymous, XII century* (?), *France*)

24. *Annunciation*. Flemish tapestry, early XV century. School of Arras, probably designed by Melchior Broederlam or a follower.

## ALLONS AU BOIS LE MAY CUEILLIR

We'll to the woods and gather may
Fresh from the footprints of the rain
We'll to the woods at every vein
To drink the spirit of the day.
The winds of spring are out at play
The needs of spring in heart and brain.
We'll to the woods and gather may
Fresh from the footprints of the rain.

The world's too near her end, you say—
Hark to the blackbird's mad refrain,
It waits for her, the vast Inane?

Then, girls, to help her on her way,
We'll to the woods and gather may.

(*Anonymous, XII century, France*)

## THE EARTH LIES OPEN-BREASTED

The earth lies open-breasted
In gentleness of spring,
Who lay so close and frozen
In winter's blustering.
The northern winds are quiet,
The west wind winnowing,
In all this sweet renewing
How shall a man not sing?

Now go the young men singing,
And singing every bird,
Harder is he than iron
Whom beauty hath not stirred.
And colder than the rocks is he
Who is not set on fire,
When cloudless are our spirits,
Serene and still the air.

Behold, all things are springing
 With life come from the dead,
The cold that wrought for evil
Is routed now and fled.
The lovely earth hath brought to birth
 All flowers, all fragrancy.
Cato himself would soften
At such sweet intimacy.

The woods are green with branches
 And sweet with nightingales,
With gold and blue and scarlet
All flowered are the dales.
Sweet it is to wander
In a place of trees,
Sweeter to pluck roses
And the fleur-de-lys,
But dalliance with a lovely lass
Far surpasseth these.

And yet when all men's spirits
 Are dreaming on delight
My heart is heavy in me,
And troubled at her sight;
If she from whom I travail
 Should still be cold to me
The birds sing unavailing
'Tis winter still for me.

(*Anonymous, XIII century, France*)

# WOULD I MIGHT GO FAR OVER THE SEA

## Marie de France

Would I might go far over the sea
My Love, or high above the air,
And come to land or heaven with thee,
Where no law is, and none shall be,

Against beholding the most rare
Strange beauty that thou hast for me.

Alas, for, in this bitter land
Full many a written curse doth stand
Against the kiss thy lips should bear
Against the sweet gift of thy hands;
Against the knowing that thou art fair,
And too fond loving of thy hair.

## DAVID'S LAMENT FOR JONATHAN

### Peter Abelard

Low in the grave with thee
    Happy to lie,
Since there's no greater thing left Love to do;
    And to live after thee
    Is but to die
For with but half a soul what can Life do?

So share thy victory
    Or else thy grave,
Either to rescue thee, or with thee lie;
    Ending that life for thee,
    That thou didst save,
So Death that sundereth might bring more nigh.

Peace, O my stricken lute!
    Thy strings are sleeping.
Would that my heart could still
    Its bitter weeping!

## ON MARRIAGE

### John of Salisbury

. . .

However honorable and useful marital union may be, it is more fecund in worry than in joy. For example it begets children in pain nor does it produce any fruit which bitterness does not precede or follow. Consequently when, as Valerius relates the incident, Socrates, that earthly oracle of human wisdom if we may so call him, was asked by a young man whether he should take unto himself a wife or abjure marriage entirely, he replied that whichever he did, he would regret it. "On the one hand" he continued "loneliness, childlessness, the dying out of your stock, and an outsider as your heir will be your destiny; on the other eternal worry, one quarrel after another, her dower cast in your face, the haughty disdain of her family, the garrulous tongue of your mother-in-law, the lurking paramour, and worry as to how the children will turn out." In the chain of trying circumstances he left to the young man no opportunity for a happy choice.

The whole chorus of correct thinkers chant the same tune, with the result that if any are repelled by the strict doctrine of the Christian religion they may learn chastity from the pagans. Not that I would at all depreciate conjugal chastity, but I am not at all inclined to think that the fruit of the hundredth or sixtieth part should be united with that of the thirtieth.

Zeno, Epictetus, Aristotle, Critolaus, and many Epicureans are said to have expressed this opinion. On the authority of Jerome there is said to be a Golden Book on marriage by Theophrastus. In this the question whether a wise man should take a wife is raised. The author, after having explained that were she beautiful, of good disposition, honorable birth, and if he were healthy and wealthy, under such circumstances a wise man marries. However he immediately adds "But such a combination is rarely found in marriage; therefore a wise man should not take a wife."

He goes on to state that in the first place the study of philosophy is hampered, and no one can serve two masters, wisdom and wife. Married women make many demands; costly garments, gold and gems, allowance, much furniture, couches, and gilded salons. Then night after night a never ending plaint: "So-and-so is better dressed than I am when she goes out; another is honored by all; I, poor thing, am looked down upon in the company of other women. Why were you ogling the woman next door? What was that you were saying to the maid? What were you bringing home when you came from the forum?" We can't have a friend or companion. She mistrusts the affection of another and yet she mistrusts her own hatred.

If there should be a teacher of renown in any of the cities, we can neither leave our wife nor take our burden with us. It is difficult to support a poor one; it is a torment to put up with a rich one. Add the fact that there is no choice, but whoso falls to one's lot has to be taken, be she bad tempered, be she a fool, ugly, haughty, or disgusting; whatever the defect, we find it out after marriage. A horse, an ass, an ox, a dog, and the cheapest slaves, clothing too and basins, a wooden chair, a goblet, and earthen pitcher are first examined and then bought. The only article not shown is a wife before marriage, for fear that she may displease.

Attention must always be given to her appearance, and her beauty praised for fear if you look at another she may think herself unattractive. She must be called My Lady; notice must be taken of her birthday; one must swear by her life; she must be wished many happy returns of the day; respect must be shown her nurse and personal maid, the family man-servant, her handsome flunkey and her marcelled steward; for a protracted and safe liaison her eunuch too, under which names adulterers lurk. All who have her favor must be loved, however distasteful they are to us.

If you entrust your whole establishment to her, you are reduced to a state of servitude; if you reserve some department for your personal direction she thinks you lack confidence in her. Her feelings will change; she will hate and abuse you and if you are not soon on your guard, she will have recourse to poison. If you admit beldames, goldsmiths, soothsayers, tradesmen in jewels and silks, her chastity is imperiled; if you shut the door on them, there is your unjust suspicion. After all what does a strict guard avail, as a lewd wife cannot be watched and a chaste one does not have to be? Necessity is but a poor protection for chastity and only she is to be called pure who has had the opportunity to sin did she so desire.

A beautiful woman is quick to inspire love; an ugly one's passions are easily stirred. What many love is hard to protect; what no one desires to have is a humility to possess. It involves less misery to possess an unattractive than to keep under surveillance a beautiful woman. No one is safe for whom everyone languishes. One pays court with his handsome presence, another with his wit, a third with his talent, and still another with his generosity. A person assailed from all sides will in some way have to yield the stronghold. Now if a wife is taken to provide a housekeeper for your establishment or to care for your ailing health or to banish your loneliness, a faithful slave will run a house better and obey his master's authority and regulations better than a wife will, for she imagines that she is mistress in proportion as she thwarts the will of her husband; that is to say, does as she pleases, not as she is ordered.

Friends and favorite slaves who are bound by benefits are better qualified to sit by the sickbed than she who charges up against us her tears in hope of a legacy and lets them flow to secure her aim, and by making a show of her solicitude destroys our tranquillity of mind when ill. If she be indisposed, we must be sick with her and never leave her side. If, on the other hand, she be a good, sweet wife, a *rara avis* indeed, we suffer with her the pangs of her labor and are tortured by her peril.

A man of wisdom however can never be lonely; he has the company of all who are or ever have been good men, and he is free to transfer his thoughts wherever he desires. What he cannot embrace in the flesh he can in the spirit, and if men fail him he will converse with God. Never will he be less alone than when he is alone. Furthermore, to marry for the purpose of begetting children, either that our name may not die out or to have a refuge in old age and natural heirs, is utter folly; for how can it affect us when we depart from this world if another is not addressed by our name, since even sons are not for that reason always given the father's name and since there are countless others who go by the same name? What safeguard against old age is it to bring up one who may perhaps die before you or turn out badly, or certainly, when he attains manhood, will feel that you are slow to die? The best and more dependable heirs are friends and connections whom you yourself select rather than those whom, whether you want them or not, you are forced to have. A safe legacy is possible as long as you are alive: namely to use wisely your substance rather than to leave for uncertain purposes what you have acquired by your own efforts.

Such and similar are the remarks of Theophrastus. They in themselves are sufficient to explain the perplexities of the married state and the calamities that overtake its cherished joy. Publius Clodius is said to have wittily remarked that it is arrogant in one who has been twice shipwrecked to blame Neptune. It may with equal discrimination be said that it is arrogant for one who has taken a second wife to accuse Venus of hostility. Who would pity the man who once freed from fetters fled back to chains? He is assuredly unworthy of the honor of liberty and leisure who rushes back to the yoke of servitude he has but just thrown off. Consequently they seem hardly human who, serving not only under the banner of philosophy but as well under that of religion, are unable to keep from the embraces of women. Often one who before he has enrolled under either banner (if indeed philosophy and religion can be considered separately, since no one can be a force in philosophy without religion) has lived a life of self-restraint, as soon as he has made a place for himself and has acquired leisure, exercises all his ingenuity in selecting and marrying a wife or, what is more vile, does not shrink from courting and seducing the wives of his neighbors.

from *Policraticus*)

## I AM EVE, WIFE OF ADAM

I am Eve, wife of Adam.
I condemned Jesus through my greed.
Greedy, I snatched Eden from my children:
I have sinned; I should be stretched upon the tree.

I ruled a kingly place.
Deadly is the evil choice which disgraced me.
Deadly is the toll of the crime which withered me:
Alas, my hands are not clean.

I picked the apple from the bough,
Scruples lost in the longing of my moist mouth:
As long as women live in sunlight
They shall not escape Your wrath.

There would be no ice glazing ground;
There would be no glistening windswept winter;
There would be no hell; there would be no sorrow;
There would be no fear, were it not for me.

(*Anonymous, X century, Ireland*)

## STABAT MATER

### Jacopo da Todi

### Sequence for the Feast of the Sorrowful Mother

| | |
|---|---|
| Stabat Mater dolorosa, | At the cross her station keeping |
| Juxta crucem lacrimosa | Stood the mournful Mother weeping |
| Dum pendebat Filius. | Close to Jesus to the last. |

Cujus animan gementem
Contristatem et dolentem
Pertransivit gladius.

Through her heart, His sorrow sharing,
All His bitter anguish bearing,
Now at length the sword has passed.

O quam tristis et afflicta
Fuit illa benedicta
Mater Unigeniti.

O how sad and sore distressed
Was that Mother, highly blest
Of the sole-begotten One!

Quae maerebat et dolebat
Pia Mater, dum videbat,
Nati poenas inclyti.

Christ above in torment hangs;
She beneath beholds the pangs
Of her dying glorious Son.

Quis est homo qui non fleret,
Matrem Christi si videret
In tanto supplicio?

Is there one who would not weep
Whelm'd in miseries so deep
Christ's dear Mother to behold?

Quis non posset contristari,
Christi Matrem contemplari
Dolentem cum Filio?

Can the human heart refrain
From partaking in her pain,
In that Mother's pain untold?

Pro peccatis suae gentis
Vidit Jesum in tormentis,
Et flagellis subditum.

Bruised, derided, cursed, defiled,
She beheld her tender child;
All with bloody scourges rent.

Vidit suum dulcem natum
Moriendo desolatum,
Dum emissit spiritum.

For the sins of His own nation
Saw Him hang in desolation,
Till His spirit forth He sent.

Eia Mater, fons amoris,
Me sentire vim doloris
Fac, ut tecum lugeam.

O thou Mother! fount of love!
Touch my spirit from above;
Make my heart with thine accord.

Fac ut ardeat cor meum,
In amando Christum Deum
Ut sibi complaceam.

Make me feel as thou hast felt;
Make my soul to glow and melt
With the love of Christ the Lord.

Sancta Mater, istud agas,
Crucifixi fige plagas
Cordi meo valide.

Holy Mother, pierce me through;
In my heart each wound renew
Of my Saviour crucified.

Tui Nati vulnerati,
Tam dignati pro me pati,
Poenas mecum divide.

Let me share with thee His pain,
Who for all my sins was slain,
Who for me in torments died.

Fac me tecum pie flere,
Crucifixo condolere,
Donec ego vixero.

Let me mingle tears with thee,
Mourning Him who mourn'd for me,
All the days that I may live.

| | |
|---|---|
| Juxta crucem tecum stare,<br>Et me tibi sociare,<br>In planctu desidero. | By the cross with thee to stay,<br>There with thee to weep and pray,<br>Is all I ask of thee to give. |
| Virgo virginum praeclara;<br>Mihi jam non sis amara;<br>Fac me tecum plangere. | Virgin of all virgins best,<br>Listen to my fond request,<br>Let me share thy grief divine. |
| Fac ut portem Christi mortem,<br>Passionis fac consortem,<br>Et plagas recolere. | Let me, to my latest breath,<br>In my body bear the death<br>Of that dying Son of thine. |
| Fac me plagis vulnerari,<br>Fac me cruce inebriari,<br>Et cruore Filii. | Wounded with His every wound,<br>Steep my soul till it hath swooned<br>In His very blood away. |
| Flammis ne urar succensus,<br>Per te, Virgo, sim defensus,<br>In die judicii. | Be to me, O Virgin, nigh,<br>Lest in flames I burn and die,<br>In His awful judgment day. |
| Christe, cum sit hinc exire,<br>Da per Matrem me venire<br>Ad palman victoriae. | Christ, when Thou shalt call me hence,<br>Be Thy Mother my defense,<br>Be Thy cross my victory. |
| Quando corpus morietur,<br>Fac ut animae donetur,<br>Paradisi gloria. | While my body here decays,<br>May my soul Thy goodness praise,<br>Safe in Paradise with Thee. |
| Amen. | Amen. |

## STAR OF THE SEA

### Bernard of Clairvaux

O you who find yourself storm-tossed by winds and waves of this world and in danger of shipwreck, look to the Star of the Sea.

If the winds of temptation blow, if troubles rise like cliffs before you, look to the Star, call to Mary.

If waves of pride, ambition, dishonesty and envy threaten to engulf your soul, look to the Star, call to Mary.

If anger, avarice or self-indulgence threaten disaster to your voyage, call to Mary.

25. *Rucellai Madonna,* Duccio. Florence, Uffizi.

If remorse, an unquiet conscience and fear of the Judgment draw you down to the depths of despair, call to Mary.

In danger, anguish and fear, think of Mary, call to Mary.

Let her name be on your lips and in your heart; seek Mary and follow her shining example. Guided by Mary, you can never lose the way. While you pray to Mary, hope is ever your companion. Think of Mary and you will keep a true course. While she supports you, stand upright; while she protects you, fear not. If she grants you her favor, you shall come to the port of safety in triumph.

# PART III

# The Journey

*Medieval civilization was young, colorfully experimental and vigorously adventurous. At every level of experience, the humanism of the Christian faith had released tremendous stores of energy and imbued western man with a fresh sense of confidence and of drama. This was a civilization on the move. From the theologians' "faith seeking understanding" to the ascetical itineraria, from the pilgrimages to the Crusades and merchant expansion, life was the great adventure.*

## *The Pilgrim*

*The age had a passion for color, pomp and pageantry. Whether it was the coronation of the king or the turning of the first shovel of earth in the spring, there were appropriate ceremonies. But the favorite ceremony was the pilgrimage. Mile after mile pilgrims wended their way to shrines, perhaps to Canterbury in England, to Holywell in Wales, St. James in Spain, or most of all, to Rome. In the year 1033 when it was popularly believed that the world would end, the millennium after Christ's death having arrived, the dust never settled on the old Roman-built roads across the Apennines. Each monastery had a pilgrim-inn, and hostels and hospitals were established for the travellers. Knights made the journey before wars, merchants before ventures across the sea. In one year alone there were 200,000 pilgrims to Canterbury, and this in a country of two million people.*

*They went to pay homage and often they went in hope of favors. There were innumerable reports of miraculous cures, some certainly due to the exercise and healthful diet. Enough, however, appeared genuine to foster hope in many a cripple brought to the shrines where the intercession of Mary and the saints was begged for physical and spiritual remedies. Among the wealthy, it became common to leave bequests in wills to have pilgrimages made in their behalf so that the professional pilgrim or palmer became customary.*

# PROLOGUE TO THE CANTERBURY TALES

## Geoffrey Chaucer

### Here bygynneth the Book of the Tales of Caunterbury

Whan that Aprille with his shoures soote
The droghte of March hath perced to the roote,
And bathed every veyne in swich licour
Of which vertu engendred is the flour;
When Zephirus eek with his sweete breeth
Inspired hath in every holt and heeth
The tendre croppes, and the yonge sonne
Hath in the Ram his halve cours yronne,
And smale foweles maken melodye,
That slepen al the nyght with open ye
(So priketh hem nature in hir corages);
Thanne longen folk to goon on pilgrimages,
And palmeres for to seken straunge strondes,
To ferne halwes, kowthe in sondry londes;
And specially from every shires ende
Of Engelond to Caunterbury they wende,
The hooly blisful martir for to seke,
That hem hath holpen whan that they were seeke.
Bifil that in that seson on a day,
In Southwerk at the Tabard as I lay
Redy to wenden on my pilgrymage
To Caunterbury with ful devout corage,
At nyght was come into that hostelrye
Wel nyne and twenty in a compaignye,

Of sondry folk, by aventure yfalle
In felaweshipe, and pilgrimes were they alle,
That toward Caunterbury wolden ryde.
The chambres and the stables weren wyde,
And wel we weren esed atte beste.
And shortly, whan the sonne was to reste,
So hadde I spoken with hem everichon
That I was of hir felaweshipe anon,
And made forward erly for to ryse,
To take oure wey ther as I yow devyse.
  But natheless, whil I have tyme and space,
Er that I ferther in this tale pace,
Me thynketh it acordaunt to resoun
To telle yow al the condicioun
Of ech of hem, so as it seemed me,
And whiche they weren, and of what degree,
And eek in what array that they were inne;
And at a knyght than wol I first bigynne.
  A Knyght ther was, and that a worthy man,
That fro the tyme that he first bigan
To riden out, he loved chivalrie.
Trouthe and honour, freedom and curteisie.
Ful worthy was he in his lordes werre,
And thereto hadde he riden, no man ferre,
As wel in cristendom as in hethenesse,
And evere honoured for his worthynesse.
At Alisaundre he was whan it was wonne.
Ful ofte tyme he hadde the bord bigonne
Aboven alle nacions in Pruce;
In Lettow hadde he reysed and in Ruce,
No Cristen man so ofte of his degree.
In Gernade at the seege eek hadde he be
Of Algezir, and riden in Belmarye.
At Lyeys was he and at Satalye,
Whan they were wonne; and in the Grete See
At many a noble armee hadde he be.
At mortal batailles hadde he been fiftene,
And foughten for oure feith at Tramyssene
In lystes thries, and ay slayn his foo.

This ilke worthy knyght hadde been also
Somtyme with the lord of Palatye
Agayn another hethen in Turkye.
And everemoore he hadde a sovereyn prys;
And though that he were worthy, he was wys,
And of his port as meeke as is a mayde.
He nevere yet no vileynye ne sayde
In al his lyf unto no maner wight.
He was a verray, parfit gentil knyght.
But, for to tellen yow of his array,
His hors were goode, but he was nat gay.
Of fustian he wered a gypon
Al bismotered with his habergeon,
For he was late ycome from his viage,
And wente for to doon his pilgrymage.
With hym ther was his sone, a yong SQUIER,
A lovyere and a lusty bacheler,
With lokkes crulle as they were leyd in presse.
Of twenty yeer of age he was, I gesse.
Of his stature he was of evene lengthe,
And wonderly delyvere, and of greet strengthe.
And he hadde been somtyme in chyvachie
In Flaundres, in Artoys, and Pycardie,
And born hym weel, as of so litel space,
In hope to stonden in his lady grace.
Embrouded was he, as it were a meede
Al ful of fresshe floures, whyte and reede.
Syngynge he was, or floytynge, al the day;
He was as fressh as in the month of May.
Short was his gowne, with sleves longe and wyde.
Wel koude he sitte on hors and faire ryde.
He koude songes make and wel endite,
Juste and eek daunce, and weel purtreye and write,
So hoote he lovede that by nyghtertale
He sleep namoore than dooth a nyghtyngale.
Curteis he was, lowely, and servysable,
And carf biforn his fader at the table.
A YEMAN hadde he and servantz namo
At that tyme, for hym liste ride so;

And he was clad in cote and hood of grene.
A sheef of pecok arwes, bright and kene,
Under his belt he bar ful thriftily,
(Wel koude he dresse his takel yemanly:
His arwes drouped noght with fetheres lowe)
And in his hand he baar a myghty bowe.
A not heed hadde he, with a broun visage.
Of wodecraft wel koude he al the usage.
Upon his arm he baar a gay bracer,
And by his syde a swerd and a bokeler,
And on that oother syde a gay daggere
Harneised wel and sharp as point of spere;
A Cristopher on his brest of silver sheene.
An horn he bar, the bawdryk was of grene;
A forster was he, soothly, as I gesse.
  Ther was also a Nonne, a PRIORESSE,
That of hir smylyng was ful symple and coy;
Hire gretteste ooth was but by Seinte Loy;
And she was cleped madame Eglentyne.
Ful weel she soong the service dyvyne,
Entuned in hir nose ful semely,
And Frenssh she spak ful faire and fetisly,
After the scole of Stratford atte Bowe,
For Frenssh of Parys was to hire unknowe.
At mete wel ytaught was she with alle:
She leet no morsel from hir lippes falle,
Ne wette hir fyngres in hir sauce depe;
Wel koude she carie a morsel and wel kepe
That no drope ne fille upon hir brest.
In curteisie was set ful muchel hir lest.
Hir over-lippe wyped she so clene
That in hir coppe ther was no ferthyng sene
Of grece, whan she dronken hadde hir draughte.
Ful semely after hir mete she raughte.
And sikerly she was of greet desport,
And ful plesaunt, and amyable of port,
And peyned hire to countrefete cheere
Of court, and to been estatlich of manere,
And to ben holden digne of reverence.

But, for to speken of hire conscience,
She was so charitable and so pitous
She wolde wepe, if that she saugh a mous
Kaught in a trappe, if it were deed or bledde.
Of smale houndes hadde she that she fedde
With rosted flessh, or milk and wastel-breed.
But soore wepte she if oon of hem were deed,
Or if men smoot it with a yerde smerte;
And al was conscience and tendre herte.
Ful semyly hir wympul pynched was;
Hir nose tretys, hir eyen greye as glas,
Hir mouth ful smal, and therto softe and reed;
But sikerly she hadde a fair forheed;
It was almoost a spanne brood, I trowe;
For, hardily, she was nat undergrowe.
Ful fetys was hir cloke, as I was war.
Of smal coral aboute hire arm she bar
A peire of bedes, gauded al with grene,
And theron heng a brooch of gold ful sheene,
On which ther was first write a crowned A,
And after *Amor vincit omnia.*
  Another NONNE with hir hadde she,
That was hir chapeleyne, and preestes thre.
  A MONK ther was, a fair for the maistrie,
An outridere, that lovede venerie,
A manly man, to been an abbot able.
Ful many a deyntee hors hadde he in stable,
And whan he rood, men myghte his brydel heere
Gynglen in a whistlynge wynd als cleere
And eek as loude as dooth the chapel belle.
Ther as this lord was kepere of the celle,
The reule of seint Maure or of seint Beneit,
By cause that it was old and somdel streit
This ilke Monk leet olde thynges pace,
And heeld after the newe world the space.
He yaf nat of the text a pulled hen,
That seith that hunters ben nat hooly men,
Ne that a monk, when he is recchelees,
Is likned til a fissh that is waterless,—

This is to seyn, a monk out of his cloystre.
But thilke text heeld he nat worth on oystre;
And I seyde his opinion was good.
What sholde he studie and make hymselven wood,
Upon a book in cloystre alwey to poure,
Or swynken with his handes, and laboure,
As Austyn bit? How shal the world be served?
Lat Austyn have his swynk to hym reserved!
Therfore he was a prikasour aright:
Grehoundes he hadde as swift as fowel in flight;
Of prikyng and of huntyng for the hare
Was al his lust, for no cost wolde he spare.
I seigh his sleves purfiled at the hond
With grys, and that the fyneste of a lond;
And, for to festne his hood under his chyn,
He hadde of gold ywroght a ful curious pyn;
A love-knotte in the gretter ende ther was.
His heed was balled, that shoon as any glas,
And eek his face, as he hadde been enoynt.
He was a lord ful fat and in good poynt;
His eyen stepe, and rollynge in his heed,
That stemed as a forneys of a leed;
His bootes souple, his hors in greet estaat.
Now certeinly he was a fair prelaat;
He was nat pale as a forpyned goost.
A fat swan loved he best of any roost.
His palfrey was as broun as is a berye.
A FRERE ther was, a wantowne and a merye,
A lymytour, a ful solempne man.
In alle the ordres foure is noon that kan
So muchel of daliaunce and fair langage.
He hadde maad ful many a mariage
Of yonge wommen at his owene cost.
Unto his ordre he was a noble post.
Ful wel biloved and famulier was he
With frankeleyns over al in his contree,
And eek with worthy wommen of the toun;
For he hadde power of confessioun.
As seyde hymself, moore than a curat,

For of his ordre he was licenciat.
Ful swetely herde he confessioun,
And plesaunt was his absolucioun:
He was an esy man to yeve penaunce,
Ther as he wiste to have a good pitaunce.
For unto a povre ordre for to yive
In signe that a man is wel yshryve;
For if he yaf, he dorste make avaunt,
He wiste that a man was repentaunt;
For many a man so hard is of his herte,
He may nat wepe, althogh hym soore smerte.
Therfore in stede to wepynge and preyeres
Men moote yeve silver to the povre freres.
His typet was ay farsed ful of knyves
And pynnes, for to yeven faire wyves.
And certeinly he hadde a murye note:
Wel koude he synge and pleyen on a rote;
Of yeddynges he baar outrely the pris.
He nekke whit was as the flour-de-lys;
Therto he strong was as a champioun.
He knew the tavernes wel in every toun
And everich hostiler and tappestere
Bet than a lazar or a beggestere;
For unto swich a worthy man as he
Acorded nat, as by his facultee,
To have with sike lazars aqueyntaunce.
It is nat honest, it may nat avaunce,
For to deelen with no swich poraille,
But al with riche and selleres of vitaille.
And over al, ther as profit sholde arise,
Curteis he was and lowely of servyse.
Ther nas no man nowher so vertuous.
He was the beste beggere in his hous;
For thogh a wydwe hadde noght a sho,
So pleasaunt was his *"In principio,"*
Yet wolde he have a ferthyng, er he wente.
His purchas was wel bettre than his rente.
And rage he koude, as it were right a whelp.
In love-dayes ther koude he muchel help,

For ther he was nat lyk a cloysterer
With a thredbare cope, as is a povre scoler,
But he was lyk a maister or a pope.
Of double worstede was his semycope,
That rounded as a belle out of the presse.
Somwhat he lipsed, for his wantownesse,
To make his Englissh sweete upon his tonge;
And in his harpyng, whan that he hadde songe,
His eyen twynkled in his heed aryght,
As doon the sterres in the frosty nyght.
This worthy lymytour was cleped Huberd.
A MARCHANT was ther with a forked berd,
In mottelee, and hye on horse he sat;
Upon his heed a Flaundryssh bever hat,
His bootes clasped faire and fetisly.
His resons he spak ful solempnely,
Sownynge alwey th' encrees of his wynnyng.
He wolde the see were kept for any thyng
Bitwixe Middelburgh and Orewelle.
Wel koude he in eschaunge sheeldes selle.
This worthy man ful wel his wit bisette.
Ther wiste no wight that he was in dette,
So estatly was he of his governaunce
With his bargaynes and with his chevyssaunce.
For sothe he was a worthy man with alle,
But, sooth to seyn, I noot how men hym calle.
A CLERK ther was of Oxenford also,
That unto logyk hadde longe ygo.
As leene was his hors as is a rake,
And he nas nat right fat, I undertake,
But looked holwe, and therto sobrely.
Ful thredbare was his overeste courtepy;
For he hadde geten hym yet no benefice,
Ne was so worldly for to have office.
For hym was levere have at his beddes heed
Twenty bookes, clad in blak or reed,
Of Aristotle and his philosophie,
Than robes riche, or fithele, or gay sautrie.
But al be that he was a philosophre,

Yet hadde he but litel gold in cofre;
But al that he myghte of his freendes hente,
On bookes and on lernynge he it spente,
And bisily gan for the soules preye
Of hem that yaf hym wherwith to scoleye.
Of studie took he moost cure and moost heede.
Noght o word spak he moore than was neede,
And that was seyd in forme and reverence,
And short and quyk and ful of hy sentence;
Sownynge in moral vertu was his speche,
And gladly wolde he lerne and gladly teche.

A SERGEANT OF THE LAWE, war and wys,
That often hadde been at the Parvys,
Ther was also, ful riche of excellence.
Discreet he was and of greet reverence—
He semed swich, his wordes weren so wise.
Justice he was ful often in assise,
By patente and by pleyn commissioun.
For his science and for his heigh renoun,
Of fees and robes hadde he many oon.
So greet a purchasour was nowher noon:
Al was fee symple to hym in effect;
His purchasyng myghte nat been infect.
Nowher so bisy a man as he ther nas,
And yet he semed bisier than he was.
In termes hadde he caas and doomes alle
That from the tyme of kyng William were falle.
Therto he koude endite, and make a thyng,
Ther koude no wight pynche at his writyng;
And every statut koude he pleyn by rote.
He rood but hoomly in a medlee cote,
Girt with a ceint of silk, with barres smale;
Of his array telle I no lenger tale.

A FRANKELEYN was in his compaignye.
Whit was his berd as is the dayesye;
Of his complexioun he was sangwyn.
Wel loved he by the morwe a sop in wyn;
To lyven in delit was evere his wone,
For he was Epicurus owene sone,

That heeld opinioun that pleyn delit
Was verraily felicitee parfit.
An housholdere, and that a greet, was he;
Seint Julian he was in his contree.
His breed, his ale, was alweys after oon;
A bettre envyned man was nowher noon.
Withoute bake mete was nevere his hous
Of fissh and flessh, and that so plentevous,
It snewed in his hous of mete and drynke,
Of alle deyntees that men koude thynke.
After the sondry sesons of the yeer,
So chaunged he his mete and his soper.
Ful many a fat partrich hadde he in muwe,
And many a breem and many a luce in stuwe.
Wo was his cook but if his sauce were
Poynaunt and sharp, and redy al his geere.
His table dormant in his halle alway
Stood redy covered al the longe day.
At sessiouns ther was he lord and sire;
Ful ofte tyme he was knyght of the shire.
An anlaas and a gipser al of silk
Heeng at his girdel, whit as morne milk.
A shirreve hadde he been, and a countour.
Was nowher swich a worthy vavasour.
  An Haberdasshere and a Carpenter,
A Webbe, a Dyere, and a Tapycer,—
And they were clothed alle in o lyveree
Of a solempne and a greet fraternitee.
Ful fressh and newe hir geere apiked was;
Hir knyves were chaped noght with bras
But all with silver; wroght ful clene and weel
Hire girdles and hir pouches everydeel.
Wel semed ech of hem a fair burgeys
To sitten in a yeldehalle on a deys.
Everich, for the wisdom that he kan,
Was shaply for to been an alderman.
For catel hadde they ynogh and rente,
And eek hir wyves wolde it wel assente;
And elles certeyn were they to blame.

It is ful fair to been ycleped "madame,"
And goon to vigilies al bifore,
And have a mantel roialliche ybore.
 A COOK they hadde with hem for the nones
To boille the chiknes with the marybones,
And poudre-marchant tart and galyngale.
Wel koude he knowe a draughte of Londoun ale.
He koude rooste, and sethe, and broille, and frye,
Maken mortreux, and wel bake a pye.
But greet harm was it, as it thoughte me,
That on his shyne a mormal hadde he.
For blankmanger, that made he with the beste.
 A SHIPMAN was ther, wonynge fer by weste;
For aught I woot, he was of Dertemouthe.
He rood upon a rouncy, as he kouthe,
In a gowne of faldyng to the knee.
A daggere hangynge on a laas hadde he
Aboute his nekke, under his arm adoun.
The hoote somer hadde maad his hewe al broun;
And certeinly he was a good felawe.
Ful many a draughte of wyn had he ydrawe
Fro Burdeux-ward, whil that the chapman sleep
Of nyce conscience took he no keep.
If that he faught, and hadde the hyer hond,
By water he sente hem hoom to every lond.
But of his craft to rekene wel his tydes,
His stremes, and his daungers hym bisides,
His herberwe, and his moone, his lodemenage,
Ther nas noon swich from Hulle to Cartage.
Hardy he was and wys to undertake;
With many a tempest hadde his berd been shake.
He knew alle the havenes, as they were,
Fro Gootlond to the cape of Fynystere,
And every cryke in Britaigne and in Spayne.
His barge ycleped was the Maudelayne.
 With us ther was a DOCTOUR OF PHISIK;
In al this world ne was ther noon hym lik,
To speke of phisik and of surgerye,
For he was grounded in astronomye.

He kepte his pacient a ful greet deel
In houres by his magyk natureel.
Wel koude he fortunen the ascendent
Of his ymages for his pacient.
He knew the cause of everich maladye,
Were it of hoot, or coold, or moyste, or drye,
And where they engendred, and of what humour.
He was a verray, parfit praktisour:
The cause yknowe, and of his harm the roote,
Anon he yaf the sike man his boote.
Ful redy hadde he his apothecaries
To sende hym drogges and his letuaries,
For ech of hem made oother for to wynne—
Hir frendshipe nas nat newe to bigynne.
Wel knew he the olde Esculapius,
And Deyscorides, and eek Rufus,
Olde Ypocras, Haly, and Galyen,
Serapion, Razis, and Avycen,
Averrois, Damascien, and Constantyn,
Bernard, and Gatesden, and Gilbertyn.
Of his diete mesurable was he,
For it was of no superfluitee,
But of greet norissyng and digestible.
His studie was but litel on the Bible.
In sangwyn and in pers he clad was al,
Lyned with taffata and with sendal;
And yet he was but esy of dispence;
He kepte that he wan in pestilence.
For gold in phisik is a cordial,
Therefore he lovede gold in special.
A good Wif was ther of biside Bathe,
But she was somdel deef, and that was scathe.
Of clooth-makyng she hadde swich an haunt,
She passed hem of Ypres and of Gaunt.
In al the parisshe wif ne was ther noon
That to the offrynge bifore hire sholde goon;
And if ther dide, certeyn so wrooth was she,
That she was out of alle charitee.
Hir coverchiefs ful fyne weren of ground;

26. Illustrations from *The Ellesmere Chaucer*.

¶ Heere bigynneth the Cookes tale

A Prentys whilom dwelled in oure Citee
And of a craft of vitaillers was hee
Gaillard he was as goldfynch in the shawe
Broun as a berye a propre short felawe
With lokkes blake ykembd ful fetisly
Dauncen he koude so wel and iolily
That he was cleped Perkyn Reuelour
He was as ful of loue and paramour
As is the hyue ful of hony sweete
Wel was the wenche with hym myghte meete
At euery bridale wolde he synge and hoppe
He loued bet the Tauerne than the shoppe
ffor whan ther any ridyng was in Chepe
Out of the shoppe thider wolde he lepe
Til that he hadde al the sighte yseyn
And daunced wel he wolde nat come ageyn
And gadered hym a meynee of his sort
To hoppe and synge and maken swich disport
And ther they setten steuene for to meete
To pleyen at the dys in swich a strete

ffor to declare thy grete worthynesse
That I ne may the weighte nat susteene
But as a child of twelf monthe oold or lesse
That kan vnnethe any word expresse
Right so fare I and therfore I yow preye
Gydeth my song yt I shal of yow seye

¶ Explicit

¶ Heere bigynneth the Prioresses tale

Ther was in Asye in a greet Citee
Amonges cristene folk a Iewerye
Sustened by a lord of that contree
ffor foul vsure and lucre of vileynye ¶ Usure lucrum
Hateful to Crist and to his compaignye
And thurgh this strete men myghte ride or wende
ffor it was free and open at eyther ende

I dorste swere they weyeden ten pound
That on a Sonday weren upon hir heed.
Hir hosen weren of fyn scarlet reed,
Ful streite yteyd, and shoes ful moyste and newe.
Boold was hir face, and fair, and reed of hewe.
She was a worthy womman al hir lyve:
Housbondes at chirche dore she hadde fyve,
Withouten oother compaignye in youthe,—
But therof nedeth nat to speke as nowthe.
And thries hadde she been at Jerusalem;
She hadde passed many a straunge strem;
At Rome she hadde been, and at Boloigne,
In Galice at Seint Jame, and at Coloigne.
She koude muchel of wandrynge by the weye.
Gat-tothed was she, soothly for to seye.
Upon an amblere esily she sat,
Ywympled wel, and on hir heed an hat
As brood as is a bokeler or a targe;
A foot-mantel aboute hir hipes large,
And on hir feet a paire of spores sharpe.
In felaweshipe wel koude she laughe and carpe.
Of remedies of love she knew per chaunce,
For she koude of that art the olde daunce.
  A good man was ther of religioun,
And was a povre PERSOUN OF A TOUN,
But riche he was of hooly thoght and werk.
He was also a lerned man, a clerk,
That Cristes gospel trewely wolde preche;
His parisshens devoutly wolde he teche.
Benygne he was, and wonder diligent,
And in adversitee ful pacient,
And swich he was ypreved ofte sithes.
Ful looth were hym to cursen for his tithes,
But rather wolde he yeven, out of doute,
Unto his povre parisshens aboute
Of his offryng and eek of his substaunce.
He koude in litel thyng have suffisaunce.
Wyd was his parisshe, and houses fer asonder,
But he ne lefte nat, for reyn ne thonder,

In siknesse nor in meschief to visite
The ferreste in his parisshe, muche and lite,
Upon his feet, and in his hand a staf.
This noble ensample to his sheep he yaf,
That first he wroghte, and afterward he taughte.
Out of the gospel he tho wordes caughte,
And this figure he added eek therto,
That if gold ruste, what shal iren do?
For if a preest be foul, on whom we truste,
No wonder is a lewed man to ruste;
And shame it is, if a prest take keep,
A shiten shepherde and a clene sheep.
Wel oghte a preest ensample for to yive,
By his clennesse, how that his sheep sholde lyve.
He sette nat his benefice to hyre
And leet his sheep encombred in the myre
And ran to Londoun unto Seinte Poules
To seken hym a chaunterie for soules,
Or with a bretherhed to been withholde;
But dwelte at hoom, and kepte wel his folde,
So that the wolf ne made it nat myscarie;
He was a shepherde and noght a mercenarie.
And though he hooly were and vertuous,
He was to synful men nat despitous,
Ne of his speche daungerous ne digne,
But in his techyng discreet and benygne.
To drawen folk to hevene by fairnesse,
By good ensample, this was his bisynesse.
But it were any persone obstinat,
What so he were, of heigh or lough estat,
Hym wolde he snybben sharply for the nonys.
A bettre preest I trowe that nowher noon ys.
He waited after no pompe and reverence,
Ne maked him a spiced conscience,
But Cristes loore and his apostles twelve
He taughte, but first he folwed it hymselve.
With hym ther was a PLOWMAN, was his brother,
That hadde ylad of dong ful many a fother;
A trewe swynkere and a good was he,

Lyvynge in pees and parfit charitee.
God loved he best with al his hoole herte
At alle tymes, thogh him gamed or smerte,
And thanne his neighebor right as hymselve.
He wolde thresshe, and therto dyke and delve,
For Cristes sake, for every povre wight,
Withouten hire, if it lay in his myght.
His tithes payde he ful faire and wel,
Boothe of his propre swynk and his catel.
In a tabard he rood upon a mere.
  Ther was also a REVE, and a MILLERE,
A SOMNOUR, and a PARDONER, also,
A MAUNCIPLE, and myself—ther were namo.
  The MILLERE was a stout carl for the nones;
Ful byg he was of brawn, and eek of bones.
That proved wel, for over al ther he cam,
At wrastlynge he wolde have alwey the ram.
He was short-sholdred, brood, a thikke knarre;
Ther was no dore that he nold heve of harre,
Or breke it at a rennyng with his heed.
His berd as any sowe or fox was reed,
And therto brood, as though it were a spade.
Upon the cop right of his nose he hade
A werte, and theron stood a toft of herys,
Reed as the brustles of a sowes erys;
His nosethirles blake were and wyde.
A swerd and bokeler bar he by his syde.
His mouth as greet was as a greet forneys.
He was a janglere and a goliardeys,
And that was moost of synne and harlotries.
Wel koude he stelen corn and tollen thries;
And yet he hadde a thombe of gold, pardee.
A whit cote and a blew hood wered he.
A baggepipe wel koude he blowe and sowne,
And therwithal he broghte us out of towne.
  A gentil MAUNCIPLE was ther of a temple,
Of which achatours myghte take exemple
For to be wise in byynge of vitaille;
For wheither that he payde or took by taille,

Algate he wayted so in his achaat
That he was ay biforn and in good staat.
Now is nat that of God a ful fair grace
That swich of lewed mannes wit shal pace
The wisdom of an heep of lerned men?
Of maistres hadde he mo than thries ten,
That weren of lawe expert and curious,
Of which ther were a duszeyne in that hous
Worthy to been stywardes of rente and lond
Of any lord that is in Engelond,
To make hym lyve by his propre good
In honour dettelees (but if he were wood),
Or lyve as scarsly as hym list desire;
And able for to helpen al a shire
In any caas that myghte fall or happe;
And yet this Manciple sette hir aller cappe.
The REVE was a sclendre colerik man.
His berd was shave as ny as ever he kan;
His heer was by his erys ful round yshorn;
His top was dokked lyk a preest biforn.
Ful longe were his legges and ful lene,
Ylyk a staf, ther was no calf ysene.
Wel koude he kepe a gerner and a bynne;
Ther was noon auditour koude on him wynne.
Wel wiste he by the droghte and by the reyn
The yeldynge of his seed and of his greyn.
His lordes sheep, his neet, his dayerye,
His swyn, his hors, his stoor, and his pultrye
Was hoolly in this Reves governyng,
And by his covenant yaf the rekenyng,
Syn that his lord was twenty yer of age.
Ther koude no man brynge hym in arrerage.
Ther nas baillif, ne hierde, nor oother hyne,
That he ne knew his sleighte and his covyne;
They were adrad of hym as of the deeth.
His wonyng was ful faire upon an heeth;
With grene trees yshadwed was his place.
He koude bettre than his lord purchace.
Ful riche he was astored pryvely:

His lord wel koude he plesen subtilly,
To yeve and lene hym of his owene good,
And have a thank, and yet a cote and hood.
In youthe he hadde lerned a good myster;
He was a wel good wrighte, a carpenter.
This Reve sat upon a ful good stot,
That was al pomely grey and highte Scot.
A long surcote of pers upon he hade,
And by his syde he baar a rusty blade.
Of Northfolk was this Reve of which I telle,
Biside a toun men clepen Baldeswelle.
Tukked he was as is a frere aboute,
And evere he rood the hyndreste of oure route.

A SOMONOUR was ther with us in that place,
That hadde a fry-reed cherubynnes face,
For saucefleem he was, with eyen narwe.
As hoot he was and lecherous as a sparwe,
With scalled browes blake and piled berd.
Of his visage children were aferd.
Ther nas quyk-silver, lytarge, ne brymstoon,
Boras, ceruce, ne oille of tartre noon;
Ne oynement that wolde clense and byte,
That hym myghte helpen of his whelkes white,
Nor of the knobbes sittynge on his chekes.
Wel loved he garleek, oynons, and eek lekes,
And for to drynken strong wyn, reed as blood;
Thanne wolde he speke and crie as he were wood.
And whan that he wel dronken hadde the wyn,
Thanne wolde he speke no word but Latyn.
A fewe termes hadde he, two or thre,
That he had lerned out of som decree—
No wonder is, he herde it al the day;
And eek ye knowen wel how that a jay
Kan clepen "Watte" as wel as kan the pope.
But whoso koude in oother thyng hym grope,
Thanne hadde he spent al his philosophie;
Ay *"Questio quid iuris"* wolde he crie.
He was a gentil harlot and a kynde;

A bettre felawe sholde men noght fynde.
He wolde suffre for a quart of wyn
A good felawe to have his concubyn
A twelf month, and excuse hym atte fulle;
Ful prively a fynch eek koude he pulle.
And if he foond owher a good felawe,
He wolde techen him to have noon awe
In swich caas of the ercedekenes curs,
But if a mannes soule were in his purs;
For in his purs he sholde ypunysshed be.
"Purs is the ercedekenes helle," seyde he.
But wel I woot he lyed right in dede;
Of cursyng oghte ech gilty man him drede,
For curs wol slee right as assoillyng savith,
And also war hym of a *Significavit*.
In daunger hadde he at his owene gise
The yonge girles of the diocise,
And knew hir conseil, and was al hir reed.
A gerland hadde he set upon his heed
As greet as it were for an ale-stake.
A bokeleer hadde he maad hym of a cake.
With hym ther rood a gentil PARDONER
Of Rouncivale, his freend and his compeer,
That streight was comen fro the court of Rome.
Ful loude he soong "Com hider, love, to me!"
This Somonour bar to hym a stif burdoun;
Was nevere trompe of half so greet a soun.
This Pardoner hadde heer as yelow as wex,
But smothe it heeng as dooth a strike of flex;
By ounces henge his lokkes that he hadde,
And therwith he his shuldres overspradde;
But thynne it lay, by colpons oon and oon.
But hood, for jolitee, wered he noon,
For it was trussed up in his walet.
Hym thoughte he rood al of the newe jet;
Dischevelee, save his cappe, he rood al bare.
Swiche glarynge eyen hadde he as an hare.
A vernycle hadde he sowed upon his cappe.

His walet lay biforn hym in his lappe,
Bretful of pardoun, comen from Rome al hoot.
A voys he hadde as smal as hath a goot.
No berd hadde he, ne nevere sholde have;
As smothe it was as it were late shave.
I trowe he were a geldyng or a mare.
But of his craft, fro Berwyk into Ware,
Ne was ther swich another pardoner.
For in his male he hadde a pilwe-beer,
Which that he seyde was Oure Lady veyl:
He seyde he hadde a gobet of the seyl
That Seint Peter hadde, whan that he wente
Upon the see, til Jhesu Crist hym hente.
He hadde a croys of latoun ful of stones,
And in a glas he hadde pigges bones.
But with thise relikes, whan that he fond
A povre person dwellynge upon lond,
Upon a day he gat hym moore moneye
Than that the person gat in monthes tweye;
And thus, with feyned flaterye and japes,
He made the person and the peple his apes.
But trewely to tellen atte laste,
He was in chirche a noble ecclesiaste.
Wel koude he rede a lessoun or a storie,
But alderbest he song an offertorie;
For wel he wiste, whan that song was songe,
He moste preche and wel affile his tonge
To wynne silver, as he ful wel koude;
Therefore he song the murierly and loude.
  Now that I toold you shortly, in a clause,
Th'estaat, th'array, the nombre, and eek the cause
Why that assembled was this compaignye
In Southwerk at this gentil hostelrye
That highte the Tabard, faste by the Belle.
But now is tyme to yow for to telle
How that we baren us that ilke nyght,
Whan we were in that hostelrie alyght,
And after wol I telle of our viage
And al the remenaunt of oure pilgrimage.

# THE VOYAGE OF ST. BRENDAN

St. Brendan the holy man was a monk of Ireland and there he was abbot of a house of a thousand monks and there he led a strait and holy life in great penitence and abstinence and he governed his monks virtuously. And there came to him a holy abbot named Beryne [Barint, nephew of King Niall] and each was joyfull to see the other; and Beryne began to tell of many wonders that he had seen in diverse places. . . .

And then St. Brendan purposed soon after to seek that place, by God's help and began to search out a good ship, which he provisioned for seven years and then he took leave of his brethern and took seventeen monks with him. But before they entered the ship, they fasted forty days and lived devoutly and each received the sacraments. And when St. Brendan with his seventeen monks entered the ship, there came two other of the monks and prayed him that they might go with him. And then he said, "You may go with me, but one of you shall go to hell before you come again." But for all that, they would go with him. . . .

Soon after, as God would, they saw a fair island, full of flowers, grass and trees, whereof they thanked God for His grace and went on land. And when they had gone a long way, they found a fair well and by it stood a fair tree, full of boughs and on every bough sat a fair bird and they sat so thick on the tree that hardly a twig could be seen. They sang so merrily that it was a heavenly sound to hear. Whereupon St. Brendan knelt down and wept for joy and prayed devoutly to God to know what those birds meant. And then one of the birds flew from the tree to St. Brendan and fluttering his wings made a merry sound like a fiddle so that it seemed to him that he had never heard so joyful a melody. And then St. Brendan commanded the bird to tell him why they sat on the tree and sang so merrily. And then the bird said, "At one time we were angels in heaven but when our master Lucifer fell down into hell for his high pride, we fell with him for our offences, some higher, some lower, according to the quality of their trespass, and because our sin is but little, therefore Our Lord set us here out of all pain in joy and mirth, after his pleasure, here to serve Him on this tree in the best manner that we can. The Sunday is a day of rest from all worldly occupations and therefore on that day we are all made white as snow, to praise our Lord in the best ways we may." And then this bird said to St. Brendan, "It is twelve months past that you departed from your abbey, and in the seven years to come you shall see the place that you wish to come into, and all this seven years you shall keep your Easter here with us, and in the end of the seventh year, you shall come into the Land of the Blessed." And this was on Easter day that the bird said this to St. Brendan. And then this fowl flew again to his fellows who sat on the tree. And then all the birds began to sing evensong so merrily, that it was a heavenly noise to hear; and after supper St. Brendan and his fellows went to bed and slept well, and on the morrow they rose early and then those birds began Matins, Prime and Hours, and all such services as Christian men used to sing.

. . .

And there he and his monks stayed from Easter till Trinity Sunday, as they did the year before, in great joy and mirth; and daily they heard the service of the birds singing on the tree. And then the bird told St. Brendan that he should return again at Christmas to the abbey of the monks, and at Easter thither again, and the other part of the year labour in the ocean in great perils, "and from year to year till the seven years are accomplished, and then shall you come to the joyful place of Paradise, and dwell there forty days in great joy and mirth; and after that you shall return home to your own abbey in safety, and there end your life and come to the bliss of heaven, to which our Lord brought you with his precious blood." And then the angel of our Lord ordained all things which were needful to St. Brendan and his monks, in food and other provisions. And then they thanked our Lord for his great goodness that he had shown to them often in their need, and then sailed forth in the great ocean abiding in the mercy of the Lord in great trouble and tempests, and soon after came to them a horrible fish which followed the ship a long time, casting so much water out of his mouth into the ship that they expected to be drowned. Wherefore they prayed devoutly to God to deliver them from that great peril. And soon after came another fish, greater than the first, out of the western sea, and fought with him, and at the last cleaved him in three places and then departed. And they thanked our Lord for their deliverance from this great danger; but they were in great trouble, for their food was almost gone. But, by the ordinance of the Lord, there came a bird and brought to them a great branch of a vine full of red grapes, by which they lived fourteen days; and then they came to a little island, wherein were many vines full of grapes on which they landed and thanked God and gathered as many grapes as they could eat for forty days after, always sailing in the sea in many a storm and tempest. And as they thus sailed, suddenly came toward them a great gryphon, which assailed them and was likely to destroy them; wherefore they prayed devoutly to our Lord Jesus Christ for help and aid. And then the bird of the tree of the island came to the gryphon and smote out both his eyes and afterward slew him; whereof they thanked our Lord and then sailed forth continually till St. Peter's day, and then they sang a solemn service in honour of the feast. And in that place the water was so clear that they could see all the fishes that were about them, and they were aghast and the monks counselled St. Brendan to sing no more for all the fishes lay then as they were asleep. And then St. Brendan said, "Fear not for you have kept two Easters celebrating the feast of the Resurrection on the back of the great fish and therefore fear not these little fishes." And then St. Brendan made himself ready and went to Mass and bade his monks to sing in the best way that they could. And then the fishes awoke and came about the ship so thickly that they could not see the water for the fishes. And when the mass was done, all the fishes departed and were seen no more.

And seven days they sailed in that clear water. And then there came a south wind and drove the ship northward, where they saw an island dark and full of stench and smoke; and there they heard a great blowing and blasting of bellows, but they could see nothing although they heard great thundering so they were very terribly frightened and blessed themselves often. And soon after there came one starting out all burning in fire and stared horribly at them and at his leaving he made the worst cry that ever was heard. And soon there came a great number of fiends and assailed them with hooks and burning iron mallets which floating on the water following the ship seemed to be all on fire but by the power of God they had no power to wound them or hurt their ship. Wherefore the fiends began to roar and cry and threw their mallets at them. And they were so afraid and prayed to God for comfort and help; for they saw the fiends all about the ship and it seemed that all the island and all the sea was on fire. And with a sorrowful cry all the fiends departed from them and returned to the place they had come from. And then St. Brendan told them that this was part of hell and he charged them to be steadfast in the faith for they would see many a dreadful place before they came home again. And then came the south wind and drove them further into the north, where they saw a hill all on fire and a foul smoke and stench coming from thence and the fire stood on each side of the hill like a burning wall. And then one of his monks began to cry and weep sadly, and said that his end was come and that he might no longer abide in the ship and then he leaped out of the ship into the sea and then he cried and roared piteously, cursing the time that he was born and also the father and mother who begat him because they did not see to his correction in his youth, "for now I must go to perpetual pain." And then the saying of St. Brendan was verified that he said to him when he entered the ship. Therefore it is good for a man to do penance and forsake sin, for the hour of death is uncertain.

And then the wind turned into the north and drove the ship into the south, so it sailed seven days continually; and they came to a great rock standing in the sea and thereon sat a naked man in great misery and pain; for the waves of the sea had so beaten his body that all the flesh was gone and nothing left but sinews and bare bones. And when the waves were gone, there was a canvas that hung over his head which beat his body with the blowing of the wind; and there were two ox tongues and a great stone that he sat on which gave him great ease. And then St. Brendan charged him to tell who he was. And he said, "My name is Judas, who sold our Lord Jesus for thirty pence, who sitteth here most wretchedly although I am worthy to be in the greatest pain that there is; but our Lord is so merciful that he has rewarded me better than I deserved, for of right my place is in the burning hell; but I am here certain times of the year, from Christmas till Twelfth Night and from Easter till Whitsuntide be past, and every feastday of our Lady and every Saturday at noon till Sunday evensong be done; but all other times I lie still in hell in burning fire with Herod, Pilate and Caiphas; therefore accursed be the time that I ever knew them." And then Judas prayed St. Brendan to abide there all the night and to keep him there so that the fiends should not take him back to hell. And he said, "With God's help you shall abide here all this night." And then he asked Judas what cloth it was that hanged over his head. And he said it was a cloth that he gave to a leper, which was bought with the money that he stole from our Lord when he carried his purse "wherefore it does great pain to me now in beating my face with the blowing of the wind; and these two ox tongues that hang above me are ones that I gave to two priests to pray for me. I bought them with my own money and therefore they ease me, because the fishes of the sea gnaw on them and spare me. And this stone that I sit on at one time lay in a desolate place where it did no good and I took it thence and laid it in a muddy way where it helped those who went by and so it eases me now; for every good deed shall be rewarded and every evil deed shall be punished." And on Sunday toward evening there came a great multitude of fiends blasting and roaring and bade St. Brendan go away, that they might have their servant Judas, "for we dare not come in the presence of our master unless we bring him to hell with us." And St. Brendan said, "I will not let you do your master's commandment but by the power of our lord Jesus Christ I charge you to leave him tonight until the morrow." "How dare you help him who sold his master for thirty pence to the Jews and caused him to die the most shameful death upon the cross?" And then St. Brendan charged the fiends by His passion that they should not annoy him that night. And the fiends went their way roaring and crying toward hell to their master, the great devil. And then Judas thanked St. Brendan so pitifully that it was sad to see, and on the morrow the fiends came with a horrible noise, saying that they had suffered great pain because they did not bring Judas and said that he should suffer double pain on the day following. And they took Judas with them. . . .

And then St. Brendan entered his ship and sailed forty days due south through a great tempest. And on Easter their procurator came to them, offering good wishes, as he had before. And then they came to the great fish where they said Easter matins and Mass. And when Mass was done, the fish began to move and swam fast into the sea so that the monks were aghast who stood on him, for it was a great marvel to see a fish as large as a country swim so fast in the water; but by the will of our Lord this fish set all the monks on land in the Paradise of Birds whole and sound and then returned to the place he came from. And then St. Brendan and his monks thanked our Lord God for their deliverance from the great fish and kept their Easter tide till Trinity Sunday as they had done before. And after this they took their ship and sailed east forty days and at the end of forty days it began to hail fast and there came a dark mist which lasted a long time, so that the monks were fearful and prayed to our Lord to keep them. And then came their procurator and urged them to be of good cheer for they had come into the Land of the Blessed. And soon after that the mist passed away and they saw eastward the fairest land that any man might see, so clear and bright that it was a heavenly sight to behold; and all the trees were laden with ripe fruit and plants full of flowers; in this land they walked forty days but they could see no end of the land; there was always day and never night and the climate never too hot or too cold. And at last they came to a river that they could not cross. And there came to them a fair young man who welcomed them courteously, calling each of them by name and did great reverence to St. Brendan and said to them: "Be ye new joyful for this is the land you have sought; but Our Lord wishes that you go hence hastily and He will show you more of His secrets when ye come again into the sea; and He wills that you load your ship with the fruit of this land and get away, for you may no longer abide here, but shall sail again to your own country and soon after thou return home, ye shall die. And this water that you see here divides the world asunder; for on that other side of the water no man may come while he is still living. And that fruit that you see is always ripe all times of the year; always it is light as you see now; and he who keeps our Lord's will at all times shall see this land when he passes out of this world."

And then St. Brendan and his monks took as much of that fruit as they would and also a plenty of precious stones. And they took their leave and went to the ship and wept sadly because they could no longer live there. And they took ship and came home to Ireland in safety, and were received by the brothers in great joy, giving thanks to our Lord who had kept them all those seven years from many perils and brought them home in safety, to whom be given honor and glory without end. And soon after, this holy man St. Brendan waxed feeble and sick and had but little joy from this world, but ever his mind and joy was on the delight of heaven. And in a short time, he being full of virtues, departed this life into everlasting life and was worshipfully buried in a fair abbey which he himself had founded, where our Lord worked for this saint many miracles. Whereupon let us devoutly pray to this holy saint that he pray for us to the Lord, that He have mercy on us, to Whom be given praise and honor world without end.

(*Anonymous, XI century, England*)

## *The Merchant*

*There was, too, the colorful life of the merchant adventurers. Especially after the Crusaders returned with their appetites whetted for the luxury goods of the East, sturdy merchants voyaged to bring cargoes of foreign goods to Europe. Overland to Venice, they might buy there from traders of the inland sea, but it was even more profitable, if more risky, to fit out a ship, borrow money against shares in the voyage and journey to the legendary lands of the East.*

*The earliest travellers had been the Vikings. They had conquered Normandy, absorbing its civilization so that there was always a hardier, more rugged strain in its people than in the other Franks. Their cathedral of Mont St. Michel was characteristic; high on its rocky cliff above stormy seas, it reflects the restlessness and hardihood of its builders. From Normandy they set out again; Tancred arrived in Sicily and Naples to establish Norman kingdoms there for his famous sons, Roger and Robert.*

*Each century brought new ventures. From Italy Marco Polo with his father made two lengthy journeys overland to the realm of the Great Khan to establish more direct trade routes. They brought back accounts of fabulous wealth, luxurious living, exotic lands, strange customs—and merchants followed their path.*

## THE TRAVELS OF MARCO POLO

### Marco Polo

*Prologue*

It came to pass in the year of Christ 1260 when Baldwin was reigning at Constantinople that Messer Nicolo Polo, the father of my lord Marco and M. Maffeo Polo, the brother of Messer Nicolo, were at the said city of Constantinople, whither they had gone from Venice with their merchant's wares. Now these two brethern, men singularly noble, wise and provident, took counsel together to cross the Greater Sea on a venture of trade; so they laid in a store of jewels and set forth from Constantinople, crossing the sea to Soldaia.

Having stayed a while at Soldaia, they considered the matter and thought it well to extend their journey further. So they set forth from Soldaia and travelled till they came to the court of a certain Tartar Prince, Banca Khan by name. . . . By reason of the war, no one could travel without peril of being taken; thus it was at least on the road the brothers had come, though there was no obstacle to their travelling

27. Village fair. Manuscript, XV century.

forward. So the brothers, finding they could not retrace their steps, determined to go forward. Quitting Bolgara, therefore, they proceeded to a city called Ucaca, which was at the extremity of the kingdom of the Lord of Ponent; and thence departing again and passing the River Tigris, they travelled across a desert which extended for seventeen days journey and wherein they found neither town nor village, falling in only with the tents of Tartars occupied with their cattle at pasture.

After they passed the desert, they arrived at a very great and noble city called Bocara, the territory of which belonged to a king whose name was Barac. The city is the best in all Persia. And when they had got thither, they found they could neither proceed further nor yet turn back again; wherefore they abode in that city of Bocara for three years. And whilst they were sojourning in that city, there came from Alan, Lord of the Levant, envoys on their way to the court of the Great Khan, the lord of all the Tartars in the world. And when the envoys beheld the two brothers they were amazed for they had never before seen Latins in that part of the world. And they said to the brothers: "Gentlemen, if ye will take our counsel, ye will find great honor and profit shall come thereof." So they replied they would be right glad to learn how. "In truth," said the envoys, "the Great Khan hath never seen any Latins and he hath a great desire to do so. Wherefore, if ye will keep us company to the court, ye may depend upon it that he will be right glad to see you and will treat you with great honor and liberality; whilst in our company ye shall travel in perfect security and need not fear to be molested by any body."

So when the two brothers had made their arrangements, they set out on their travels, in company with the envoys and journeyed for a whole year, going northward and northeastward before they reached the court of that Prince. And on their journey they saw many marvels of divers and sundry kinds. . . .

When the two brothers got to the Great Khan, he received them with great honour and hospitality and showed much pleasure at their visit, asking them a great number of questions. First, he asked about the emperors, how they maintained their dignity and administered justice in their domains and how they went forth to battle and so forth. And then he asked like questions about the kings and princes and other potentates.

And then he inquired about the Pope and the Church and about all that is done at Rome and all the customs of the Latins.

After this the prince caused letters from himself to be indited in the Tartar tongue and committed them to the two brothers and to that Baron of his own and charged them with what he wished to say to the Pope. Now the contents of the letter were to this purport: He begged that the Pope would send as many as a hundred persons of our Christian faith; intelligent men, acquainted with the Seven Arts well qualified to enter into controversy and able clearly to prove by force of argument to idolaters and other kinds of folk, that the law of Christ was best and that all other religions were false and naught; and that if they would prove this, he and all under him would become Christians and the Church's liegemen. Finally he charged his envoys to bring back to him some of the oil of the lamp which burns on the sepulchre of our Lord at Jerusalem. . . .

And when they had been honorably conducted to Acre, they proceeded to the presence of the Pope and paid their respects to him with humble reverence. He received them with great honor and satisfaction and gave them his blessing. He then appointed two friars of the Dominicans to accompany them to the Great Khan and to do whatever might be required of them, sending by them also many fine vessels of crystal as presents to the Great Khan. So when they had got all that was needful, they took leave of the Pope, receiving his benediction and the four set out together from Acre, always accompanied by Messer Nicolo's son, Marco.

## *The Crusader*

*The most typical adventure of the Middle Ages was the Crusade. Combining the religious appeal of rescuing the Holy Land with the adventurous spirit of the times, it attracted a great outpouring of men and treasure. The obstacles were formidable: problems of transport and supply, lack of cooperation from the Byzantine Empire, discoordinate aims of the leaders. Still, Jerusalem fell to the West to become the site of its first great experiment in democratic government. After the Crusaders returned home with a new world-consciousness, never again would Europe be quite so provincial.*

28. Village street with drapers. Miniature, XV century.

# THE THIRD CRUSADE

## Roger of Wendover

### How King Richard [The Lion Hearted] Took a Ship Called a Dromund

On the 21st of March in that year [1191] Philip king of the French landed at Acre and Richard following him, embarked at Cyprus with a large stock of provisions. He heard that the French king's army was suffering at Acre from hunger and scarcity to such a degree, that a quart of corn cost sixty marks, and he therefore hastened to the relief of such distress and misery with his ships loaded with large quantities of corn. Whilst he was sailing with a fair wind toward Acre, which city was formerly called Ptolemais, there came in sight on the 6th of June, a very large ship called a dromund which had been sent loaded with an immense sum of money from the city of Baruch, by Saladin's brother, Salahadin, Soldan of Babylon, to carry assistance to the pagans who were besieged in Acre. On board this vessel they had Greek fire, and many pots of fiery serpents; and the crew consisted of fifteen hundred warriors, besides fifteen hundred strong men by whose aid the ship might be strengthened. King Richard immediately ordered his followers to prepare for action, and on the galleys nearing one another a fierce attack commenced on both sides, but the hostile ship became helpless on account of the wind falling. At length one of the king's rowers, who was a skilful diver, approached the pagan vessel under water, and bored a hole in it, after doing which, under Christ's protection, he returned to his own ship and told the king what he had done. The water entering in a short time rose over the deck of the ship, and the crew, who before trusted to their bulwarks, soon lost all hope of escape; thirteen hundred of these were drowned by King Richard's order, the surviving two hundred he kept as hostages.

### Of King Richard's Arrival at Acre and the Capture of That City

King Richard, after collecting all the spoils of the pagan ship, approached the port of Acre, whither he was bound, with a favouring wind. At length on the 8th of June the king entered the harbour, and the shrill sound of clarions, the braying of trumpets, with the horrid din of the horns filled the air near the shore, and resounded for a distance round inland; this event animated the Christians for battle, but struck terror into the besieged Saracens, for it proclaimed the arrival of the great chief. King Richard showed his generous feelings to all by supplying food to the famished army. The two kings, then, attended by crowds of knights and soldiers, arranged stone engines and other machines around the city, and by the weight of their missiles, and constant use of these engines day and night, they battered the walls of the city so that the infidels were panic-struck, lost all confidence in their power of resistance, and at length held a council and began to treat of peace. The conditions of the agreement were, that, for the ransom of the garrison, Saladin should restore the true cross, which he had taken in battle, and should release fifteen hundred captive Christians, to be chosen by them, and in addition to the above stated agreement should pay seven thousand bezants. Thus the city, with the arms and everything in it, excepting only the persons of the Saracens, was happily surrendered to the two kings on the 12th of July. When the appointed day of payment arrived, Saladin did not fulfil his agreement. To punish this great transgression, therefore, about two thousand six hundred were beheaded, only a few of the most noble were saved and placed in prison at the disposal of the kings.

## Of King Richard's Progress

After these events, on the eve of the assumption of the blessed Mary, king Richard, with his fellow warriors, led the way from the gates of Acre, and boldly set out on his march to besiege and take the cities on the sea coast; and he ordered his camp to be pitched near and in sight of Saladin's army, at the place where he had caused the two thousand six hundred of the Saracens, whom the two kings had taken prisoners at Ptolemais, to be beheaded, as has been before related. When the report of this event reached the Saracens, they were alarmed lest the king in his anger should inflict to them a similar punishment to that of the Ptolemaidans, and having no confidence in Saladin's assisting them, since he had refused to pay what was demanded of him for the ransom of the others, they evacuated their cities and fled immediately on hearing of the approach of the king. This was the case with the inhabitants of Caiphas, Caesarea, Assur, Joppa, Gaza and Ascalon, and thus, by the will of God, all the maritime district in that part of the country fell into the hands of the Christians. This however did not result without some severe fighting; for the army of Saladin followed closely on the Christian flanks and in the defiles dreadfully harassed the outposts, from which cause great slaughter often ensued in both armies. King Richard, therefore, after he had fortified the cities above named, returned in triumph to Acre.

But this account which we have given will be more clearly understood by our giving the letter which Richard sent to Walter archbishop of Rouen, on this same subject. "Richard, by the grace of God, king of England, etc—Know that our lord the king of the French has returned home; and we, after repairing the damage and breaches of the city of Acre, in order to promote the Christian cause and to fulfil the purpose of our vow, marched to Joppa, in company with the duke of Burgundy and his French followers, count Henry and his troops, and many other counts and barons. Whereas between Acre and Joppa the country is extensive and the way long; we at length, with much sweat and toil, came down to Caesarea; Saladin too lost several of his followers in this same march. When the army of God had rested some time at Joppa, we set out again on our proposed march; and when our advanced guard had gone forward and was pitching the camp near Assur, Saladin, with a large host of pagans, made an attack on our rear guard; but, by the divine favour, though only four battalions were opposed to him face to face, he was put to flight; they pursued him for one league, and made such a slaughter of the Saracen nobles on that day, St. Mary's Eve, at Assur, as Saladin has not in one day sustained for forty years. After this, under God's guidance, we came to the city of Joppa, and strengthened it with trenches and walls; it being our purpose, whenever we could, to promote the cause of Christianity as much as lay in our power. Saladin, indeed, since the day of the above-mentioned engagement with the Christians, secretly laid snares for destroying the friends of the cross, as a lion in his den awaits sheep destined for slaughter. On hearing, however, that we were marching with haste on Ascalon, he razed that city to the ground, and how, as if deprived of all plan and deliberation, he leaves all Syria to its fate; on which account we take courage, being in good hopes that in a short time the inheritance of our Lord will be entirely regained. Farewell."

## The Discovery of Arthur, the Most Famous King of the Britons

In the same year the bones of Arthur, a renowned king of Britain, were found buried at Glastonbury, in a very old sarcophagus, near which two pyramids stood, and on these, letters had been carved out, but which were scarcely legible on account of their roughness and shapelessness. The occasion of their being found was as follows: Certain people who were digging a grave in the same place to bury there a monk, who had during his life earnestly desired to be buried there, found a kind of sarcophagus, on which was placed a leaden cross with these words carved on it: "Here lies the renowned Arthur, king of the Britons, buried in the island of Avalon." The place is surrounded on all sides by marshes, and was formerly called the "island of Avalon" that is, the isle of apples. In this year, too, Robert, a canon of the church of Lincoln, and son of William, seneschal of Normandy, was at Canterbury consecrated bishop of Winchester, by William, legate of the apostolic see.

## How King Richard Forced Saladin to Raise the Siege of Joppa

King Richard, after the death of the duke of Burgundy, embarked on board his ships of war with a small force, and hastened to Joppa to render assistance to the besieged; but owing to the violence of the winds and the heavy sea his ships were driven in a contrary direction towards Cyprus, and the inhabitants of Acre, seeing this, suspected that the king was returning home. But the king and those with him, in spite of the fury of the winds, by means of strong rowing, made an oblique course and on the third day, at glimmer of dawn, they arrived with but three ships at Joppa. In the meantime Saladin, after frequent assaults had now taken the city, and had slain all the infirm and wounded soldiers, who, on account of their weakness remained there; but five of them bolder than the rest, whom Richard had placed there in charge of the city, left it and betook themselves to the castle, where they were debating about surrendering the castle before they should be compelled to do so by assaults of the enemy. This they would quickly have done had they not been warned by the patriarch, who was allowed free passage between the two armies, that the army of Saladin had, to avenge the deaths of their friends and relatives whom the English king had beheaded without mercy in many places, sworn to slay them all, notwithstanding they should have Saladin's free permission to depart. Thus they were in great danger of death and were in doubt as to what they should do, considering the number and ferocity of their enemies, and the few there were of themselves, and having no confidence in the king's coming to assist them;

when however, they learned that the king had arrived they became bolder and defended themselves courageously. The king, knowing from the fierce struggles both of besiegers and besieged, that the castle of the city was not yet taken, leaped nimbly into the sea armed as he was, and with his followers, boldly threw himself like a raging lion into the thickest of the enemy's troops, hewing them down right and left. The Turks being unable to endure this sudden attack, and thinking that he had brought a more numerous army with him, soon abandoned the siege, exhorting each other to fly, and announcing the inopportune arrival of the king; and their panic was such that their flight could not be checked till they entered the city of Ramula, Saladin all the time leading their rapid flight in his chariot. King Richard having thus put the enemy to flight, pitched his camp in the plain outside the city, to the great and unexpected joy of the besieged.

## How King Richard with a Small Force Defeated Sixty-two Thousand Pagans at Joppa

On the day after his defeat Saladin was told that the king had come with only a very small army, and that he had no more than eighty knights, besides four hundred of his crossbowmen in company with him, on hearing which he was greatly enraged and indignant with his army, because they, so many thousands, had been put to rout by such a few. He thereupon, to the confusion of his army, counted them out, and issued his imperial edict that sixty-two thousand of them should return immediately to Joppa, take the king himself prisoner, and bring him alive on the following day into his presence. The king and his army were resting that night in security, and without fear of any inopportune attack, when at daybreak the whole army of the infidels came up and entirely surrounded the king's camp, and that they might have no chance of escaping into the city, an immense force had stationed themselves between it and the royal camp. The king and all the Christian forces, aroused by their bustle and shouting, were wonder-struck at seeing themselves hemmed in on every side by the enemies of Christ. The king, however, perceiving their imminent danger, immediately armed himself, and laying aside all fear of death, as if he were emboldened by the number of his enemies, encouraged by his voice his men to the combat; he himself with eleven knights, who alone out of the whole number were mounted, boldly broke through the ranks of the enemy, with his drawn sword and quivering lance, and dealt thundering blows with his clashing sword on the helmed heads of the enemy, and freeing the Arab horses from their proper riders, he distributed them to his own knights, who were on foot. They, nimbly mounting them, with the king always leading the way, dispersed the troops of the enemy on all sides, and put to death without mercy all that came in their way. The pagans falling under the stroke of the enemy uttered miserable cries and yielded their souls to Tartarus. In this battle the crossbowmen took the lead, and behaved most praiseworthily, for their incomparable valour repelled the enemy's attack, and humbled him by their fierce audacity. How much the king's valour shone in this battle, and how much the prowess of his men, how many thousands of the enemy he put to flight, would seem incredible, were it not that the divine hand protected him. For who would ever believe that eighty knights could so invincibly cope with sixty-two thousand men for almost an entire day, could endure the showers of their missiles, and the attacks of their javelins without retreating a foot from their first position, but could moreover disperse their adversaries in all directions, and after putting them to flight, have thus gained a joyful and unlooked-for victory over them, unless they relied on the assistance of God, and believed that they were under the protection of heaven? At length the garrison of Joppa, beholding the invincible bravery of the king and his followers, boldly sallied forth, and suddenly falling upon the enemy in the rear, by repeated attacks on their part as well as on that of the king, the infidels turned their backs and fled in confusion, with great loss, taking to woods and caves for safety.

## How the Army of the Christians Arrived to the Assistance of King Richard

In the meantime news had reached the army, which had been left at Ptolemais by the king, that he was hemmed in on all sides at Joppa by the enemy, and was placed in great peril, unless they went speedily to his succour. This news struck fear and grief into all, and they all had thoughts of flight; but the more courageous part of the army assembled to deliberate on their being able to render the king any assistance. They therefore by common consent marched to Caesarea, not daring to go further for fear of the enemy; and being there told of the unexpected victory of the king, they were overcome with joy, and gave praises to

God as the preserver of them all. This battle took place at the feast of St. Peter *ad vincula*. . . .

(from *Flowers of History*)

## *The Artist*

*The episode of the Crusades sparked the commercial advance necessary to maintain a leisure class so essential to cultural development. For as these bourgeois and religious patrons of the arts came forth, a new sense of freedom and experiment entered into the arts. Contemptuously dubbed "Gothic" by the classical purists of later times, this experimental style has now achieved its deserved place in our cultural heritage. In painting came dramatic changes that would lead into the great quattrocento art of the Renaissance. Cimabue and Giotto in Italy broke with the Byzantine tradition of stiff hieratic forms; to public acclaim they stressed naturalness of form, facial expression and drapery. In Flanders the van Eycks rejected gold base tempera painting to explore the use of oils. With their colleagues they experimented with light and shadow, movement, foreshortening of figures. The religious mysticism of the earlier medieval painters remained but with a new realism and delicacy. Similar experiments were attempted in sculpture, both in adornment of buildings and the novel statues in the round.*

*In the Gothic cathedrals experimentation was dramatic. Higher and higher the roofs soared; indeed, in the building of Beauvais the builders outran their engineering abilities and the roof collapsed. The jagged leaping roofline came to be characteristic of the best work of its time. Geography was a factor as the steep roofs withstood the heavy snows of the North and wide windows admitted light to the dark interiors. But, beyond necessity, there was the determination to achieve a structure reflecting the aspirations of the builders. The stress of high pillars and ribbed vaulting would have been too great but for the innovation of flying buttresses supporting the building from the outside. In theory, these should have made the buildings hideous; instead they were peculiarly adapted to the unfinished, asymmetrical approach of the whole.*

29. Nave, Beauvais Cathedral.

# GIOTTO

## Lorenzo Ghiberti

The art of painting began to rise in Tuscany in a village near the city of Florence called Vespignano. There was born a child of marvellous talent who drew a sheep from nature. Cimabue, the painter, passing along the road to Bologna saw the boy sitting on the ground, drawing a sheep on a flat stone. He was seized with great wonder that the child, being of such a tender age, could do so well, seeming to have the gift from nature, and he asked the boy what he was called. He replied, "I am called Giotto, and my father is named Bondoni and lives in that house which is close by." Cimabue went with Giotto to the father; he had a very fine appearance and he asked the father for the boy. And the father was very poor. He gave the boy to Cimabue who took Giotto with him and Giotto became the pupil of Cimabue.

He [Cimabue] followed the "Greek manner"; in this style he had won very great fame in Tuscany. Giotto made himself great in the art of painting. He brought in the new art, abandoned the stiffness of the Greeks, rose to fame most excellently in Tuscany. And he made the most notable works, especially in the city of Florence, and in many other places, and about him there were a number of disciples, all learned like the ancient Greeks. Giotto saw in art what the others did not add to it; he brought into being art according to nature and gentleness with it, not exceeding measure. He was most expert in all aspects of art; he was an inventor and a discoverer of much knowledge which had been buried about the year 600. When nature wishes to grant anything, she grants it in truth without any stint. Giotto was prolific in everything; he worked in murals, he worked in oil, he worked on wood. He made in mosaic the Navicella of St. Peter in Rome and with his own hand painted the chapel and altarpiece of St. Peter. He painted most nobly the hall of King Robert with pictures of famous men. In Naples he painted in the Castello dell' Uovo. He painted, that is, all by his own hand, in the church of the Arena of Padua, and by his own hand a Last Judgment. And in the Palazzo della Parte he did a story of the Christian faith, and many other things in the said palace. He painted in the church of Assisi of the order of Friars Minor almost all the lower part. He also painted in Santa Maria degli Angeli in Assisi and in Santa Maria della Minerva in Rome a crucifix and a panel. . . .

30. *Descent from the Cross,* Giotto. Padua, Arena Chapel.

He painted for many lords. He painted in the palace of the podesta in Florence; within he represented the commune, showing how it was robbed, and the chapel of Santa Maria Maddalena.

Giotto deserved the highest praise. He was most worthy in all branches of art, even in the art of sculpture. The first compositions in the edifice which was built by him, of the bell tower of Santa Reparata, were sculptured and designed by his hand. In my time I have seen the models of these reliefs in his hand, most nobly designed. He was skilled in the one kind of art and in the other. Since from him came and developed such great knowledge, he is the one to whom the highest praise should be given, because nature is seen to produce in him every skill. He led art to its greatest perfection. He had very many disciples of the greatest fame. . . .

## THE VARIOUS ARTS

### Theophilus

The processes of the various arts are learned gradually. To paint, first learn how to make up colors; then apply yourself with care to mixing them well. Practice your work, and bring the greatest precision to everything; your paintings should be ornamented without sacrificing the natural; then, the many teachings of the masters will lay open the domain of art: this book will furnish the proof.

### Preface to The First Book

Theophilus—humble priest, servant of the servants of God, unworthy of the name and profession of monk—wishes to all, who are willing to avoid and spurn idleness and the shiftlessness of the mind by the useful occupation of their hands and the agreeable contemplation of new things, the recompense of a heavenly reward!

In the account of the creation of the world, we read that man was created in the image and likeness of God and was animated by the Divine breath, breathed into him. By the eminence of such distinction, he was placed above the other living creatures, so that, capable of reason, he acquired participation in the wisdom and skill of the Divine Intelligence, and, endowed with free will, was subject only to the will of his Creator, and revered His sovereignty. Wretchedly deceived by the guile of the Devil, through the sin of disobedience he lost the privilege of immortality, but, however, so far transmitted to later posterity the distinction of wisdom and intelligence, that whoever will contribute both care and concern is able to attain a capacity for all arts and skills, as if by hereditary right.

Human skill sustained this purpose and, in its various activities, pursued profit and pleasure and, finally, with the passage of time transmitted it to the predestined age of Christian religion. So, it has come about that, what God intended to create for the praise and glory of His name, a people devoted to God has restored to His worship.

Therefore, let not the pious devotion of the faithful neglect what the wise foresight of our predecessors has transmitted to our age; what God has given man as an inheritance, let man strive and work with all eagerness to attain. When this has been attained, let no one glorify himself, as if it were received of himself and not Another, but let him humbly render thanks to God, from Whom and through Whom all things are, and without Whom nothing is. Nor let him conceal what has been given in the cloak of envy, or hide it in the closet of a grasping heart. But, repelling all vain-glory, let him with a joyful heart and with simplicity dispense to all who seek, in fear of the Gospel judgment on that merchant who failed to restore to his master his talent with added interest, and, deprived of all reward, merited the censure from his master's lips of being a wicked servant.

Fearful of incurring this judgment, I, an unworthy and frail mortal of little consequence, freely offer to all, who wish to learn with humility, what has freely been given me by the Divine condescension, which gives to all in abundance and holds it against no man. I exhort them to recognise God's favour towards me and to appreciate His generosity, and I would have them know that they can be quite sure that the same things are at hand for themselves if they will add their own labour. For, as it is wicked and detestable for man in any way to strive after, or take by theft, what is forbidden or not intended for him, so, to fail to strive after what is rightfully his and an inheritance from God the Father, or to hold it in contempt, must be put down to laziness and foolishness.

Therefore, dearest son—whoever you may be, whose heart is inspired by God to investigate the vast field of the various arts and apply your mind and care in order to gather from it what pleases you—do not despise useful and precious things, simply because your native earth has produced them for you of its own accord or unexpectedly. For, foolish is the merchant who suddenly finds a treasure in a hole in the ground and fails to pick it up and keep it. If the common vines were to produce myrrh, frankincense and balsam for you: if your native springs were to pour forth oil, milk and honey: if, instead of nettles and thistles and other weeds of the garden, nard, calamus and various spices grew, surely you would not still despise them as mean and homely, and voyage over lands and seas to procure foreign things, not better but probably more mean. This, you would consider to be great folly. For, however much men are accustomed to place in the first rank precious things that are sought with much toil and acquired at great expense, and to look after them with great solicitude, yet, if meanwhile they happen to find or come across things for nothing that are comparable or better, then they keep these with a similar, even greater care.

Wherefore, dearest son,—whom God has made wholly happy in this regard, in so far as those things are offered freely, for which many at the greatest peril of life plough the sea waves compelled to endure hunger and cold, or which others, wearied with long servitude in the schools and not exhausted by the desire of learning, only acquire with intolerable labour—be eager and anxious to look at this little work on the various arts, read it through with a retentive memory, and cherish it with a warm affection. If you will diligently examine it, you will find in it whatever kinds and blends of various colours Greece possesses: whatever Russia knows of workmanship in enamels or variety of niello: whatever Arabia adorns with repoussé or cast work, or engravings in relief: whatever gold embellishments Italy applies to various vessels or to the carving of gems and ivories: whatever France esteems in her precious variety of windows: whatever skilled Germany praises in subtle work in gold, silver, copper, iron, wood and stone.

When you have read through these things several times and commended them to a retentive memory, you will recompense me for the labour of instruction if every time you make good use of my work you pray to Almighty God to have mercy on me. He knows that I have written the things collected here out of no love for human approbation nor greed for temporal gain, and that I have not appropriated anything precious or rare nor kept silent about something reserved especially for myself from malice or envy, but that, to increase the honour and glory of His name, I have ministered to the necessities of the many and had regard to their advantage.

31. Birth of Christ. Stained glass window, Erhardt Klank. Bad Münster Church.

## The Mixing of Colours for Nude Bodies

The colour, which is called the flesh tone, with which the face and nude bodies are painted is composed as follows. Take flake-white—which is white made from lead—and, without grinding it, put it just as it is, dry, in a copper or iron pot, place it over a fire and heat it until it has changed to a yellow colour. Then grind it and mix with it some ordinary flake-white and vermilion until it becomes the colour of flesh. Mix these colours according to how you want them: for example, if you want to have red faces add more vermilion; if you want light faces add more white, and, if pallid ones, add instead of vermilion a little green earth.

## The Colour, Green Earth

Green earth is a pigment, which looks like viridian mixed with black. Its nature is such that it is not ground upon stone, but, when put in water, it dissolves and is then carefully strained through a cloth. On a new wall it can be very usefully employed as a green colour.

## The First Shadow Colour for Flesh

When you have mixed the flesh colour and with it filled in the faces and nude [parts of] figures, mix with it green earth and red (which is burnt from ochre) and a little vermilion, and prepare the shadow colour for flesh. With this you define the eyebrows and eyes, the nostrils and mouth, the chin, the hollows round the nostrils and the temples, the lines of the forehead and neck, the curves of the face, the beards of young men, the relief of the hands and feet, and all the parts that are separately defined in the nude figure.

## The First Rose Colour

Then mix with the plain flesh colour a little vermilion and a little red lead and prepare the colour which is called rose. With this you redden thc upper and lower jaw, the mouth and lower chin, the neck, the wrinkles of the forehead slightly, the forehead itself on each side above the temple, the length of the nose, on each side above the nostrils, and the relief of the other nude parts of the figure.

## The First Highlight

After this, with the plain flesh colour mix ground flake-white and prepare the colour which is called the highlight. With this you will paint the eyebrows, the length of the nose, on each side above the openings of the nostrils, the fine lines around the eyes, below the temples, above the chin, near the nostrils and on each side of the mouth, the upper forehead, between the wrinkles of the forehead—sparingly, the neck in the middle, around the ears, around the relief of the hands and feet and the centre of the highest relief of the hands, feet and arms.

## The Dark Grey Which Is Applied to the Eyes

Then mix black with a little white; this colour is called dark grey. With it fill in the pupils of the eyes. Add to it still more white and fill the eyes on either side. Between this colour and the pupil apply plain white and blend in with water.

## The Panels of Altars and Doors and Casein Glue

The panels of altars or doors are first carefully joined together one by one with the cramp which coopers and barrel-makers use. Then they are stuck together with casein glue, which is made in this way.

Soft cheese is cut up into small pieces and washed in warm water with a pestle and mortar until the water, which you have poured on several times, comes out unclouded. Then this cheese is thinned out by hand and placed in cold water until it becomes hard. After this it is broken up finely on a smooth wooden board with a piece of wood. It is then replaced in the mortar and carefully pounded with the pestle, and water mixed with quicklime is added until it becomes as thick as lees. With this glue the panels are fastened together. When they have dried, they stick together so firmly that they cannot be separated by damp or heat.

Later, they should be levelled with an iron spokeshave which is curved and has an edge on the inner side and two handles so that it can be used with both hands. With this, panels, doors and shields are planed down until they are perfectly smooth. These are covered with the untanned hide of a horse, an ass or a cow, which has been soaked in water until the hairs can be scraped off; then some of the water is wrung out and, while still damp, it is stuck on with the casein glue.

## Whitening Hide and Wood with Gesso

After this take some gypsum burnt like lime, or the chalk used for whitening skins, and carefully grind it on a stone with water. Then put it in an earthenware pot, pour in some of the hide-glue and place it over a fire until the glue melts. Then spread this very thinly over the hide with a paintbrush, and, when it is dry, spread it rather more thickly and, if necessary, apply a third coat. When it is completely dry, take the plant called shaveweed, which grows like a bulrush and is knotty. You gather it in the summer, dry it in the sun, and rub this whitening with it until it is completely smooth and shining. If you do not have any leather to cover the panels with, cover them in the same way with new linen or hemp cloth of medium strength, using the same glue.

## Sticky Varnish

Put some linseed oil in a small new pot and add some finely powdered gum called sandarac. This looks like very clear incense, but when broken up has a brighter glitter. When you have placed it over a fire, heat it carefully, without letting it boil, until a third part has evaporated, and be careful of the flame because it is extremely dangerous and is difficult to extinguish if it catches fire. Every painting coated with this varnish becomes bright and decorative and completely durable.

## Grinding Colours with Oil and Gum

All kinds of colours can be ground with this [linseed] oil and used on woodwork—but only on objects which can be dried in the sun, because each time that you apply a colour, you cannot apply another over it until the first has dried. On figures this is a particularly long and tedious process.

If, however, you want to speed up your work, take the gum which oozes from the cheery or plum tree, cut it up very small, and place in an earthenware pot. Pour in plenty of water, and place it in the sun, or in winter over a fire, until the gum melts, and stir carefully with a round piece of wood. Then strain it through a cloth and, with this [drying] medium, grind the colours and apply them. All colours and their combinations can be ground and used with this medium, except red lead, flake-white and vermilion, which are ground up and applied with the white of egg. Spanish green is not mixed with sap green when it is to be coated with varnish, but it can be applied by itself with the medium. You can, however, mix it with other colours if you wish.

## How Many Times the Same Colour May Be Applied

You ought to apply all colours on wood three times, whether ground with oil or the [drying] medium. When the painting is completed and dried and the work has been carried out into the sun, carefully spread over it the sticky varnish, and when this begins to run with the heat, rub it gently with the hand. Do this three times and then leave it until it is thoroughly dried.

## The Translucent Painting

A painting, which is called translucent, is also made on wood and by some it is described as lustrous. You make it in this way.

Take some tinfoil, not coated with varnish nor coloured with saffron but plain just as it is. Polish it carefully, and with it cover the area you want to paint by this method. Then very carefully grind the colours, which are to be applied, with linseed oil. When they are extremely thin, apply them with a paintbrush, and so allow them to dry.

## Vermilion

If you wish to make vermilion, take some sulphur of which there are three kinds—white, black and yellow. Break it up on a dry stone, and add to it two parts of quicksilver, weighing them on the scales. When you have carefully mixed them, put them in a glass jar, cover this on every side with clay, stop up the mouth so that no vapour can escape, and put it on a fire to dry. Then place it in a burning fire and, when it begins to get hot, you will soon hear a cracking noise inside caused by the quicksilver combining with the burning sulphur. When the noise has stopped, remove the jar at once, open it and take the colour.

## Salt Green

If you wish to make a green colour take a piece of oak of whatever length and width you like, and hollow it out in the form of a box. Then take some copper and have it beaten into thin sheets, as wide as you like but long enough to go over the width of the hollow box. After this, take a dish full of salt and, firmly compressing it, put it in the fire and cover it with coal overnight. The next day, very carefully grind it on a dry stone. Next, gather some small twigs, place them in the above-mentioned hollow box so that two parts of the cavity are below and a third above, coat the copper sheets on each side with pure honey over which you sprinkle pounded salt, place them together over the twigs and carefully cover them with another piece of wood, prepared for the purpose, so that no vapour can escape. Next, have an opening bored in a corner of this piece of wood through which you can pour warm vinegar or hot urine until a third part of it is filled, and then stop up the opening. You should put this wooden container in a place where you can cover it on every side with dung. After four weeks take off the cover and whatever you find on the copper scrape off and keep. Replace it again and cover it as above.

## Spanish Green

If you want to make Spanish green, take some plates of copper that have been beaten thin, carefully scrape them on each side, pour over them pure, warm vinegar, without honey and salt, and put them in a small hollowed out piece of wood in the above way. After two weeks, inspect and scrape them and do this until you have enough colour.

## Flake-White And Red Lead

To prepare flake-white, get some sheets of lead beaten out thin, place them, dry, in a hollow piece of wood, like the copper above, and pour in some warm vinegar or urine to cover them. Then, after a month, take off the cover and remove whatever white there is, and again replace it as at first. When you have a sufficient amount and you wish to make red lead with it, grind this flake-white on a stone without water, then put it in two or three new pots and place it over a burning fire. You have a slender curved iron rod, fitted at one end in a wooden handle and broad at the top, and with this you can stir and mix this flake-white from time to time. You do this for a long time until the red lead becomes completely red.

## Ink

To make ink, cut for yourself some wood of the hawthorn—in April or May before they produce blossom or leaves—collect them together in small bundles and allow them to lie in the shade for two, three or four weeks until they are fairly well dried out.

Then have some wooden mallets, and with them pound these thorns on a hard piece of wood until you can completely peel off the bark, which you immediately put in a barrel full of water. When you have filled two, three, four or five barrels with bark and water, allow them to stand like this for eight days until the water has drawn off all the sap of the bark. Then put this water into a very clean pot or into a cauldron, place it on the fire and heat it. From time to time, put some of this bark into the pot so that, if there is any sap left in it, it can be boiled out, and, when you have heated it for a little, take it out and put in some more. This done, boil down what remains of the water to a third [of its original quantity], pour it from this pot into a smaller one and continue to heat it until it becomes black and begins to thicken, taking particular care that you do not add any water except that which was mixed with the sap. When you see it become thick, add a third part of pure wine, put it in two or three new pots and continue to heat it until you see that it develops a kind of skin at the top.

Then lift these pots off the fire and put them in the sun until the black ink resolves itself from the red dregs. Afterwards, take some small, carefully sewn, parchment bags like bladders, pour the pure ink into them and hang them up in the sun until it is completely dried. When it is dried, take from it as much as you want, mix it with wine over a fire, add a little iron vitriol and write. If, as a result of carelessness, the ink is not black enough, take a piece of iron, an inch thick, put it on the fire until it is red hot and then throw it into the ink.

# *The Scholar*

*A counterpart to the physical and aesthetic restlessness of the age was its eager acceptance of new ideas. Medieval man had an insatiable desire to know what was on the other side of the mountain. To find the complete truth in regard to the universe of natural being was his ideal; reliance on dogma liberating rather than limiting rational inquiry.*

*The cathedral schools originated by Charlemagne had gradually eclipsed the monastic schools, whose real interest lay in training monks. A teacher like Gerbert at the cathedral school of Rheims could draw scholars from all Europe (thus the name* studium generale). *He had studied in Spain and Italy, bringing home the Arabic numerals, the use of the zero, much astronomy and some medicine, and by 980 his was the best cathedral school in Europe. It had the elements of the seven liberal arts, which Vincent of Beauvais had classified. The trivium—grammar (the science of words), logic and rhetoric (the science of thought)—were followed by the quadrivium—music, astronomy, geometry and arithmetic. These subjects were taught by a guild of masters or faculty.*

*Each school developed its unique style. Gerbert's most famous pupil, Fulbert, became bishop of Chartres in 1006 and attracted scholars there. This was the most humanistic of the schools, owing much to John of Salisbury, an accomplished Latinist with a deep love of the classics for their humanist value.*

*At Bologna, one of the three largest schools and the first to become truly a university* (Universitatis societatis magistrorum et discipulorum), *Irnerius won renown for his glosses on the* Corpus juris civilis *of Constantine. With the rising merchant class establishing businesses, the nobility struggling to hold power against the monarchs and the Church at the height of its temporal power, civil and canon law became important and respected professions.*

*The University of Padua specialized in experimental science. Prior to the twelfth century scientific theory had been based on analogy. The introduction of Aristotle was a vast improvement, but the field was limited by lack of observation and apparatus. Although astronomy was the most progressive branch, the cosmocentric universe of the Greeks remained unquestioned. In physical science, meanwhile, there were isolated voices—John of Salisbury stating that all art and science must draw its origins from the senses, and Roger Bacon insisting that without experience nothing can be known truly. Science,* however, remained largely a reorganization of existing knowledge so that Jacques Maritain can speak of medieval science as a "void of learned ignorance."

Best known of the universities was Paris. The city was expanding feverishly while the royal family consolidated its territories around this center. Political and mercantile activities abounded. At this propitious time Peter Abelard came to the schools. Exceptionally gifted, a dynamic teacher, remembered by many only for his romance with Heloise, his restless and challenging mind left a permanent imprint on his century.

Abelard joined a faculty at Paris which was already distinguished. Bernard Silvestris, for example, had won renown with the method that became the French lecture expliqué. Students were questioned on the rhetoric of the lesson, the teacher gave a commentary, the subject matter was analyzed and annotated. On the following day the students were strictly required to repeat the lesson. Such a method involved much discussion and made sharp demands on intellectual prowess. Bernard's key doctrine was a modified pantheism: the universe is an organism animated by one life which lives in all creatures. With his stress on the transcendence as well as the immanence of the Creator, Bernard was able to stay within doctrinal bounds. All of his colleagues, however, were not so fortunate.

The great philosophic question in the schools was the nature of universals: was there a universal prototype of which individual objects were replicas? John of Salisbury, who considered the problem insoluble, protested that more time was lost on it than the Caesars spent on conquering their empire. Still, theologians were concerned, since it implicated the whole question of the nature of the Trinity and the Church. Roscellinus, in holding that the only real is the singular, was forced to a position which implied that not one, but three gods exist, and he was required by the Council of Soissons to abandon this teaching. He, as well as Anselm of Laon and William of Champaux, was defeated in debate by the rising scholar Abelard. One of the most brilliant creative minds of the age, Abelard was always sought out by students but he was seldom popular with the authorities. Too far ahead of his time, he was given to antagonizing other scholars and to prac-

*ticing a brinkmanship in heresy, so that two of his books were burned by his enemies in Church councils. Yet in time his position on universals came to be accepted as the basis for the moderate realism of the scholastics, and other of his more radical views were ultimately assimilated.*

*The reaches of knowledge at the universities changed dramatically during the twelfth and thirteenth centuries. The introduction of Plato and Aristotle revolutionized the curriculum. Boethius in translating Euclid had given little more than the propositions, but in 1130 a new translation from the Arabic by Adelard of Bath opened the world of Greek geometry. Geography was scanty, but the Near East was becoming known through exploration. In the West, however, the legends of St. Brendan, the traveling Irish monk, dominated geographic thought until the time of Columbus. In medicine, too, the great advances were made when the Arabic copies of Galen and Hippocrates were received, especially at Salerno; but the barber-surgeon and herb poultices remained customary and research was mostly in pharmacology and the control of contagion.*

*At no other time prior to our own had the schools so much influence in the world. The number of students was astonishing in the relatively small population, and by our standards they were young for the exacting curriculum. Generally, the arts course required six years, theology perhaps ten, before the student could request examination. If he passed a lengthy oral examination and successfully defended his own thesis, he received a license to teach.*

*Although the majority of students were candidates for advancement in theology, many came for other reasons. The vows of the clerics were not permanent; when they chose, they could withdraw from the service of the Church but in the meantime, they enjoyed "benefit of clergy," the right to be governed by the leniency of the Church rather than by state authorities. With all their work there was time to participate in politics, to petition Popes for charters of rights, and to write songs ranging from solemn Latin elegies to pagan drinking songs—the Goliardi, for example, wandering scholars, professional adolescents, left a treasure of light verse.*

# ON THE ADMIRABLE FORCE AND EFFICACY OF ART AND NATURE

## Roger Bacon

I will speak first of the marvelous operations of nature and art, following which I will give the causes and I will indicate the manner of procedure. In all that follows one will see that there is nothing of magic and that all of magical art is not able to produce the superior or even equal of these phenomena.

Let us examine first the works of art. It is possible to build sailing ships such that, in great oceans or smaller rivers, one man could steer them, yet they would travel with a speed greater than that of many oarsmen. Cars could also be made which would not be drawn by any animal but would move with considerable speed; probably these were the "chairs of fire" on which the ancient people waged war. Then a machine to fly could be constructed; a man would sit in the center of the apparatus and make a wheel turn which would cause artificially built wings to flap the air in the manner of a flying bird. One could also make an instrument of small volume which could lift up or let down weights of unlimited amount, a very useful device. By the aid of such an instrument no longer than three fingers, a man would be able to get out of prison, to raise and lower himself and his companions.

Then, too, it is possible to construct instruments by the use of which, a man could draw himself and a thousand persons with violence and against their will; it would be the same for many kinds of traction. One could also make instruments with which a man could move through the sea or in deep rivers without any danger to his body. Alexander used such a machine to discover the secrets of the ocean, as we are told by Ethicus, the astronomer.

There have been experiments with all these things from ancient times up to our own and I affirm them to be genuine, except the flying machine, which I have never seen; neither have I known any man who has seen one, but I know the scholar who invented it. An infinite number of things of this kind would be possible, such as bridges crossing rivers without piles or other visible supports, and many other ingenious things little known.

The experiences of which we are going to speak have no connection with the preceding. We are able at our will to build a fire with the aid

32. Buttresses of Le Mans Cathedral.

of saltpeter and other matter; likewise, one can produce a roaring blaze with naphtha, grease and other ingredients as given by Pliny in his Book II. . . .

One can also build ever-burning lamps and baths continually warm. We know there are substances that fire does not burn; the skin of salamanders, talcum, for instance; to these we could add certain substances to render them luminous but, instead of burning them, the fire would purify them. Thunder and lightning can be imitated in a manner more terrifying than that of nature. If one takes as much as an inch (or thumb length) of a certain preparation, it makes a terrible noise and a fearful brightness. These results can be achieved in several ways and used to destroy a city or an army, as Gideon did, with three hundred men carrying lamps and pots of earth which they threw with a frightful noise of flames to destroy the great city of the Modianites. . . .

(from *A Letter to a Friend*)

## LETTER TO HIS COURT ASTROLOGER

### FREDERICK II

When Frederick, emperor of Rome and always enlarger of the empire, had long meditated according to the order which he had established concerning the various things which are and appear to be on the earth, above, within, and beneath it, on a certain occasion he privately summoned me, Michael Scot, faithful to him among all astrologers, and secretly put to me at his pleasure a series of questions concerning the foundations of the earth and the marvels within it, as follows:

"My dearest master, we have often and in divers ways listened to questions and solutions from one another concerning the heavenly bodies, that is, the sun, moon, and fixed stars, the elements, the soul of the world, peoples, pagan and Christian, and other creatures above and on the earth, such as the plants and metals; yet we have heard nothing respecting those secrets which pertain to the delight of the spirit and the wisdom thereof, such as paradise, purgatory, hell, and the foundations and marvels of the earth. Wherefore we pray you, by your love of knowledge and the reverence you bear our crown, explain to us the foundations of the world, that is to say, how it is established over the abyss and how the abyss stands beneath the earth, and whether there is anything else than air and water which supports the earth, and whether it stands of itself or rests on the heaven beneath it. Also how many heavens there are and who are their rulers and principal inhabitants, and exactly how far one heaven is from another, and by how much one is greater than another, and what is beyond the last heaven if there are several; and in which heaven God is in the person of His divine majesty and how He sits on His throne, and how He is accompanied by angels and saints, and what these continually do before God. Tell us also how many abysses there are and the names of the spirits that dwell therein, and just where are the hell, purgatory, and heavenly paradise, whether under or on or above the earth or above or in the abysses; and what is the difference between the souls who are daily borne thither and the spirits which fell from heaven; and whether one soul in the next world knows another and whether one can return to this life to speak and show one's self; and how many are the pains of hell. Tell us also the measure of this earth by thickness and length and the distance from the earth to the highest heaven and to the abyss, and whether there is one abyss or several; if several, how far one is from another; and whether the earth has empty spaces or is a solid body like a living stone; and how far is it from the surface of the earth down to the lower heaven.

Likewise tell us how it happens that the waters of the sea are so bitter and the waters are salt in many places and some waters away from the sea are sweet although they all come from the living sea. Tell us too concerning the sweet waters how they continually gush forth from the earth and sometimes from stones and trees, as from the vines when they are pruned in the paring-time, where they have their source and how it is that certain waters come forth sweet and fresh, some clear, some turbid, others thick and gummy; for we greatly wonder at these things, knowing already that all waters come from the sea, which is the bed and receptacle of all running waters. Hence, we should like to know whether there is one place by itself which has sweet water only and one with salt water only, or whether there is one place for both kinds and in this case how the two kinds of water are so unlike, since by reason of difference of color, taste, and movement there would seem to be two places. So, if there are two places for these waters, we wish to be informed which is the greater and which the smaller, and how the running waters in all their abundance seem to pour forth continually from their source, and although their flow is copious, yet they do not increase as if more were added beyond the common measure but remain constant at a flow which is uniform or nearly so. We should like to know further whence come the salt and bitter waters which gush forth in some places and the fetid waters in many baths and pools, whether they come of themselves or from elsewhere; likewise concerning those waters which come forth warm or hot or boiling as if in a cauldron on a blazing fire, whence they come and how it is that some of them are always muddy and some always clear. Also we should like to know concerning the wind which issues from many parts of the earth, and the fire which bursts from plains as well as from mountains, and likewise what produces the smoke which appears now in one place and now in another, and what causes its blasts as is seen in the region of Sicily and Messina, as Etna, Vulcano, Lipari, and Stromboli. How comes it that a flaming fire appears not only from the earth but also in certain parts of the sea of India? . . ."

## THE LONDON LAPIDARY OF KING PHILIP

### Rubie

Rubie is reed I steyneth all ze reed stones. Ze boke telleth vs the gentil rubie fyne I cleve is lorde of stones. It is also water of waters. Hit hath ze vertue of precious stones above all other. He is of suche lordeshippe zat when he zat bereth hym cometh amonge men, all ther shul bere hym honeur and grace and all shul bere hum joye of his presence. Ze bokes seyn vs hat ze bestes hat drynken of ze water where ze rubie hath been wette une shul be houle of zeir sekenes; and ze hat is discomforted hat in gode belie beholdeth zis stone, hit shul comforte and make hym to forgete his contrariousete be vertue zat god hat yeven verto. Hit fedeth ze man and comforteth ze hert and ze body, and wynneth to a man lordeshippe above other stones. Her ben gretten rubies and ben founden in lande of rubie in a flode of paradis. The book of Moyses seyn vs wot God Commanded zat ze rubie shulde be put first in ze second mouce, for he signifieth ze second lawe, and to lizte ze werkis be nyght and day. Al he lyghted yam and hugely he alyghted yam and makes yam clear, yer is no lyght yt spreddes to his gentil colour. And zough we take non hede to the significance of ze rubie and of his blissful color, yet Moyses seith zat hit signifieth Jhesu Xrist zat came in-to zis worlde for to lyghten our darkenes. The boke saith zat seint John seith of ze coming of Ihesu Xrist zat is veray lyghte zat lyghteth all men and all ze worlde. Isaie ze prophete seith of zis lyght zat ze people zat was in darkness saue a grete lyghte. Seint John seith zat he saue not ze rubie in the fundament of ze hevenly kyngdome of Iherusalem and perfore was not ze rubie named with the ii stones he named zere. Al ther zat ze rubie and ze veray bryghtnes of ze rubie beholden shulde beholde ze veray lyghte of Ihesu Xrist, whoso beholdeth ze rubie of ze lymmes of Ihesu Xrist must think on Ihesu Xrist. He shal loue ze more thoo zat ben ze clene livyng peple of zis worlde.

### Sardonyes

Sardonyes is a stone of a redisshe Reedness and blackysshe. Zis stone be hym-self swagith wrathe of a man and maketh him reste wel be nyghte and voideth much drechyng and naying tatches and doeth awey noying vices fro man and keepeth chaste and shamefast and graciouse.

### Teramus

Teramus is a stone zat falleth with ze thondre and he that bereth hit clenely, ze thondre shal neuer smyte hym in house ne in fire; he shal not be loste in debate amonges men; and gode hit is ouercome batailles and hit yeueth gode metynges and hit is of many colours.

(*Anonymous, XIII century, England*)

## BARTOLOMEUS ANGLICUS

## Medieval Lore

Glass, as Avicenna said, is among stones as a fool among men for it taketh on all manner of colour and painting. Glass was first found beside Ptolomeida in the cliff beside the river that is called Vellus that springeth out of the foot of Mount Carmel, at which shipmen arrived. For upon the gravel of that river shipmen made fire of clods medlied with bright gravel, and thereof ran streams of new liquor that was the beginning of glass. It is so suppliant that it taketh anon divers and contrary shapes by the blast of the glazier and is sometimes beaten and sometimes graven as silver. And no matter is more apt to make mirrors than is glass and to receive painting; and if it be broken it may not be amended without melting it again.

. . .

The crow is a bird of long life and diviners tell that she taketh heed of spying and awaitings and teacheth and sheweth ways and warneth what shall fall. But it is full unlawful to believe, that God sheweth his privy council to crows. It is said that crows rule and lead storks and come about them as it were in routs and fly about the storks and defend them and fight against other birds and fowl that hate storks. And take upon them the battle of other birds, to their own peril. And an open proof thereof is: for in that time, that the storks pass out of the country, crows are not to be seen in places where they were wont to be. And also for they come again with sore wounds and with voice of blood, that is well known, and with other signs and tokens and show that they have been in strong fighting.

. . .

All the planets move by double moving, by their own kind moving out of the west into the east, against the moving of the firmament; and by their moving out of the east into the west, and that by ravishing of the firmament. By violence of the firmament they are ravished every day out of the east into the west. And by their kindly moving, by the which they labour to move against the firmament, some of them fulfil their course in shorter time and some in longer time. And that is for their courses are some more and some less. For Saturn abideth in every sign xxx months and full-endeth its course in xxx years. Jupiter dwelleth in one sign every year and full-endeth its course in xij years. Mars abideth in every sign xlv days and full-endeth its course in two years. The Sun abideth in every sign xxx days and 10 hours and a half and full-endeth its course in ccclxv days and vj hours. Mercury abideth in every sign xxviij days and vj hours and endeth its course in cccxxxviij days. Venus abideth in every sign 29 days and full-endeth its course in cccxlviii days. The moon abideth in every sign two days and a half and six hours and one bisse less and full-endeth its course from point to point in 27 days and 8 hours. And by entering and out-passing of these seven stars in the twelve signs and out thereof, everything that is bred and corrupt in this nether world is varied and disposed and therefore in the philosopher's book Mesaleth it is read in this manner: The Highest made the world to the likeness of a sphere and made the highest circle above it movable in

33. Bronze doors of Bishop Bernward for St. Michael's. Hildesheim Cathedral.

the earth, pight and stedfast in the middle thereof; not withdrawing toward the left side nor toward the right side, and set the other elements moveable, and made them move by the moving of seven planets and all other stars help the planets in their working and kind. . . . The first moving is the round moving that a planet makes in its own circle and passeth never the works and bounds of that circle. The second moving is that he maketh under the zodiac and passeth away like great space in a like space of time. And the first moving of a planet is made in its own circle that is called Eccentric and it is called so for the earth is not the middle thereof as it is the middle of the circle that is called Zodiac. Epicycle is a little circle that a planet describeth and goeth about therein by the moving of its body and the body of the planet goeth about the roundness thereof. And thereof it showeth that the sun and other planets move in their own circle and first alike swift, although they move diversely in diverse circles.

## OXFORD STATUTES

Masters of the liberal arts willingly perform varied and heavy labors in lecturing and discussing, for the profit and advantage of their scholars, but on account of stinginess, which has grown up in these modern days more than formerly, they are not sufficiently rewarded by them for these labors, as is befitting and was formerly done; therefore it is made a rule that each scholar of the faculty of arts attending in the hall at the usual weekly exercises shall pay, for either the old or new logic, at least twelve pence for the whole year, dividing it in proper proportion for the separate terms.

Those who shall regularly hear lectures on books on physics must pay eighteen pence for hearing these books for a year.

. . .

The bachelors about to take their degree in a certain year must appear before certain masters and bachelors. They shall then swear, touching the sacred objects, that they have heard all the books of the old logic at least twice, except the books of Boethius, which it is enough to have read once, and the fourth book of the *Topics* of Boethius which they are not required to have read. Of the new logic they shall swear that they have read the books of *First Topics* and *Outlines* twice, the book of

*Later Topics* at least once. Of grammar they must swear that they have heard *Concerning Constructions* of Priscian twice, the *Barbarism* of Donatus once, or three books of physical matters; viz, *Physics, Of the Soul, Of Generation* and *Corruption.*

. . .

Since it is one of the works of Piety to give relief to the poverty of pious scholars, who in seeking the pearl of knowledge in the field of the Lord are exposing themselves to labor, conflict and various troubles, the executors of Lord John of Pontisara formerly bishop of Winchester, who had a special affection for the masters and scholars of this university have generously given and delivered to us 200 marks, which we acknowledge to have received from the said executors, to be converted to the use and advantage of the masters and scholars of the said university under the following regulations. Every year on Saint Nicholas Eve, in winter, shall be celebrated a solemn anniversary of the said bishop with the full service of the dead.

Scholars of each faculty, if they are needy, shall enjoy the benefits of this fund, on condition that a master who lectures may borrow forty shillings, a master who does not lecture two marks and a half, a bachelor two marks, a sophist one mark.

Each scholar receiving any of the money is required to say the Lord's Prayer and the Ave Maria each five times for the soul of the dead above mentioned.

(*Anonymous, XIII century, England*)

## HISTORY OF MY CALAMITIES

### Peter Abelard

I was born in the village of Le Pallet, near the border of Brittany, about eight miles from Nantes. To my native land I attribute a lightheartedness, but also an aptitude for learning. My father, before putting on the uniform of a soldier, had received some training in letters; later he held learning in such regard that he wished to give each of his sons an education even before training in arms, a rule to which he made no exceptions. I was the oldest child and his care for my instruction was no less than his affection for me. For my part, I advanced quickly in my studies to which I was greatly attached; finally, I relinquished the pomp of military glory and granted to my brothers my rights of inheritance as eldest son; I left the court of Mars to study at the knee of Minerva. Preferring the weapons of dialectic to all other branches of philosophy, I exchanged the arsenal of battle for that of logic, the trophies of war for the assaults of debate. I travelled through the provinces, always debating; wherever I heard that the art of disputation was cultivated, I went, becoming like the peripatetics.

At last I arrived at Paris where dialectics was already flourishing and for some time I attended the lectures of William of Champeaux who was justly regarded as the most skillful teacher of this branch of learning. At first I was welcomed; but I soon became a trial to him, as I attacked many of his ideas, I argued against him to my utmost, and, returning ever to the attack, I sometimes had the satisfaction of winning the argument. This boldness aroused the more distinguished of my fellow students to great indignation, because of my youth and the brief period of my study. In this began my calamities which have never ended; as my reputation grew, the envy increased.

At last, presuming against the established powers, I dared to aspire to become head of a school. Already I had seen the place where I would set up a rival chair. It was in Melun, an important city then and a royal residence. William suspected my design and wishing to remove my school farther from his own, used every means in his power to deter me from this venture even before I left him for a school at that site. But there were several powerful men opposed to him and only too glad to help me to accomplish my desires; his avowed enmity secured for me almost general approval. From my first lectures, my reputation in dialectics took on such proportions that the renown of my elder fellows and even that of Champeaux were surpassed. Such success made me arrogant; I wanted to be near to Paris and I moved my school to Corbeil to have my enemy near at hand and to challenge him in disputation. But after a little time, I became ill from overwork; I needed to breathe the air of my own country. Cut off from France for some years, I was missed by all those who found dialectics attractive.

Some years later when I had recovered, my former teacher William archdeacon of Paris, had changed his habit to enter the Order of Clerics Regular, with the rumored hope of obtaining, through the appearance of great piety, a rapid advancement in ecclesiastical rank; this was not long in coming, for he was made Bishop of Chalons. His new habit had not changed his taste for life in Paris or for philosophy and in the very monastery to which he had retired, he opened a new school.

I returned to study rhetoric under him. In the many disputations that followed, I refuted so vigorously his position on universals that I forced him to alter his position and finally to renounce it. In his original system he held that the universal is that which exists wholly and essentially in all individuals of a class; such individuals do not differ in essence but only in their accidents of existence. In his second attempt, he no longer considered universals as constituting the essence of individuals but as forming their identity, because in all individuals of a class, universals are found without differentiation. Now this question of universals is one of the most essential in dialectic; Porphyry himself, writing in *Isagoge* on universals, did not dare to resolve it, saying, "This is most serious." William, who had been obliged first to modify his teaching, then to abandon it, saw his course fall into such discredit that he could scarcely lecture on logic as if the entire subject consisted of the question of universals.

This victory gave such authority to my school that the most fervent disciples of William, his partisans and even some of my enemies left him to come to my lectures. The professor who had become master in the school of Paris came to offer me his place and to audit my lectures in the room where we had witnessed the good days of Champeaux. I took over the chair of dialectic. To tell you of the envy which consumed William, of the ferment of bitterness that roiled in his spirit and of his despair is not easy. Unable to bear his increasing vexation, he tried once more to destroy me by trickery; and as he did not have a plausible complaint against me, he used false accusations to bring about the discharge of the master who had ceded his chair to me and sent another in his place as a rival to me. So, returning to Melun, I again established my school and since I was obviously the victim of envious persecution, I gained consideration, as the poet says:

> All grandeur draws envy; only the summits are battered by the winds. (Ovid, *De Remedio Amoris,* I, 369)

But William soon observed that the sincerity of his religious ardor was suspected by most of his pupils and that they were murmuring loudly against his supposed conversion for he never left Paris; so he moved with his little company and his school to a country place farther from the capital. Soon I returned from Melun to Paris, hoping that now he would leave me in peace. But since he had filled my chair by a rival, I struck my camp outside the city on Mt. St. Genevieve, to besiege the usurper. At this news William, losing all discretion, hastened to return to Paris bringing his confreres and all the disciples he could attract from the cloister to save the lieutenant he had abandoned. Instead of prospering as he hoped, this move failed. For this unfortunate master had at least some students drawn by his ability to lecture on Priscian. On the arrival of his master, his school was completely deserted, and he was obliged to close it. A short time later, doubtless despairing of worldly glory, he also entered a monastery. The return of the master to Paris, the scholastic disputes between my students and his followers, the success my school achieved in these hostilities are details known to all. I can say boldly and with the modesty of Ajax:

> If you ask the issue of this combat, I have not been defeated by my enemy.

and

> If I did not say this, it would speak for itself and the outcome tells enough. (Ovid, *Metamorphoses,* XIII, 89, 90)

Meantime, my mother Lucia was urging me to return to Brittany; Berenger, my father, had entered a religious order and she was preparing to follow his example. After the ceremony of her reception, I returned to France, primarily with the intention of studying theology, which this same William of Champeaux offered with much pomp at his bishopric of Chalons. He had taken as master of this science Anselm of Laon, long regarded as the outstanding theologian in the church.

I went to hear Anselm. This old man held his great reputation rather from custom than from his genius. If you came to his door to consult him on any difficulty, your confusion increased, you went away more puzzled than you came. Excellent for simple listeners, he had no ability in the presence of an adversary. He used a marvelous abundance of language but, for all their beauty, his words were weak in wisdom. When he lighted a fire, it filled the house with smoke rather than giving light. . . .

Once disillusioned, I did not stay long in his shadow. I came rarely to his lectures and this indifference wounded his chief disciples as an insult to their great doctor. They were angry with me and their treacherous suggestions made me an enemy. One day after a session of Sentences it came about that we students were chatting; one of them asked in sidiously what I thought of the lectures on the sacred writings, I who had studied only philosophy. I answered that it was the most salutary of lectures since it taught us the care of our souls, but I was astonished to see that these lettered people were not able to explain the com mentaries of the saints from their glosses, but they needed other aids. There was general laughter. I was asked if I felt I had force and bold ness enough to attempt an equal task. I replied that I was ready, if they wished, to prove it. Crying out and laughing, "Certainly," they said, "we are indeed ready." "All right," I said, "someone seek out a difficult pass age of Scripture for which there is only one gloss and I will accept the challenge." They agreed to choose an obscure prophecy of Ezeckiel. Tak ing the book, I invited them to hear my commentary the next morning. Then, giving counsel to a man who had no taste for it, they warned me that the enterprise was serious, and should not be undertaken hastily that I ought to take my time and meditate on my interpretation a leisure. I answered angrily that my habit was not to proceed by length of work but by mental ability; and I added that I would keep my word when they came to hear my explication the next morning.

I must admit that my first lecture attracted only a small audience be cause it seemed so ridiculous that a young man who had scarcely opened the holy books would handle them with such assurance. Meanwhile those who came were so delighted with the first meeting that they praised it highly and urged me to give a commentary by the same method. Th lecture was talked about freely; those who had not come to the firs lecture hastened to attend the second and third and were as eager to take down my commentary as the early students had been. Such a triumph aroused in the aged Anselm a fury of envy. Earlier he had become hostil to me through the maneuvers of trouble-makers; now he began to plagu me in theology class as William had once done in philosophy.

There were, in Anselm's school, two disciples who seemed to hold pre eminence, Alberic of Rheims and Loculph of Lombardy. The more the admired this former genius, the more they hated me. With lying in sinuations they troubled Anselm's mind. He became so alarmed that h ordered me flatly to discontinue the commentary I had begun, allegin as a pretext that if I expressed any error, the responsibility would li with him because of my inexperience in theology. All the students wer outraged. Never was envy unmasked with more impudence, never veng ance seemed more hateful; but the lies of Anselm and his jealousy turned to my honor and his persecution to my glory.

A few days later I returned to Paris to accept the cathedral chair which had been offered me long before and from which I had been so unfairly barred. For several years I stayed in possession peacefully and there I was able to finish the commentaries begun at Laon. They were so well received by their readers that public opinion placed the theologian ahead of the philosopher. The enthusiasm roused by my two courses multiplied the number of my students, so I had money and glory.

. . .

There lived in the city of Paris a young girl named Heloise, the niece of Canon Fulbert. Her uncle's loving wish for her was that she would have the best education that he could possibly provide. She was not unattractive and in knowledge of letters she excelled all other women. Such ability is rare in women and had gained renown for her throughout the kingdom. Seeing that she possessed all the qualities which ordinarily attract lovers, I longed to draw her to me in a love affair and I believed it would be easy to do so. My name was so distinguished, the grace of my youth and perfection of form made me worthy to court any woman; any one would be honored by my attention and I had no fear of a refusal. I persuaded myself that the young lady would easily consent to my desire. The resources of my spirit and her love for study added to my hopes. Even if we were separated, we could be united through letters; the pen is braver than the spoken word and so would continue our happy intimacy.

Filled with love for the maiden, I looked for an occasion to meet her, to become acquainted through frequent visits and to persuade her to accept me. To accomplish this, I had some of my friends intervene with her uncle Fulbert. They urged him to take me into his house which was near my school, for a fixed sum. I would say, for appearance sake, that the care of domestic affairs interfered with my studies and that my expenses were too heavy. Fulbert was a greedy man and also he wished to facilitate his niece's progress in literature. For these two motives he was easily persuaded to my wishes; the old man could not resist the lure of money and the secret hope of seeing his niece profit intellectually by my presence. He even urged me with many solicitations in this regard. Indeed he was more accommodating than I had dared to hope and himself aided my suit. He gave Heloise entirely into my care, praying me to give her instruction at whatever time I should be free from my school, authorizing me to see her at any hour of day or night; if I found her negligent, I should punish her.

If I admired his good nature and simplicity on one hand, on the other I was astonished that he confided such a tender lamb to a ravening wolf. In giving Heloise to my care, he was giving free rein to my desires and granting me opportunity even if the girl did not want my lovemaking. Indeed, if caresses failed, I could resort to blows to subdue her. Two considerations kept Fulbert free of suspicion, his love for his niece and my reputation for continence. In a word, we were united first under the same roof, then in our hearts. Under the pretext of study, we gave ourselves entirely to love. In this privacy romance flourished in our studious retreat. The books were open but the words were of love rather than wisdom, kisses more common than precepts; my hands reached more often to Heloise than to the books; love was reflected in our eyes instead of the sentences before us. To avert suspicion, I even struck her lightly, blows of love rather than anger and a thousand times sweeter than the perfumes of eastern world.

What can I tell you? In our ardor we passed through all degrees of love, tried all its aspects, no sign of love was omitted. Whatever love could devise was ours. These joys were so new to us that we prolonged them, wishing never to separate. It became boring for me to work at my lectures, to spend time at school. I was weary, as well, with hours of night kept for love and those of the day for study. I prepared my lessons carelessly; my mind created nothing; I spoke from memory instead of inspiration; I was reduced to repeating old lessons. Verse I composed, but it was of love and not of philosophy. Much of it, as you know, became popular and is sung in many lands by people whose lives have been glorified by the same sentiments.

You can scarcely believe the sadness and laments of my disciples, when they saw what this preoccupation was doing to my mind. Such a visible passion could not long be overlooked. Everyone was aware of it except the one whose honor was most involved, the uncle of Heloise. Vainly people hinted to him of my intrigue but he never believed them, because of his love for his niece and his respect for the purity of my past life. We do not easily believe evil of those we love and in such deep affection there was no room for mistrust. As St. Jerome says in his epistle to Sabianus:

> We are usually last to know the evils of our own house and we ignore the faults of our children and husbands even when our neighbors bewail them. But though one learns later than others, one finally discovers and that which is known to all is with difficulty hidden from 'the one'. (*Epist.* 147, 10)

After many months, these words came true for us. Fulbert learned all. What was his sorrow at this discovery! how bitter was the parting of the lovers! what was my anger and remorse! with what a broken heart I grieved for the misery of this dear child! Picture her chagrin when I was publicly denounced. In the terrible blow which had fallen, each of us forgot himself to weep for the other and each of us grieved only for the other one.

But the separation of our bodies bound our union of spirit. Our love, deprived of joy, was the more inflamed. In time the scandal ceased to disturb us and we scarcely resented shame in return for the charms of love. We were like the mythical legend of Mars and Venus who were surprised in love. Soon Heloise found that she was pregnant and joyfully wrote to consult me on what measures to take. One night while Fulbert was away, I stole her from his house and took her to Brittany to stay with my sister. There she gave birth to a son whom she named Astrolabe.

But Fulbert! After his return he began to go mad. Everyone could see the fury raging in him. To restore his good name, revenge was necessary to him. But what he could do against me, he did not know. If he killed or wounded me, he believed that my kinfolk in Brittany would injure Heloise. To seize and imprison me was impracticable for I was carefully guarded against attack, certain that he would use any means possible. At last, pitying his excessive sorrow, and blaming myself for this treasonable love, I went to see Fulbert. I begged forgiveness and promised any atonement he would ask. I assured him that my conduct would not surprise anyone who knew the power of love or who recalled the downfalls that had come to great men through women since the beginning of time. And, to appease him, I offered him a satisfaction for which he had not even hoped, that I would marry the girl I had seduced, provided the marriage was kept secret to guard my reputation. He agreed; pledging his faith and that of his kinsmen, he kissed me to bind the reconciliation; but it was all done to betray me.

I went down to Brittany to tell my beloved and make her my wife. Instead of being pleased, she objected vehemently. She offered reasons to dissuade me; the danger and the disgrace to which I would be exposed. She swore that her uncle had not forgiven me and never would; events proved her right. She asked me how she could rejoice over a marriage which would ruin my reputation and humiliate us both. What expiation could the world rightly ask of her for extinguishing this brilliant light! She called to my attention the curses that would greet this marriage, the prejudice against me that it would cause in the church, the price it would cost the realm of philosophy. Would it not be intolerable to see a man destined by nature for the world now tied to one woman and submitting meekly to this yoke. She opposed totally any union which had as dowry the loss of my renown and the ruin of my future. She reminded me of the difficulties which would follow our marriage, difficulties that the Apostle had warned when he said:

> Art thou free from a wife; then seek no wife. If you marry, you have not sinned; if the virgin marries, she does not sin; yet I say they will have tribulations of the flesh, but I would spare you. (1 *Cor.* vii, 27)

If I would not listen to the counsel of the Apostle, nor the exhortations of those who considered marriage a heavy yoke, at least, she said, I ought to consult the philosophers and take into consideration those who had written on this matter, either of themselves or concerning others; for even the saints had given warnings on the subject. St. Jerome in the First Book against Jovinianus tells how Theophrastus after listing in detail the trials of conjugal life, proved by most rational arguments that philosophers should never marry; Jerome himself adds the counsel of his wisdom by saying:

> Who is the Christian who would not be convinced by such a dissertation as this of Theophrastus?

In the same work the saint cites the example of Cicero who was sought by Hircius to marry his sister after his divorce from Terentia; he refused formally, saying that it was impossible to care equally for a wife and philosophy. He did not say simply "to care for"; he added "equally," not wishing to do anything that would limit his study of philosophy.

Forgetting for the moment the obstacles a wife would cause to my studies, Heloise urged that I consider the situation in which this marriage would place me. What harmony can there be between the schools and the trappings of domesticity, between students and cradles, books and distaffs, pens and spindles? Is there a man, who, deep in his philosophic or theological meditations, can bear the crying of children, the songs of the nursemaid quieting them, the bustle of servants, the confusion of family life? How would he endure the continual disorder of small children? For the rich, it is one thing; they have vast houses with room for escape. The expense is nothing to their wealth and they are spared worry over daily concerns. But the state of philosophers is not that of the rich; those who seek fortune, plunging themselves into a melee of worldly affairs, seldom study at any length. The famous philosophers of former times, full of disdain for the world, fled it willingly, withdrawing from its pleasures and giving themselves wholly to the embrace of philosophy. The grandest of them all, Seneca, said in his instructions to Lucilius:

> Philosophy demands more than your leisure time. It is necessary to quit all else for this study, for which no amount of time is ever enough. (LXIII, 3) . . . .

Speaking in her own name, she reminded me that it would be dangerous for me to return to Paris, insisting that the title of mistress was more attractive to her than that of wife (and more honorable to me). She would hold me only by my love and not by the chains of a conjugal vow. Our separations would be repaid by the joy of reunion, all the dearer because of their rarity. At last, seeing that her efforts to convince me and change my resolution were not accomplishing anything, and not wishing to offend me, she said through her tears: It is the only thing that remains, to give ourselves up and prepare for sorrow as great as the love that preceded it. In this, as everyone knows, she felt the spirit of prophecy.

We left our little son in the care of my sister and returned secretly to Paris. A few days later, having spent the night in vigil in the church, at dawn we received the nuptial blessing in the presence of Heloise's uncle and a few friends. Then we left separately and with stealth. We met rarely and in great secrecy to conceal as much as possible what we had done. But Heloise's uncle and other members of his family, seeking to avenge the affront they had received, began to divulge the marriage and to break their promise to me. Heloise, for my protection, denied their allegations and swore they were false. Angered by her conduct, Fulbert began to mistreat her; when I learned of this, I decided to send her to the convent of nuns at Argenteuil, near Paris, where she had been brought up and received her early education. I had her take the religious habit suitable to convent life, but not the veil of the nun.

At this news, her uncle and kinsmen thought I had duped them and that I sent Heloise to a convent to be free of her. Outraged, they conspired against me and sought to punish me. One night, they bribed one of my servants with gold to leave open a door to my house and they attacked me during my sleep—a vengeance so savage and shameful that the world heard the news with great astonishment; they cut off the part of my body through which I had committed the fault which offended them. My friends pursued them; two who were captured suffered blindness and the same loss as I; one was the servant whose greed had caused him to betray me.

Morning came and all the town gathered outside my door. It is difficult, indeed impossible, to describe their shock, their irritating lamentation, their grief which drove me to desperation. The clergy and my disciples tormented me with their unbearable consolation, for their compassion was infinitely more painful to me than my wound. I suffered more from shame than from pain. My mind was full of sad thoughts; of the glory I had enjoyed and with what ease a single moment had destroyed it forever. The judgment of God is just and I was punished in that part of my body wherein I had sinned. The vengeance of Fulbert was just; he had repaid treason with treason. What a triumph for my enemies! How they would delight in the perfect balance between the fault and the retribution! What sorrow this blow struck at me would cause to my parents and friends! The incident would be bruited about, carrying my shame to the ends of the earth. What could I do now? What kind of public figure would I make? I had been held up to shame before all the world, demeaned in all languages, become a monster in the eyes of men.

One more consideration disturbed me—according to the deadly letter of the law, eunuchs are such an abomination in the sight of God that men reduced to this state are forbidden to enter the church, even as the unclean; even such mutilated animals are rejected as sacrifice.

> No impotent beast that hath been bruised or crushed or cut or mutilated shall you offer to the Lord. (*Lev.* XXII, 24)

> The eunuch shall not enter in the congregation of the Lord. (*Deut.* XXIII, 1)

Thus confused and shamed, it was the feeling of my pitiful disgrace rather than any sincere vocation that made me seek the shadow of the cloister, after Heloise obeyed my orders and, taking the veil, entered the convent. We donned the religious habit at the same time, I at the abbey of St. Denis, she at the convent of Argenteuil, of which I had spoken highly. Many people wished to dissuade her from bowing under the yoke of monastic rule at such an early age, urging that it was an insupportable burden from the perspective of tender years. All their sympathetic efforts were useless; she answered only through her tears in the words of Cornelia's lament:

> O noble husband! my fatal couch should never have received you! Has fortune power to strike so noble a head? What demon fury threw me in your arms, if I was only to cause you such grief? But you shall be avenged; for my heart goes to be your sacrifice. (Lucan, *Pharsalia,* viii, 94)

With these words she went to the altar, received the veil from the hands of the bishop and took the vows before them all.

*Abelard then narrates further troubles: with the monks of St. Denis, who resented his proving that the patron Denis could not possibly be Dionysius the Areopagite, disciple of Paul; with the Church council which burned his book on the Trinity as heretical without having read it; with the monks of Brittany who chose him abbot believing he would condone their evil ways and persecuted him for his integrity; with the abbot of St. Denis who laid claim to the land of Argenteuil, evicting Heloise and her nuns. Here, as he tells of finding a refuge for them, he speaks of Heloise, now an abbess:*

> God had granted to her such grace that the bishops loved her as a daughter, the abbots as a sister, the laity as a mother; and all marvelled at her piety, her wisdom and her gentle kindness.

*A series of letters passed between them, as Abelard became spiritual advisor to these nuns. In his last years Abelard lived at the monastery of Cluny; the letter written by its abbot to Heloise upon his death follows. His body was secretly transported to the convent ruled by Heloise; at her death she was buried in the same tomb.*

34. *Adoration of the Magi,* Nicola Pisano. Detail of the Marble Pulpit. Pisa, Baptistery.

# A LETTER TO HELOISE CONCERNING ABELARD

## Peter the Venerable

. . . But although this may be denied to us concerning you, by the providence of God which disposes all things, it has been granted concerning one of yours, concerning that Master Peter, I say, often and always to be named with honour, the servant and truly the philosopher of Christ, whom, in the last years of his life, that same divine providence brought to Cluny; and he enriched her in and from that gift more precious than gold and topazes. A brief word cannot tell of his holy, humble, and devout way of life among us, as Cluny bears strong witness. For, unless I am mistaken, I do not recollect that I have seen his like, in the appearance and actions of humility, so much so that, to the very discerning, neither St. Germain would appear more abject, nor St. Martin himself poorer. And when, at my command, he took a superior rank in that great assembly of our brothers, he seemed the least in the plainness of his apparel.

I wondered often, as he preceded me in processions with the others, according to custom, nay, I was almost astounded that a man of so great and so famous a name could thus belittle himself, could thus humble himself. And while there are certain of those who profess religion, who desire that the religious garments which they wear should be exceedingly sumptuous, he was completely sparing in these, and, content with a simple garment of any kind, he asked for nothing more. He observed this practice also in food, and in drink, and in all care of his own body, and he condemned in his words and in his life, I do not say the superfluous only, but everything except what was really necessary, both for himself and for everyone. His reading was continual, his prayer frequent, his silence perpetual, except when familiar intercourse with the brothers or public discussion in their assembly pressed him to speak to them about divine things. He frequented the divine sacraments as much as he was able, offering the sacrifice of the immortal Lamb of God; and indeed, after the apostolic favour had been granted, by letters and through my effort, he frequented them almost constantly.

And what more can I say? His mind, his tongue, his labour, always serving God, always philosophical, ever more learned, he meditated, taught, and spoke. Living thus with us for some time, this simple and upright man, fearing God, and withdrawing from evil, consecrated the last days of his life to God, and to end them (for more than usual, he was troubled by scabies and certain discomforts of body), he was sent by me to (St. Marcelies) Chalons. For because of the pleasant situation of that place, which surpasses almost all regions of our Burgundy, I thought to provide a suitable place for him, near the city indeed, but yet near where the Saone flows. There, as much as his illness permitted, he renewed his former studies, always bending over his books, and he did not, as Gregory the Great wrote, allow a single moment to be wasted, but always he prayed, or read, or wrote, or dictated. In these holy exercises, the coming of that angelic visitor found him, not as the foolish, but as the wise virgin, to the marriage feast of eternity. For he brought with him a lamp full of oil, that is, a conscience filled with the testimony of a holy life. For, in order that the common debt of mortal life should be paid, he was seized by illness, and suffering in it, he was in a short time brought to his end. Then truly, how holy, how devout, how Catholic, was the confession he made, first, of his faith, and then of his sins. With what longing of his loving heart he received the last repast of the journey, and the pledge of eternal life, the body of the Lord our Redeemer, how faithfully he commended to Him his body and soul here and forever, the brothers are witnesses, and all the members of that monastery where the body of the holy martyr Marcellus lies. Thus Master Peter brought his days to a close, and he who known throughout almost the whole world for his unique mastery of knowledge, was everywhere famous, persevering, meek and humble, in the discipleship of Him who said: "Learn of Me, for I am meek and humble of heart," thus passed over to Him, as it should be believed. Him, then, venerable and dearest sister in the Lord, to whom you clung in the bonds of the flesh, and later in the so much stronger and better bond of divine love, with whom and under whom you have long served the Lord; him, I say, in your place, and as another you, Christ cherishes in His own embrace, and He preserves him to be restored to you by His grace, at the coming of the Lord, when He descends from heaven, with the singing of archangels and the sound of the trumpet. Be mindful of him, then, in the Lord; be mindful also of me, if it pleases you, and solicitously commend to those holy sisters who serve the Lord with you, the brothers of our congregation, and the sisters, who everywhere in the world, as much as they can, are serving the same Lord as you do.

## *The Philosopher*

*Philosophy and theology were the golden studies of the intellectual pilgrims. In the ninth century, the Irish Scotus Erigena pioneered in the reconciliation of the two fields, appealing to reason to support the truths of revelation. In his book* On the Division of Nature, *he had listed three states in regard to truth. From the fall of Adam to the coming of Christ, reason was under a cloud and limited to establishing a physics of nature and its Maker. With the Incarnation, the second state began when reason receives truth from an infallible source so that "faith must precede the exercise of reason." Yet faith, rather than limiting reason, begets the desire for intellectual knowledge and aids reason. "Light shines in the darkness of believing souls and it shines more and more while, starting from faith, it tends toward the sight of God." Only after death, when the soul receives the light of the Beatific Vision, does it attain to the third state.*

*The decline of Carolingian culture affected the study of Erigena, however, but in the eleventh century another churchman, Anselm of Canterbury, revived the same theme. "For I do not seek to understand that I may believe, but I believe that I may know." "Faith seeking understanding" became a wide-ranging program of the intellectual pilgrimage. It symbolized the spiritual value of the adventure of the mind and gave meaning to the thirst for universal knowledge.*

*Within this general framework, as each scholar followed his own bent, certain major schools of theology developed. At the Augustinian house of St. Victor, Hugh, the heir of Augustine's historical sense, taught an organically developing doctrine while his student Richard of Saint Victor, was the outstanding psychologist of his century. But the Victorine school, too mystical for the philosophers and too philosophical for the mystics, had only limited effect on its age. A far more significant development was the dialogue, often dispute, between the Franciscan schools and the followers of St. Thomas Aquinas. For example, Augustine had taught that the intellect of man is able by divine illumination to possess immediate knowledge of supernatural reality, and so held the great Franciscan of the thirteenth century, St. Bonaventure. On the other hand, the mighty mind of the Dominican Thomas Aquinas, while accepting Augustinian theology, questioned his philosophy and took the Aristotelian view that man's knowledge is always mediated through the senses: knowledge of divine things is by inference from or analogy with his knowledge of material things. On many other points, the Platonic-Augustinian outlook of the Franciscans came into opposition with Aquinas: they found his God too mechanistic, his system dualistic; and against his emphasis on reason they asserted the primacy of will and of love over the intellect. Thus were formed the two great mainstreams of Catholic philosophy.*

*In no sense, then, was medieval culture a static thing. In every field there was quest, all life was a pilgrimage. And no area of life was alien to this religious orientation. The growth of medieval culture was medieval man's pilgrimage toward God so that between the adventurous activities of merchant and pilgrim, between the saint and scholar, there was a difference of quality but not of purpose.*

## THE PROSLOGION

### St. Anselm of Canterbury

Up now, slight man! Flee, for a little while, thy occupations; hide thyself, for a time, from thy disturbing thoughts. Cast aside, now, thy burdensome cares and put away thy toilsome business. Yield room for some little time to God; and rest for a little time in him. Enter the inner chamber of thy mind; shut out all thoughts save that of God, and such as can aid thee in seeking him; close thy door and seek him. Speak now, my whole heart! speak now to God, saying, I seek thy face; thy face, Lord, will I seek. And come thou now, O Lord my God, teach my heart where and how it may find thee.

Lord, if thou art not here, where shall I seek thee, being absent? But if thou art everywhere, why do I not see thee present? Truly thou dwellest in unapproachable light. But where is unapproachable light, or how shall I come to it? Or who shall lead me to that light and into it, that I may see thee in it? Again, by what marks, under what form, shall I seek thee? I have never seen thee, O Lord, my God; I do not know thy form. What, O most high Lord, shall this man do, an exile far from thee? What shall thy servant do, anxious in his love of thee, and cast out afar from thy face? He pants to see thee, and thy face is too far from him. He longs to come to thee, and thy dwelling-place is inaccessible. He is eager to find thee, and knows not thy place. He desires to seek thee and does not know thy face. Lord, thou art my God, and thou art my Lord, and never have I seen thee. It is thou that hast made me, and hast made me anew, and hast bestowed upon me all the blessings I enjoy; and not yet do I know thee. Finally, I was created to see thee, and not yet have I done that for which I was made.

O wretched lot of man, when he hath lost that for which he was made! O hard and terrible fate! Alas, what has he lost, and what has he found? What has departed, and what remains? He has lost the blessedness for which he was made, and has found the misery for which he was not made. That has departed without which nothing is happy, and that remains which, in itself, is only miserable. Man once did eat the bread of angels, for which he hungers now; he eateth now the bread of sorrows, of which he knew not then. Alas for the mourning of all mankind, for the universal lamentation of the sons of Hades! He choked with satiety, we sigh with hunger. He abounded, we beg. He possessed in happiness, and miserably forsook his possession; we suffer want in unhappiness, and feel a miserable longing, and alas, we remain empty.

Why did he not keep for us, when he could so easily, that whose lack we should feel so heavily? Why did he shut us away from the light and cover us over with darkness? With what purpose did he rob us of life, and inflict death upon us? Wretches that we are, whence have we been driven out; whither are we driven on? Whence hurled? Whither consigned to ruin? From a native country into exile, from the vision of God into our present blindness, from the joy of immortality into the bitterness and horror of death. Miserable exchange of how great a good, for how great an evil! Heavy loss, heavy grief, heavy all our fate!

But alas! Wretched that I am, one of the sons of Eve, far removed from God! What have I undertaken? What have I accomplished? Whither was I striving? How far have I come? To what did I aspire? Amid what thoughts am I sighing? I sought blessings, and lo, confusion. I strove toward God, and I stumbled on myself. I sought calm in privacy and I found tribulation and grief in my inmost thoughts. I wished to smile in the joy of my mind, and I am compelled to frown by the sorrow of my heart. Gladness was hoped for, and lo, a source of frequent sighs.

And thou too, O Lord, how long? How long, O Lord, dost thou forget us; how long dost thou turn thy face from us? When wilt thou enlighten our eyes, and show us thy face? When wilt thou restore thyself to us? Look upon us, Lord; hear us, enlighten us, reveal thyself to us. Restore thyself to us, that it may be well with us—thyself, without whom it is so ill with us. Pity our toilings and strivings toward thee, since we can do nothing without thee. Thou dost invite us; do thou help us. I beseech thee, O Lord, that I may not lose hope in sighs, but may breathe anew in hope. Lord, my heart is made bitter by its desolation; sweeten thou it, I beseech thee, with thy consolation. Lord, in hunger I began to seek thee; I beseech thee that I may not cease to hunger for thee. In hunger I have come to thee; let me not go unfed. I have come in poverty to the Rich, in misery to the Compassionate; let me not return empty and despised. And if, before I eat, I sigh, grant, even after sighs, that which I may eat. Lord, I am bowed down and can only look downward; raise me up that I may look upward. My iniquities have gone over my head; they overwhelm me; and, like a heavy load, they weigh me down. Free me from them; unburden me, that the pit of iniquities may not close over me.

Be it mine to look up to thy light, even from afar, even from the depths. Teach me to seek after thee, and reveal thyself to me, when I seek thee; for I cannot seek thee, except thou teach me, nor find thee, except thou reveal thyself. Let me seek thee in longing, let me long for thee in seeking; let me find thee in love, and love thee in finding. Lord, I acknowledge and I thank thee that thou hast created me in this thine image, in order that I may be mindful of thee, may conceive of thee, and love thee; but that image has been so consumed and wasted away by vices, and obscured by the smoke of wrong-doing, that it cannot achieve that for which it was made, except thou renew it, and create it anew. I do not endeavor, O Lord, to penetrate thy sublimity, for in no wise do I compare my understanding with that; but I long to understand in some degree thy truth, which my heart believes and loves. For I do not seek to understand that I may believe, but I believe in order to understand. For this also I believe—that unless I believe, I should not understand.

And so, Lord, do thou, who dost give understanding to faith, give me, so far as thou knowest it to be profitable, to understand that thou art as we believe; and that thou art that which we believe. And, indeed, we believe that thou art a being than which nothing greater can be conceived. Or is there no such nature, since the fool hath said in his heart, there is no God? But, at any rate, this very fool, when he hears of this being of which I speak—a being than which nothing greater can be conceived—understands what he hears, and what he understands is in his understanding; although he does not understand it to exist.

For, it is one thing for an object to be in the understanding, and another to understand that the object exists. When a painter first conceives of what he will afterwards perform, he has it in his understanding, but he does not yet understand it to be, because he has not yet performed it. But after he has made the painting, he both has it in his understanding, and he understands that it exists, because he has made it.

Hence, even the fool is convinced that something exists in the understanding, at least, than which nothing greater can be conceived. For, when he hears of this, he understands it. And whatever is understood, exists in the understanding. And assuredly that, than which nothing greater can be conceived, cannot exist in the understanding alone. For, suppose it exists in the understanding alone; then it can be conceived to exist in reality, which is greater.

Therefore, if that, than which nothing greater can be conceived, exists in the understanding alone, the very being, than which nothing greater can be conceived, is one, than which a greater can be conceived. But obviously this is impossible. Hence, there is no doubt that there exists a being, than which nothing greater can be conceived, and it exists both in the understanding and in reality. . . .

But how has the fool said in his heart what he could not conceive; or how is it that he could not conceive what he said in his heart since it is the same to say in the heart, and conceive?

But, if really, nay, since really, he both conceived, because he said it in his heart, because he could not conceive; there is more than one way in which a thing is said in the heart or conceived. For, in one sense, an object is conceived, when the word signifying it is conceived; and in another, when the very entity, which the object is, is understood.

In the former sense, then, God can be conceived not to exist; but in the latter, not at all. For no one who understands what fire and water are can conceive fire to be water, in accordance with the nature of the facts themselves, although this is possible according to the words. So, then, no one who understands what God is can conceive that God does not exist;

although he says these words in his heart, either without any, or with some foreign signification. For, God is that than which a greater cannot be conceived. And he who thoroughly understands this, assuredly understands that this being so truly exists, that not even in concept can it be non-existent. Therefore, he who understands that God so exists, cannot conceive that he does not exist. . . .

## THE GRADES OF KNOWLEDGE

### Hugh of St. Victor

There are three modes of cognition belonging to the rational soul: cogitation, meditation and contemplation. It is cogitation when the mind is touched with the idea of things and the thing itself is by its image presented suddenly, either entering the mind through sense or rising from memory. Meditation is the assiduous and sagacious revision of cogitation and strives to explain the involved and penetrate the hidden. Contemplation is the mind's perspicacious and free attention, diffused everywhere throughout the range of whatever may be explored. There is this difference between meditation and contemplation; meditation related always to things hidden from our intelligence; contemplation related to things made manifest, according to either their nature or our capacity. Meditation always is occupied with some one matter to be investigated; contemplation spreads abroad for the comprehending of many things, even the universe. Thus meditation is a certain inquisitive power of the mind, sagaciously striving to look into the obscure and unravel the perplexed. Contemplation is that acumen of intelligence which, keeping all things open to view, comprehends all with clear vision.

## BENJAMIN MINOR

### Richard of St. Victor

"Benjamin a youth, in ecstasy of mind." Let the young men hear a sermon about youth, let them wake up to the words of the prophet: "There is Benjamin a youth, in ecstasy of mind." Many know who this Benjamin is, some by learning and some by experience. Let those who know from teaching listen patiently and those who know by experience, listen willingly. For he who has once come to know Benjamin by experience as a master, will never be satisfied with a sermon about him, however lengthy. But who can be fit to speak worthily of him? For he was fair of form among all the children of Jacob, even he who was worthy to be born of Rachel. For Leah, although she had many children, could not have fairer ones. Jacob, as we read, had two wives. One was called Leah, the other Rachel. Leah was more fruitful, Rachel more beautiful; Leah though fruitful was blear-eyed, Rachel though sterile was well favored. Now let us see what these two wives of Jacob signify that we may more easily understand what their sons mean. Rachel is the teaching of truth, Leah the discipline of virtue. Rachel is the search for wisdom, Leah the desire for righteousness. But we know that Jacob served seven years for Rachel and yet the days seemed few for the greatness of his love. Do you wonder at this? According to the greatness of her beauty was the greatness of his love. I should like to attempt something in praise of wisdom, whatever I shall say it will be but little. For what is loved more ardently than wisdom or is sweeter to possess? For her comeliness is beyond all beauty and her sweetness beyond all delight. For one says "she is more lovely than the sun and above all the order of the stars; being compared with the light she is found before it" (Wisdom vii, 29). For the day is followed by night but wisdom is not overcome by evil. "She reacheth therefore from end to end mightily and ordereth all things sweetly. I have loved her and have sought her out from my youth and have desired to take her for my spouse; and I became a lover of her beauty" (Wisdom viii, 1,2). What wonder is it then if Jacob burned with love for such a bride, if he was unable to temper the flames of such a fire, of such love. "I have loved wisdom above health and beauty" (Wisdom vii, 10). As we have said, nothing is loved more ardently than wisdom, nothing is sweeter to possess. Hence it is that all men wish to be wise but very few can attain wisdom.

Now if you please, we will carefully examine the subject of Jacob and his two wives and manifest openly whatever our mind suggests. Every rational spirit is given two powers by the Father of Lights from whom comes every good and perfect gift. The one is the reason, the other the affections; the reason for truth, the affection for virtue. . . . They are the two wives of a rational being which produce numerous offspring and are the heirs of the heavenly kingdom. Of reason springs right counsel, of affection holy desires. Of the first spiritual senses, of the second ordered affections. The latter produces all the virtues, the former all truth. Therefore, we must realize that the affection begins truly to be Leah when it strives to conform to the pattern of righteousness. And reason can definitely be identified with Rachel when it is illumined by the light of the true and highest wisdom. But we shall not forget how laborious is the one and how joyous the other. For the affection of the soul is not withdrawn from illicit things and set upon right things without great labour, so that this wife Leah is rightly called laborious. Can anything be happier than to fix the mind's eye in contemplation of the highest wisdom? Therefore, when wisdom is directed to this contemplation, it deserves to be honoured by the name of Rachel. The word Rachel is interpreted as meaning "seeing the beginning" or "a sheep." To be worthy of this name she must fulfill what is written, "Think of the Lord in goodness, and seek Him in simplicity of heart." For he who thinks of the Lord in goodness discerns Him who is the beginning of all things. And in a true sense he is a sheep if he seeks with simplicity. See then that it is not any ordinary wisdom but the highest wisdom pursued in simplicity which makes one to be Rachel.

Each of them [Leah and Rachel] receives her handmaid; the servant of the affections is sensation, that of reason is the imagination. But each of these handmaids is known to be necessary to her mistress for without them the whole world would not be of use to them. For the reason would know nothing without the imagination and the affections would feel nothing without the sensibility. For why is Leah so moved by the love of transitory things, if it be not that the services of her handmaid, the outer senses, give her a variety of delights? As it is written "For the invisible things of Him from the creation of the world are clearly seen being understood by the things that are made" (Rom. I, 20). From this we may clearly see that the reason would never rise to the knowledge of invisible things, unless her handmaid the imagination were to represent to her the form of visible things. For by the image of visible things she rises to a knowledge of invisible things as often as she draws up a likeness between them in her mind. Clearly without the imagination she would have no knowledge of bodily things and without it she could not rise to the contemplation of heavenly things. For the outer sense alone perceives visible things and the eye of the heart alone, sees the invisible. . . .

The rational soul finds in itself the chief and principal mirror for seeing God. If the invisible things of God are clearly seen, being understood by the things that are made, where, I ask, are the traces of knowledge distinctly impressed to be found, but in this image of God (in the soul)? Man is made after the likeness of God we read and believe and therefore, as long as we walk by faith and not by sight and as long as we still see Him in a glass darkly, we cannot find a better mirror for seeing Him in the imagination, so to say, than the rational spirit. Let him who desires to see God wipe his mirror and cleanse his heart. . . . But when the mirror has been cleansed and examined for a long time carefully, a brightness of the divine light begins to shine through to him and a great beam of illumination not known hitherto, appears before his eyes. It was this light which enlighteneth the eye of him who said: "The light of Thy countenance is sealed upon us O Lord, Thou hast given gladness in my heart" (Ps. IV, 7). Therefore by the sight of this light which is wonderful in itself, the soul is marvellously enflamed and given the power to see the light which is above itself. I say, from this vision it conceives a flame of desire to see God and it takes courage. So the mind burning already with the desire of this vision, if it hopes for its desire may now know that it has conceived Benjamin. It conceives in hope, it bears with desire, and the greater the desire, the nearer the birth.

# RETRACING THE ARTS TO THEOLOGY

## St. Bonaventure

*Every best gift and every perfect gift is from above, coming down from the Father of lights,* James in the first chapter of his Epistle. These words of Sacred Scripture not only reveal the source of all illumination but they likewise point out the generous flow of manifold rays which issue from that Font of light. Notwithstanding the fact that every illumination of knowledge is within, still, we can with propriety distinguish what we call the *external* light, or the light of mechanical skill; the *lower* light, or the light of sense perception; the *inner* light, or the light of grace and of Sacred Scriptures. The first light illumines in the consideration of the *arts and crafts;* the second, in regard to *natural form;* the third, in regard to *intellectual truth;* and the fourth and last, in regard to *saving truth.*

The first light, then, since it enlightens the mind for an appreciation of the *arts and crafts,* which are, as it were, exterior to man and intended to supply the needs of the body, is called the light of *mechanical skill.* This [skill] being, in a certain sense, servile and of a lower nature than philosophical knowledge, [such light] can rightly be termed *external.* It has seven divisions corresponding to the seven mechanical arts enumerated by Hugh in his Didascalicon, namely, weaving, fabrication, agriculture, hunting, navigation, medicine, and the dramatic art. That the above mentioned arts *suffice* is shown in the following way. Every mechanical art is intended for man's *consolation* or his *comfort;* its purpose, therefore, is to banish either *sorrow* or *want;* it either *benefits* or *delights,* according to the words of Horace:

> Either to serve or to please is the wish of the poets.

And again:

> He hath gained universal applause who hath combined the profitable with the pleasing.

If its aim is to afford *consolation* or amusement, it is *dramatic* art, or the art of exhibiting plays, which embraces every form of entertainment, be it song, music, drama, or pantomime. If, however, it is intended for the *comfort* or betterment of the exterior man, it can accomplish its purpose by providing either *covering* or *food,* or by *serving as an aid in the acquisition of either.*

. . .

Furthermore, as an aid in the *acquisition of either* [*shelter or food*], the mechanical skills help in two ways: either by *supplying a want,* and this is *navigation,* which includes all commerce of articles of covering or of food; or by *removing impediments* and ills of the body, and this is *medicine,* whether it is concerned with the preparation of drugs, potions, or ointments, or with the amputation of members, in which later case it is called surgery. Dramatic art, on the other hand, is in a class by itself. Considered in this light, the classification of the mechanical arts seems adequate.

The second light, which enables us to discern *essential forms,* is the light of *sense perception.* Rightly it is called the *lower light* because sense perception begins from below and takes place by the aid of physical light. It has five divisions corresponding to the five senses. In his third book on

Genesis, St. Augustine, in the following way bases the *adequacy* of the senses on the nature of the light present in the elements: if the light or brightness, which makes possible the discernment of things corporeal, exists in a *high degree of its own property* and in a certain purity, it is the sense of *sight; commingled with the air,* it is *hearing; with vapor,* it is *smell; with a fluid,* it is *taste; with a solid, earthly substance,* it is *touch.* Now the sensitive life of the body partakes of the nature of light, for which reason it thrives in the nerves which are naturally unobstructed and capable of transmitting impressions, and in these five senses it possesses more or less vigor according to the greater or less soundness of the nerves. Therefore, since there are in the world five simple substances, namely, the four elements and the fifth essence, man has for the perception of all these corporeal forms five senses well adapted to these substances, because, on account of the well-defined nature of each sense, apprehension can take place only when there is a certain conformity and rapport between the faculty and the object. There is another way of determining the adequacy of the senses, but St. Augustine sanctions this method and it seems reasonable, as proving sufficiency by means of the simultaneous correspondence of medium, organ and object.

The third light which guides man in the investigation of *intelligible truths* is the light of *philosophical knowledge.* It is called *inner* because it inquires into inner and hidden causes through principles of knowledge and essential truth, which are inherent in man. It is a threefold light diffusing itself over the three divisions of philosophy: *rational, essential,* and *moral,* a classification which seems suitable, since there is truth of *speech,* truth of *beings,* and truth of *morals. Rational* philosophy considers the truth of *speech; essential* philosophy the truth of *beings;* and *moral* philosophy, the truth of *morals.* Or considering it in a different light: just as we may see the principle of the efficient, the formal or the exemplary, and the final causes in the Most High God, since "He is the Cause of being, the Principle of knowledge, and the Pattern of human life," so may we see it in the illumination of philosophy which enlightens the mind to discern the *causes of being* in which case it is *essential* philosophy (metaphysics); or to understand *principles of reasoning* in which case it is *discursive* philosophy (logic); or to learn the right way *of living* in which case it is *moral* or practical philosophy.

Considering it under a third aspect: the light of philosophical knowledge illumines the intellect itself and this enlightenment may be threefold: if it governs the *motive* faculty, it is *moral* philosophy; if it sways

35. Balthasar, one of the Three Kings from an Adoration group. Linden wood. From Baden, Convent of Lichtentahl. Late XV century.

*itself,* it is *essential* philosophy; if it directs the *interpretive* faculty it is *discursive* philosophy. As a result, man is enlightened as regards the truth of life, the truth of knowledge, and the truth of doctrine.

And since one may, through the medium of *speech,* give expression to his thoughts with one of three purposes: namely, to communicate his ideas, or to arouse love or hatred, for this reason, *discursive* or rational philosophy has three subdivisions: *grammar, logic* and *rhetoric.* Of these sciences the first aims to express; the second, to teach; the third, to persuade. The first considers the mind as *apprehending;* the second, as *judging;* the third, as *motivating,* and since the mind apprehends by means of *correct* speech, judges by means of *true* speech, and persuades by means of *eloquent* speech, with good reason does this triple science consider these three qualities in speech.

Again, since it is proper to our intellect to be guided in its judgment by formal principles, these principles, likewise, must be considered under three aspects; when they pertain to *matter,* they are termed *formal causes;* when they pertain to the *mind,* they are termed *intellectual causes;* and when they pertain to *Divine Wisdom,* they are called *ideal causes.* Essential philosophy, therefore, is subdivided into *physics properly so-called,* into *mathematics,* and *metaphysics.* Physics, accordingly, treats of the generation and corruption of matter in terms of essential properties and seminal principles; *mathematics* considers abstract forms through intellectual principles; *metaphysics* treats of the knowledge of all entities, which leads back to one ultimate Principle from which they proceed according to ideal principles, that is, to God, since He is the Beginning, the End, and the Exemplar. Concerning these ideal principles, however, there has been some controversy among metaphysicists.

Finally, since there are three approaches to ethical principles, namely, those governing the *individual,* the *family* and the *state,* so are there three corresponding divisions of moral philosophy, namely, the *individual,* the *domestic,* and the *political,* divided in the manner shown above, as may be seen clearly in the names themselves.

Now the fourth light, which illumines the mind for the understanding of *saving truth,* is the light of *Sacred Scripture.* This light is called *higher* because it leads to things above by the manifestation of truths which are beyond reason and also because it is not acquired by human research, but comes down by inspiration from the "Father of lights." Although in a literal sense, it is *one,* still, in a spiritual and mystical sense, it is *threefold,* for in all the books of Sacred Scripture, in addition to the *literal* meaning which the words clearly express, there is implied a threefold *spiritual* meaning: namely, the *allegorical,* by which we are taught how to keep close to God. Hence all of Sacred Scripture teaches these three truths: namely, the eternal generation and *the* Incarnation of Christ, the pattern of human life, and the union of the soul with God. The first regards *faith;* the second, *morals;* the third, the *purpose of both.* To the study of the first, the doctors should devote themselves; on that of the second, the preachers should concentrate; and to the attainment of the third, the contemplatives should aspire. Augustine is the chief exponent of the first class; Gregory, of the second; Dionysius, of the third. Anselm follows Augustine; Bernard follows Gregory; Richard (of St. Victor) follows Dionysius; for Anselm excels in reasoning, Bernard in preaching, Richard in contemplation. But Hugh (of St. Victor) excels in all three.

From the foregoing statements, it is evident that although, according to our first classification, the light coming down from above is *fourfold,* still, it admits of *six* modifications: namely, the light of *Sacred Scripture,* the light of *sense perception,* the light of *mechanical knowledge,* the light of *rational philosophy,* the light of *natural philosophy,* and the light of *moral philosophy.* And for that reason there are in this life six illuminations and they have their twilight, for all science will be destroyed; for that reason, too, there follows a seventh day of rest, a day which knows no evening, the *illumination of glory.*

. . .

And thus it is clear how the *manifold Wisdom of God,* which is clearly revealed in Sacred Scripture, lies hidden in all knowledge and in all nature. It is clear also how all divisions of knowledge are handmaids of theology and it is for this very reason that theology makes use of illustrations and terms pertaining to every branch of knowledge. It is likewise evident how wide is the way of enlightenment and how in everything which is perceived or known, God Himself lies hidden within. And this is the advantage of all sciences, that in all, faith is strengthened, *God is honored,* character is formed, and consolation is derived, and all this is obtained from the union of the Spouse with his bride, a union which takes place through charity, to the attainment of which the whole purpose of Sacred Scripture, and, consequently, every illumination descending from above, is directed—a union without which all knowledge is vain because the Son is never attained except through the Holy Ghost who teaches us *all truth, and who is blessed for ever and ever. Amen.*

# PHILOSOPHY THE HANDMAID OF THEOLOGY

## St. Thomas Aquinas

. . . Sacred doctrine is a science. We must bear in mind that there are two kinds of sciences. There are some which proceed from principles known by the natural light of the intellect, such as arithmetic and geometry and the like. There are some which proceed from principles known by the light of a higher science: thus the science of optics proceeds from principles established by geometry, and music from principles established by arithmetic. So it is that sacred doctrine is a science because it proceeds from principles made known by the light of higher science, namely, the science of God and the blessed. Hence, just as music accepts as authority the principles taught by the arithmetician, so sacred science accepts the principles revealed by God.

. . .

*We proceed thus to the Fifth Article:*

*Objection* 1. It seems that sacred doctrine is not nobler than other sciences, for the nobility of a science depends on its certitude. But other sciences, the principles of which cannot be doubted, seem to be more certain than sacred doctrine; for its principles—namely, articles of faith—can be doubted. Therefore other sciences seem to be nobler.

*Objection* 2. Further, it is the part of a lower science to draw upon a higher; as music draws upon arithmetic. But sacred doctrine does draw upon philosophical sciences; for Jerome observes, in his Epistle to Magnus, that *the ancient doctors so enriched their books with doctrines and thoughts of the philosophers, that thou knowest not what more to admire in them, their profane erudition or their scriptural learning.* Therefore sacred doctrine is inferior to other sciences.

*On the contrary,* Other sciences are called the handmaids of this one: *Wisdom sent her maidens to invite to the tower* (Prov. ix. 3).

*I answer that,* Since this science is partly speculative and partly practical, it transcends all other sciences, speculative and practical. Now one speculative science is said to be nobler than another either by reason of its greater certitude, or by reason of the higher dignity of its subject-matter. In both these respects this science surpasses other speculative sciences: in point of greater certitude, because other sciences derive their certitude from the natural light of human reason, which can err, whereas this derives its certitude from the light of the divine knowledge, which cannot err; in the point of the higher dignity of its subject-matter, because this science treats chiefly of those things which by their sublimity transcend human reason, while other sciences consider only those things which are within reason's grasp. Of the practical sciences, that one is nobler which is ordained to a more final end, as political science is nobler than military science; for the good of the army is directed to the good of the state. But the purpose of this science, in so far as it is practical, is eternal beatitude, to which as to an ultimate end the ends of all the practical sciences are directed. Hence it is clear that from every standpoint it is nobler than other sciences.

*Reply to Objection* 1. It may well happen that what is in itself the more certain may seem to us the less certain because of the weakness of our intellect, *which is dazzled by the clearest objects of nature; as the owl is dazzled by the light of the sun*. Hence the fact that some happen to doubt about the articles of faith is not due to the uncertain nature of the truths, but to the weakness of the human intellect; yet the slenderest knowledge that may be obtained of the highest things is more desirable than the most certain knowledge obtained of the lowest things, as is said in *De Animalibus* xi.

*Reply to Objection* 2. This science can draw upon the philosophical sciences, not as though it stood in the need of them, but only in order to make its teaching clearer. For it accepts its principles, not from the other sciences, but immediately from God, by revelation. Therefore it does not draw upon the other sciences as its superiors, but uses them as its inferiors and handmaidens: even so the master sciences make use of the subordinate sciences, as political science of military science. That it thus uses them is not due to its own defect or insufficiency, but to the defect of our intellect, which is more easily led by what is known through natural reason (from which proceed the other sciences), to that which is above reason, such as are the teachings of this science.

PART IV

# The City

*The dominant image in the building of medieval culture was that of the "City of God," the imaginative symbol which St. Augustine had provided and which was to fire the imaginations of the great leaders of medieval society from Charlemagne to King Louis. This City was to be the society of all men of good will from the moment of creation to the end of the world, moving through time toward its ultimate destiny in the Eternal City, when beyond history, it will be perfectly ordered.*

*It is in this image that we find the medieval emphasis on* summa *and structure—the attempt, in building social, literary, intellectual and architectural works, to embrace organically a whole universe of experience* (summa) *and to manifest its organic structure (architectonic).*

# ST. AUGUSTINE

## FROM THE CITY OF GOD

. . .

Accordingly, two cities have been formed by two loves; the earthly by the love of self, even to the contempt of God; the heavenly by the love of God, even to the contempt of self. The former, in a word, glories in itself, the latter in the Lord. For the one seeks glory from men; but the greatest glory of the other is God, the witness of conscience. The one lifts up its head in its own glory; the other says to its God, "Thou art my glory, and the lifter up of mine head." In the one, the princes and the nations it subdues are ruled by the love of ruling; in the other, the princes and the subjects serve one another in love, the latter obeying, while the former take thought for all. The one delights in its own

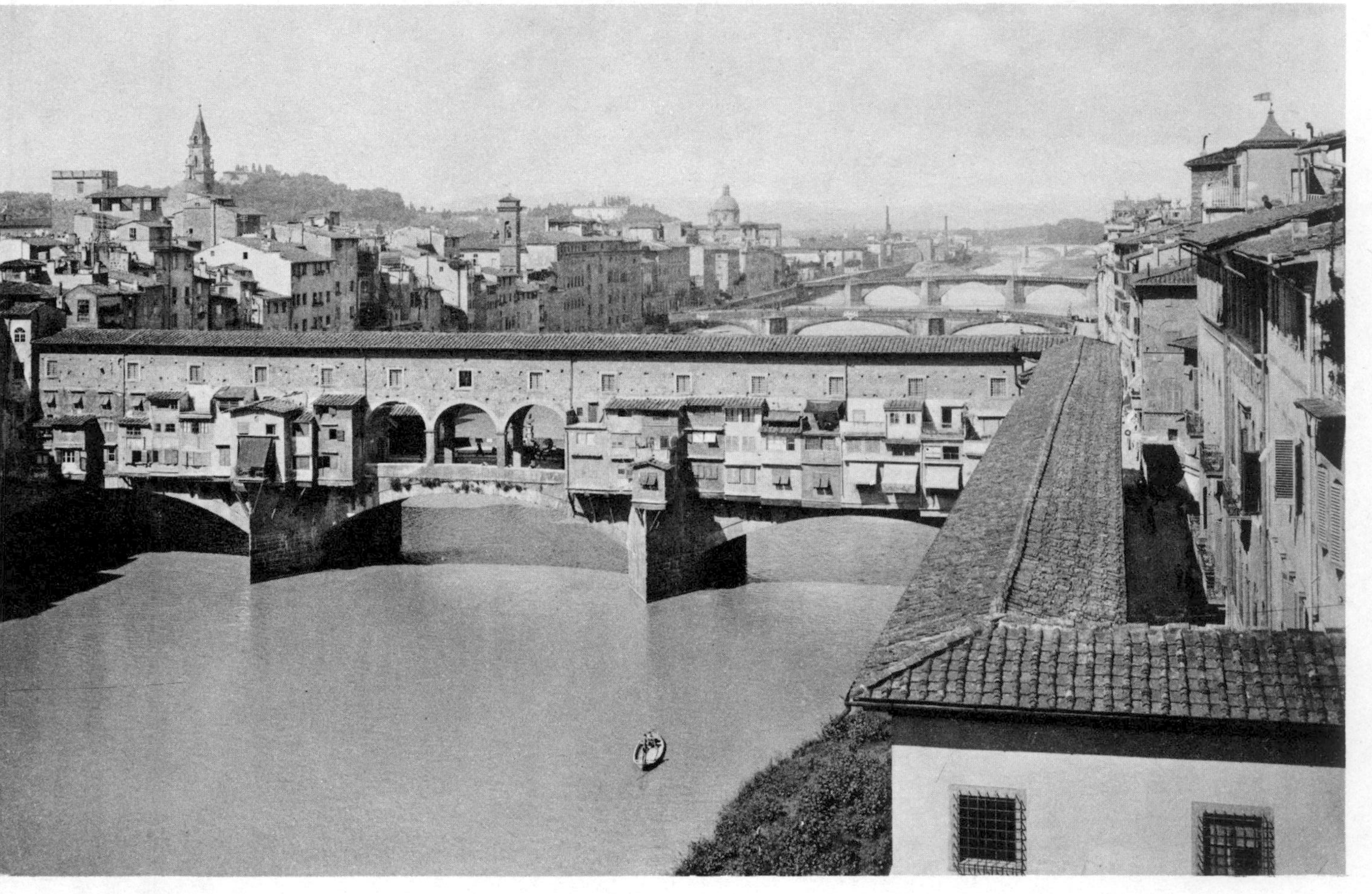

36. Ponte Vecchio, Florence.

strength, represented in the persons of its rulers; the other says to its God, "I will love thee, O Lord, my strength." And therefore the wise men of the one city, living according to man, have sought for profit to their own bodies or souls, or both, and those who have known God "glorified Him not as God, neither were thankful, but became vain in their imaginations, and their foolish heart was darkened; professing themselves to be wise"—that is, glorying in their own wisdom, and being possessed by pride—"they became fools, and changed the glory of the incorruptible God into an image made like to corruptible man, and to birds, and four-footed beasts, and creeping things." For they were either leaders or followers of the people in adoring images, "and worshipped and served the creature more than the Creator, who is blessed for ever." But in the other city there is no human wisdom, but only godliness, which offers due worship to the true God, and looks for its rewards in the society of the saints, of holy angels as well as holy men, that God may be all in all. (XIV, 28)

. . .

But the families which do not live by faith seek their peace in the earthly advantages of this life; while the families which live by faith look for those eternal blessings which are promised; and use as pilgrims such advantages of time and of earth as do not fascinate and divert them from God, but rather aid them to endure with greater ease, and to keep down the number of those burdens of the corruptible body which weigh upon the soul. Thus the things necessary for this mortal life are used by both kinds of men and families alike, but each has its own peculiar and widely different aim in using them. The earthly city, which does not live by faith, seeks an earthly peace, and the end it proposes, in the well-ordered concord of civic obedience and rule, is the combination of men's wills to attain the things which are helpful to this life. The heavenly city, or rather the part of it which sojourns on earth and lives by faith, makes use of this peace only because it must, until this mortal condition which necessitates it shall pass away. Consequently, so long as it lives like a captive and a stranger in the earthly city, though it has already received the promise of redemption, and the gift of the Spirit as the earnest of it, it makes no scruple to obey the laws of the earthly city, whereby the things necessary for the maintenance of this mortal life are administered; and thus, as this life is common to both cities, so there is a harmony be-

37. *Adoration of the Lamb*, Hubert and Jan van Eyck. Part of the Ghent Altarpiece. Ghent, St. Bavo.

tween them in regard to what belongs to it. But, as the earthly city has had some philosophers whose doctrine is condemned by divine teaching, and who, being deceived either by their own conjectures or by demons, supposed that many gods must be invited to take an interest in human affairs, and assigned to each a separate function and a separate department—to one the body, to another the soul; and in the body itself, to one the head, to another the neck, and each of the other members to one of the gods; and in like manner, in the soul, to one god the natural capacity was assigned, to another education, to another anger, to another lust, and so the various affairs of life were assigned—cattle to one, corn to another, wine to another, oil to another, the woods to another, marriages to another, birth and fecundity to another, money to another, navigation to another, wars and victories to another, and other things to other gods: and as the celestial city, on the other hand, knew that one God only was to be worshiped, and that to Him alone was due that service which the Greeks called *hatpeia,* and which can be given only to a god, it has come to pass that the two cities could not have common laws of religion, and the heavenly city has been compelled in the matter to dissent, and to become obnoxious to those who think differently, and to stand the brunt of their enemies who have been alarmed by the multitude of Christians and quelled by the manifest protection of God according to them. This heavenly city, then, while it sojourns on earth, calls citizens out of all nations, and gathers together a society of pilgrims of all languages, not scrupling about diversities in the manners, laws, and institutions whereby earthly peace is secured and maintained, but recognizing that, however various these are, they all tend to one and the same end of earthly peace. It therefore is so far from rescinding and abolishing all these diversities, that it even preserves and adopts them, so long only as no hindrance to the worship of the one supreme and true God is thus introduced. Even the heavenly city, therefore, while in its state of pilgrimage, avails itself of the peace of the earth, and, so far as it can without injuring faith and godliness, desires and maintains a common agreement among men regarding the acquisition of the necessaries of life, and makes this earthly peace bear upon the peace of heaven; for this alone can be truly called and esteemed the peace of the reasonable creatures, consisting as it does in the perfectly ordered and harmonious enjoyment of God and of one another in God. When we shall have reached this peace, this mortal life shall give place to one that is eternal, and our body shall be no more this animal body which by its corruption weighs down the soul, but a spiritual body feeling no want, and in all its members subjected to the will. In its pilgrim state the heavenly city possesses this peace by faith; and by this faith it lives righteously when it refers to the attainment of that peace every good action towards God and man; for that life of the city is a social life. (XIX, 17)

## FROM THE TWO CITIES

### Bishop Otto of Freising

. . . Since, then, the changeable nature of the world is proved by this and like evidence, I thought it necessary . . . to compose a history whereby through God's favor I might display the miseries of the citizens of Babylon and the glory of the kingdom of Christ to which the citizens of Jerusalem are to look forward with hope, and of which they are to have a foretaste even in this life. I have undertaken therefore to bring down as far as our own time, according to the ability that God has given me, the record of the conflicts and miseries of the one city, Babylon; and furthermore, not to be silent concerning our hopes regarding the other city, so far as I can gather hints from the Scriptures, but to make mention also of its citizens who are now sojourning in the worldly city. In this work I follow most of all those illustrious lights of the Church, Augustine and Orosius, and I have planned to draw from their fountains what is pertinent to my theme and my purpose. The one of these (Augustine) has discoursed most keenly and eloquently on the origin and the progress of the glorious City of God and its ordained limits, setting forth how it has ever spread among the citizens of the world, and showing which of its citizens or princes stood forth pre-eminent in the various epochs of the princes or citizens of the world. The other (Orosius), in answer to those who, uttering vain babblings, preferred the former times to Christian times, has composed a very valuable history of the fluctuations and wretched issues of human greatness, the wars and the hazards of wars, and the shifting of thrones, from the foundation of the world down to his own time. Following in their steps I have undertaken to speak of the Two Cities in such a way that we shall not lose the thread of history, that the devout reader may observe what is to be avoided in mundane affairs by reason of the countless miseries wrought by their unstable character, and that the studious and painstaking investigator may find a record of past happenings free from all obscurity.

. . .

It remains now to tell in this eighth book about the third state, namely, how the one City is to attain to the highest blessedness, the other to fail and to descend to the utmost misery, when the most righteous Judge shall, at the last judgment, examine and shall decide the case of each city. Because, as Solomon says, before destruction the heart is constantly exalted, before honor is constantly humbled, I think it appropriate to tell by way of preface what humiliation precedes the glory of His City, what transient exaltation under Antichrist goes before this downfall of the evil city—insofar as it is possible to reach conclusions from the authoritative books. For thus after the dense darkness of the persecutions the eternal day of eternal peace will appear the most delightful, and after the approving smile of this world the grievous storm of punishments and the eternal night will appear the more terrible, inasmuch as the hope of that glory makes present troubles light, the fear of that doom detracts from this temporal pleasure (if there be any such) because it is fleeting.

. . . That the time of persecution is to continue for three years and a half—just as long, indeed, as the Lord's ministry—is indicated in veiled fashion by the fact that it is stated, also by a prophet: "Until a time and times and half a time." It is more clearly declared on the authority of the Apocalypse: "the holy city shall they tread under foot forty and two months." The Lord intimates that, by reason of the enormity of the persecution, this short time has been provided by a most merciful judge for the elect's sake, when He says, "Except those days had been shortened, no flesh would have been saved; for the sake of the elect those days shall be shortened."

When the head of the impious city shall be smitten, the Jews, that unbelieving people, seeing that they have been deceived will, it is believed, be converted, in accordance with the following saying of the prophet: "If the number of the children of Israel be as the sand of the sea, it is the remnant shall be saved." After this a time for repentance remains—a time whose length is hidden from all mortals. Then when all those things which have been foretold shall have been brought to com-

38. *Kiss of Judas* group. Naumberg Cathedral.

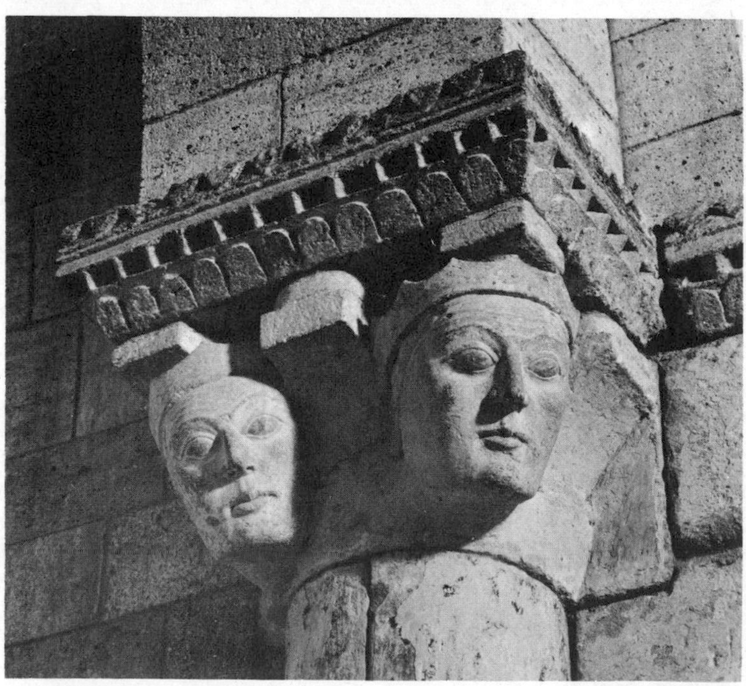

39. Limestone capital with two crowned heads, possibly Henry II and Eleanor of Aquitaine. From Church of Notre Dame Du Bourg, Langon, XII century.

pletion, and strange signs shall have been revealed in the sun, the moon, the stars and the sea—when all men shall be fainting for fear, and for expectation of the things which are to come upon the whole world—then the destruction of the evil city, and the increase of the City of Christ, and the day of the Lord are at hand, in accordance with the word of truth which, sweetly consoling God's own people, says: "When ye see these things coming to pass, know ye that the kingdom of God is nigh." . . .

After these things shall have come to pass the Lord will, no doubt, come for the judgment and for the final sifting of both cities. He will come to judge, moreover, in the form in which he previously came to be judged, that with even justice the world may find a severe judge in Him whom previously with haughty mind it despised when He came humbly in the flesh.

. . .

Finally, having by laborious argument made our way through the fate of the wicked, let us relying on God's grace, come to the sweet and joyous end of His city. Now that Babylon, the city of the world, has been miserably brought to destruction let us hear how the Holy Jerusalem, the City of Christ, is to be glorified. When John in the Apocalypse had said of the former city that with its seducers, the devil and its false prophet, Antichrist, it had been cast into the furnace "of fire and brimstone, where they shall be tormented day and night for ever and ever," after a moment he added, "And I saw the holy city, the New Jerusalem, coming down out of heaven, made ready by God as a bride adorned for her husband." . . .

Next we must note what is elsewhere stated that the City itself is made of pure gold, its foundations of every sort of precious stone, its twelve gates each one of pearl, its streets of pure gold, as it were translucent glass. How great and how delightful an abode do these things promise for us in the heavenly city! If such things are beautiful and comely when they are interpreted literally, how much the more are they found to be joyous and delightful far beyond compare when they are spiritually interpreted. If gold is precious, how much more precious is that which is signified by gold! . . .

Now we must inquire what the blessedness of that country is; for we must not suppose that souls, after they have been stripped from the body, or after they have taken up spiritual bodies and are not inferior to angelic spirits in purity and rank, find delight in external things as men do in this life. Accordingly when Holy Scripture says that their spirits are refreshed and affected by flowering and verdant meadows, by pleasant places, by the singing of birds, by fragrant things (such as cinnamon and balsam), such expressions should, it is clear, be interpreted spiritually rather than carnally. And yet, for the sake of the simple, who must be nourished on mild, not on solid food, whose understanding is not yet exercised and who cannot as yet comprehend spiritual delights —these things are frequently set down by certain teachers that the simple may thus be directed through the visible to the understanding and discovery of the invisible. The blessedness of the saints then lies in beholding their Creator, in accordance with that saying of the Lord, "This is life eternal, that they should know thee the true God, and him whom thou didst send, even Jesus Christ;" of course, we must understand the words "with the Holy Spirit" who proceedeth from both. "This," he says, "is life eternal." For what else is life eternal than purest blessedness? For if the life were temporary, it would not be blessed since it would be rendered anxious lest it come to an end. Again, however long in duration, it could not be called blessed unless it were free from the defect of misery of every kind and abounded in every sort of happiness, or if it were marred by any sort of blemish. That life therefore, is eternal and blessed, blessed and eternal "that they should know thee, the true God, and Him whom thou didst send, even Jesus Christ."

## THE TWO KINDS OF MEN

### St. Augustine

Observe two kinds of men; the one of men labouring, the other of those among whom they labour; the one of men thinking of earth, the other of heaven; the one of men weighing down their heart into the deep, the other of men with angels their heart conjoining; the one trusting in earthly things, the other confiding in heavenly; which God who lieth not hath promised. But mingled are these kinds of men. We see now the citizen of Jerusalem, citizen of the kingdom of heaven, have some office upon earth; to wit, one weareth purple, is a magistrate, is aedile, is proconsul, is emperor, doth direct the earthly republic; but he hath his heart above, if he is a Christian, if he is a believer, if he is godly, if he is despising those things wherein he is and trusteth in that wherein he is not yet. . . . Despair not we then of the citizens of the kingdom of heaven when we see them engaged in any of Babylon's matters, doing something earthly in republic earthly; nor again let us forthwith congratulate all men that we see doing matters heavenly; because even the sons of pestilence sometimes sit in the seat of Moses of whom is said "What things they say, do ye; but what things they do, do not; for they say and do not." Those, amid earthly things lift up heart to heaven; these amid heavenly words, trail heart upon earth. But there will come time of winnowing, when both are to be severed with greatest diligence, in order that no grain may pass over into the heap of chaff that is to be burned, that not one single straw may pass over into the mass that is to be stored in the barn. So long as then now it is mingled, hear we thence our voice, that is voice of the citizens of the kingdom of heaven (for to this we ought to aspire, to bear with evil men here). . . .

(from *Enarrationes in Psalmos* LII, 2)

## *The Social Image*

*Medieval society was seen organically as a body analogous to the human body, composed of members in essential relation to each other, the whole somehow more than the sum of its parts. Within its hierarchy, from the king as head to the servant as foot, each person held a unique role in the scheme of salvation for the body social. This structuring of layers of society established harmony between the individual and the social and accounts for centuries of stability in the medieval period. It was, however, not a totally static society: the ambitious youth of the lower classes could rise through prowess on the battlefield as did the parliamentary leader Simon de Montfort, or through clerical positions to the heights as did the commoner-chancellor Thomas Becket. Only in the years of decline, when growth of commerce made mobility through wealth the likely road to advancement, did discontent seep into the foundations of the structure and weaken its bases.*

40. Nave. Cathedral of Notre-Dame, Paris.

# THE BODY SOCIAL

## John of Salisbury

The prince is first of all to make a thorough survey of himself and diligently study the condition of the whole body of the commonwealth of which he is the representative, and in whose place he stands. A commonwealth, according to Plutarch, is a certain body which is endowed with life by the benefit of divine favor, which acts at the prompting of the highest equity, and is ruled by what may be called the moderating power of reason. Those things which establish and implant in us the practice of religion, and transmit to us the worship of God (here I do not follow Plutarch who says "of the gods") fill the place of the soul in the body of the commonwealth. And therefore those who preside over the practice of religion should be looked up to and venerated as the soul of the body. For who doubts that the ministers of God's holiness are His representatives? Furthermore, since the soul is, as it were, the prince of the body, and has rulership over the whole thereof, so those whom our author calls the prefects of religion preside over the entire body. . . . The place of the head in the body of the commonwealth is filled by the prince, who is subject only to God and to those who exercise His office and represent Him on earth, even as in the human body the head is quickened and governed by the soul. The place of the heart is filled by the Senate, from which proceeds the initiation of good works and ill. The duties of eyes, ears and tongue are claimed by the judges and the governors of provinces. Officials and soldiers correspond to the hands. Those who always attend upon the prince are likened to the sides. Financial officers and keepers (I speak not of those who are in charge of the prisons but of those who are keepers of the privy chest) may be compared with the stomach and intestines, which, if they become congested through excessive avidity, and retain too tenaciously their accumulations, generate innumerable and incurable diseases, so that through their ailment the whole body is threatened with destruction. The husbandmen correspond to the feet, which always cleave to the soil and need more especially the care and foresight of the head, since while they walk upon the earth doing service with their bodies, they meet the more often with stones of stumbling and therefore deserve the aid and protection all the more justly since it is they who raise, sustain, and move forward the weight of the entire body. Take away the support of the feet from the strongest body, and it cannot move forward by its own power, but must creep painfully and shamefully on its hand, or else be moved by means of brute animals. . . . Therefore Plutarch says that that course is to be pursued in all things which is of advantage to the humbler classes, that is to say to the multitudes; for small numbers always yield to great. Indeed the reason for the institution of magistrates was to the end that subjects might be protected from wrongs, and that the commonwealth itself might be "shod" so to speak, by means of their services. For it is, as it were, "unshod," when it is exposed to wrongs,—than which there can be no more disgraceful pass of affairs to those who fill the magistracies. For an afflicted people is a sign and proof of the goutiness, so to speak, of the prince. Then and only then will the health of the commonwealth be sound and flourishing when the higher members shield the lower, and the lower respond faithfully and fully in like measure to the just demands of their superiors, so that each and all are as it were members one of another by a sort of reciprocity and each regards his own interest as best served by that which he knows to be most advantageous for the others. . . .

Next in order comes the simile of eyes, ears and tongue which, as above mentioned, is applied to provincial governors. A governor is one who presides over the administration of justice among the people of a province. He therefore should have knowledge of the just and the unjust and should have the means and the will to enforce justice. . . . So if a governor knows and wishes to do equity, but has not adequate power, the fault is not so much his own as it is the fault of the prince. It is, however, most certain that the duty of a judge and his religion should include the following things: he ought to have a knowledge of law, a will disposed toward good and adequate power to enforce his decisions, and he should be bound by an oath to keep the laws so that he may know that it is not permissible for him to depart in any particular from the purity thereof. . . .

But what is the office of the fully ordained soldiery? To defend the Church, to assail infidelity, to venerate the priesthood, to protect the poor from injuries, to pacify the province, to pour out their blood for their brothers (as the formula of the oath instructs them), and, if need be, to lay down their lives. The high praises of God are in their throat, and two-edged swords are in their hands to execute punishment on the nations and rebuke upon the peoples, and to bind their kings in chains and their nobles in links of iron. But to what end? To the end that they may serve madness, vanity, avarice, or their own private self-will? By no means. Rather to the end that they may execute the judgment that is committed to them to execute; wherein each follows not his own will but the deliberate decision of God, the angels, and men, in accordance with equity and the public utility.

. . .

Those are called the feet who discharge the humbler offices and by whose services the members of the whole commonwealth walk upon solid earth. Among these are to be counted the husbandmen, who always cleave to the soil, busied about their plough-lands or vineyards or pastures or flower-gardens. To these must be added the many species of cloth-making, and the mechanic arts, which work in wood, iron, bronze, and the different metals; also the menial occupations, and the manifold forms of getting a livelihood and sustaining life, or increasing household property, all of which, while they do not pertain to the authority of the governing power, are yet in the highest degree useful and profitable to the corporate whole of the commonwealth. All these different occupations are so numerous that the commonwealth in the number of its feet exceeds not only the eight-footed crab but even the centipede, and because of their very multitude they cannot be enumerated; for while they are not infinite by nature, they are yet of so many different varieties that no writer on the subject of offices or duties has ever laid down particular precepts for each special variety. But it applies generally to each and all of them that in their exercise they should not transgress the limits of the law, and should in all things observe constant reference to the public utility. For inferiors owe it to their superiors to provide them with service, just as the superiors in their turn owe it to their inferiors to provide them with all things needful for their protection and succour.

. . .

Between a tyrant and a prince there is this single or chief difference, that the latter obeys the law and rules the people by its dictates, accounting himself as but their servant. It is by virtue of the law that he makes good his claim to the foremost and chief place in the management of the affairs of the commonwealth and in the bearing of its burdens; and his elevation over others consists in this, that whereas private men are held responsible only for their private affairs, on the prince fall the burdens of the whole community. Wherefore deservedly there is conferred on him, and gathered together in his hands, the power of all his subjects, to the end that he may be sufficient unto himself in seeking and bringing about the advantage of each individually, and of all; and to the end that the state of the human commonwealth may be ordered in the best possible manner, seeing that each and all are members of another. Wherein we indeed but follow nature, the best guide of life; for nature has gathered all the senses of her microcosm or little world, which is man, into the head, and has subjected all the members in obedience to it, in such wise that they will all function properly so long as they follow the guidance of the head, and the head remains sane. Therefore the prince stands on a pinnacle which is exalted and made splendid with all the great and high privileges which he deems necessary for himself. And rightly so, because nothing is more advantageous to the people than that the needs of the prince should be fully satisfied; since it is impossible that his will should be found opposed to justice. Therefore, according to the usual definition, the prince is the public power, and a kind of likeness on earth of the divine majesty. . . .

Princes should not deem that it detracts from their princely dignity to believe that the enactments of their own justice are not to be preferred to the justice of God, whose justice is an everlasting justice, and His law is equity. Now equity, as the learned jurists define it, is a certain fitness of things which compares all things rationally, and seeks to apply like rules of right and wrong to like cases, being impartially disposed toward all persons, and allotting to each that which belongs to him. Of this equity the interpreter is the law, to which the will and intention of equity and justice are known. Therefore Crisippus asserted that the power of the law extends over all things, both divine and human, and that it accordingly presides over all goods and ills, and is the ruler and guide of material things as well as of human beings. To which Papinian, a man most learned in the law, and Demosthenes, the great orator, seem to assent, subjecting all men to its obedience because all law is, as it were, a discovery, and a gift from God, a precept of wise men, the corrector of excesses of the will, the bond which knits together the fabric of the state, and the banisher of crime; and it is therefore fitting that all men should live according to it who lead their lives in a corporate political body. . . .

His [the prince's] shield is strong, but it is a shield for the protection of the weak, and one which wards off powerfully the darts of the wicked from the innocent. Those who derive the greatest advantage from his performance of the duties of his office are those who can do least for themselves, and his power is chiefly exercised against those who desire to do harm. Therefore not without reason he bears a sword, wherewith he sheds blood blamelessly, without becoming thereby a man of blood, and frequently puts men to death without incurring the name or guilt of homicide. . . .

This sword, then, the prince receives from the hand of the Church, although she herself has no sword of blood at all. Nevertheless she has this sword, but she uses it by the hand of the prince, upon whom she confers the power of bodily coercion, retaining to herself authority over spiritual things in the person of the pontiff. The prince is, then, as it were, a minister of the priestly power, and one who exercises that side of the sacred offices which seems unworthy of the hands of the priesthood. . . . But if one who has been appointed prince has performed faithfully the ministry which he has undertaken, as great honour and reverence are to be shown to him as the head excels in honour all the members of the body. Now he performs his ministry faithfully when he is mindful of his true status, and remembers that he bears the person of the *universitas* of those subject to him; and when he is fully conscious that he owes his life not to himself but to others, and allots it to them accordingly, with duly ordered charity and affection. Therefore he owes the whole of himself to God, most of himself to his country, much to his relatives and friends, very little to foreigners, but still somewhat. He has duties to the very wise and the very foolish, to little children and to the aged. Supervision over these classes of persons is common to all in authority, both to those who have care over spiritual things and those who exercise temporal jurisdiction. And so let him be both father and husband to his subjects, or, if he has known some affection more tender still, let him employ that; let him desire to be loved rather than feared, and show himself to them as such a man that they will out of devotion prefer his life to their own, and regard his preservation and safety as a kind of public life; and then all things will prosper well for him, and a small bodyguard will, in case of need, prevail by their loyalty against innumerable adversaries. For love is as strong as death; and the wedge which is held together by strands of love is not easily broken.

# FROM THE LIFE OF CHARLEMAGNE

## EINHARD

Charles was large and strong, and of lofty stature, though not disproportionately tall (his height is well known to have been seven times the length of his foot): the upper part of his head was round, his eyes very large and animated, nose a little long, hair fair, and face laughing and merry. Thus his appearance was always stately and dignified, whether he was standing or sitting; although his neck was thick and somewhat short, and his belly rather prominent; but the symmetry of the rest of his body concealed these defects. His gait was firm, his whole carriage manly, and his voice clear, but not so strong as his size led one to expect. His health was excellent, except during the four years preceding his death, when he was subject to frequent fevers; at the last he even limped a little with one foot. Even in those years he consulted rather his own inclinations than the advice of physicians, who were almost hateful to him, because they wanted him to give up roasts, to which he was accustomed and to eat boiled meat instead. In accordance with the national custom, he took frequent exercise on horseback and in the chase, accomplishments in which scarcely any people in the world can equal the Franks. He enjoyed the exhalations from natural warm springs, and often practiced swimming, in which he was such an adept that none could surpass him; and hence it was that he built his palace at Aix-la-Chapelle, and lived there constantly during his latter years until his death. He used not only to invite his sons to his bath, but his nobles and friends, and now and then a troop of his retinue or bodyguard, so that a hundred or more persons sometimes bathed with him.

He used to wear the national, that is to say, the Frank, dress—next his skin a linen shirt and linen breeches, and above these a tunic fringed with silk; while hose fastened by bands covered his lower limbs, and shoes his feet, and he protected his shoulders and chest in winter by a close-fitting coat of otter or marten skins. Over all he flung a blue cloak, and he always had a sword girt about him, usually one with a gold or silver hilt and belt; he sometimes carried a jeweled sword, but only on great feastdays or at the reception of ambassadors from foreign nations. He despised foreign costumes, however handsome, and never allowed himself to be robed in them, except twice in Rome, when he donned the Roman tunic, chlamys and shoes; the first time at the request of Pope

Hadrian, the second to gratify Leo, Hadrian's successor. On great feastdays he made use of embroidered clothes and shoes bedecked with precious stones, his cloak was fastened by a golden buckle, and he appeared crowned with a diadem of gold and gems, but on other days his dress varied little from the common dress of the people.

Charles was temperate in eating, and particularly so in drinking, for he abominated drunkenness in anybody, much more in himself and those of his household; but he could not easily abstain from food, and often complained that fasts injured his health. He very rarely gave entertainments, only on great feastdays, and then to large numbers of people. His meals ordinarily consisted of four courses, not counting the roast, which his huntsmen used to bring in on the spit; he was more fond of this than of any other dish. While at table, he listened to reading or music. The subjects of the readings were the stories and deeds of olden times; he was fond, too, of St. Augustine's books, and especially of the one entitled "The City of God." He was so moderate in the use of wine and all sorts of drink that he rarely allowed himself more than three cups in the course of a meal. In summer after the midday meal, he would eat some fruit, drain a single cup, put off his clothes and shoes, just as he did for the night, and rest for two or three hours. He was in the habit of awaking and rising from bed four or five times during the night. While he was dressing and putting on his shoes, he not only gave audience to his friends, but if the Count of the Palace told him of any suit in which his judgment was necessary, he had the parties brought before him forthwith, took cognizance of the case and gave his decision, just as if he were sitting on the judgment seat. This was not the only business that he transacted at this time, but he performed any duty of the day whatever, whether he had to attend to the matter himself, or to give commands concerning it to his officers.

Charles had the gift of ready and fluent speech, and could express whatever he had to say with the utmost clearness. He was not satisfied with command of his native language merely, but gave attention to the study of foreign ones, and in particular was such a master of Latin that he could speak it as well as his native tongue; but he could understand Greek better than he could speak it. He was so eloquent, indeed, that he might have passed for a teacher of eloquence. He most zealously cultivated the liberal arts, held those who taught them in great esteem, and conferred great honors upon them. He took lessons in grammar of the deacon Peter of Pisa, at that time an aged man. Another deacon, Albin of Britain, surnamed Alcuin, a man of Saxon extraction, who was the greatest scholar of his day, was his teacher in other branches of learning. The king spent much time and labor with him studying rhetoric, dialectics, and especially astronomy; he learned to reckon, and used to investigate the motions of the heavenly bodies most curiously, with an intelligent scrutiny. He also tried to write, and used to keep tablets and blanks in bed under his pillow, that at leisure hours he might accustom his hand to form the letters; however, as he did not begin his efforts in due season, but late in life, they met with ill success.

He cherished with the greatest fervor and devotion the principles of the Christian religion, which had been instilled into him from infancy. Hence it was that he built the beautiful basilica at Aix-la-Chapelle, which he adorned with gold and silver and lamps, and with rails and doors of solid brass. He had the columns and marbles for this structure brought from Rome and Ravenna, for he could not find such as were suitable elsewhere. He was a constant worshipper at this church as long as his health permitted, going morning and evening, even after nightfall, besides attending mass; and he took care that all the services there conducted should be administered with the utmost possible propriety, very often warning the sextons not to let any improper or unclean thing be brought into the building or remain in it. He provided it with a great number of sacred vessels of gold and silver and with such a quantity of clerical robes that not even the doorkeepers who fill the humblest office in the church were obliged to wear their everyday clothes when in the exercise of their duties. He was at great pains to improve the church reading and psalmody, for he was well skilled in both, although he neither read in public nor sang, except in a low tone and with others.

He was very forward in succoring the poor, and in that gratuitous generosity which the Greeks call alms, so much so that he not only made a point of giving in his own country and his own kingdom, but when he discovered that there were Christians living in poverty in Syria, Egypt, and Africa, at Jerusalem, Alexandria and Carthage, he had compassion on their wants, and used to send money over the seas to them. The reason that he zealously strove to make friends with the kings beyond seas was that he might get help and relief to the Christians living under their rule. He cherished the Church of Saint Peter the Apostle at Rome above all other holy and sacred places and heaped its treasury with a vast wealth of gold, silver, and precious stones. He sent great and countless gifts to the popes, and throughout his whole reign the wish that he had nearest at heart was to re-establish the ancient authority of the city of Rome under his care and by his influence, and to defend and protect the Church of St. Peter and to beautify and enrich it out of his own store above all other churches. Although he held it in such veneration, he only repaired to Rome to pay his vows and make his supplications four times during the whole forty-seven years that he reigned.

When he made his last journey thither, he had also other ends in view. The Romans had inflicted many injuries upon the Pontiff Leo, tearing out his eyes and cutting out his tongue, so that he had been compelled to call upon the King for help. Charles accordingly went to Rome, to set in order the affairs of the Church, which were in great confusion, and passed the whole winter there. It was then that he received the titles of Emperor and Augustus, to which at first he had such an aversion that he declared that he would not have set foot in the Church the day they were conferred, although it was a great feastday, if he could have foreseen the design of the Pope. He bore very patiently with the jealousy which the Roman emperors showed upon his assuming these titles, for they took this step very ill; and by dint of frequent embassies and letters, in which he addressed them as brothers, he made their haughtiness yield to his magnanimity, a quality in which he was unquestionably the superior.

It was after he had received the imperial name that, finding the laws of his people very defective (the Franks have two sets of laws very different in many particulars), he determined to add what was wanting, to reconcile the discrepancies, and to correct what was vicious and wrongly cited in them. However, he went no further in this matter than to supplement the laws by a few capitularies, and these imperfect ones; but he caused the unwritten laws of all the tribes that came under his rule to be compiled and reduced to writing. He also had the old rude songs that celebrate the deeds and wars of the ancient kings written out for transmission to posterity. He began a grammar of his native language. He gave the months names in his own tongue, in place of the Latin and barbarous names by which they were formerly known among the Franks. He likewise designated the winds by twelve appropriate names; there were hardly more than four distinctive ones in use before. . . .

Toward the close of his life, when he was broken by ill health and old age, he summoned Louis, King of Aquitania, his only surviving son by Hildegard, and gathered together the chief men of the Franks in a solemn assembly. He appointed Louis, with their unanimous consent, to rule with himself over the whole kingdom, and constituted him heir to the imperial name; then, placing the diadem upon his son's head, he bade him be proclaimed Emperor and Augustus. This step was hailed by all present with great favor, for it really seemed as if God had prompted him to it for the kingdom's good; it increased the King's dignity and struck no little terror into foreign nations. After sending his son back to Aquitania, although weak from age, he set out to hunt, as usual, near his palace at Aix-la-Chapelle, and repassed the rest of the autumn in the chase, returning thither about the first of November. While wintering there he was seized, in the month of January, with a high fever, and took to his bed. As soon as he was taken sick, he prescribed for himself abstinence from food, as he always used to do in case of fever, thinking that the disease could be driven off, or at least mitigated, by fasting. Beside the fever, he suffered from a pain in the side, which the Greeks call pleurisy; but he still persisted in fasting and in keeping up his strength only by draughts taken at very long intervals. He died January 28th, the 7th day from the time that he took to his bed, at nine o'clock in the morning, after partaking of the holy communion, in the 72nd year of his age and the 47th of his reign. . . . He had a summary drawn up of his wishes regarding the distribution of his property, the terms and text of which are as follows:

In the name of the Lord God, the Almighty Father, Son and Holy Ghost. This is the inventory and division dictated by the most glorious and most pious Lord Charles, Emperor Augustus, in the 811th year of the Incarnation of our Lord Jesus Christ, in the 43rd year of his reign in France and 37th in Italy, the 11th of his empire, and the 4th Indiction, which considerations of piety and prudence have determined him, and the favor of God enabled him, to make of his treasures and money ascertained this day to be in his treasure chamber. In this division he is especially desirous to provide not only that the largess of alms which Christians usually make of their possessions shall be made for himself in due course and order out of his wealth, but also that his heirs shall be free from all doubt, and know clearly what belongs to them, and be able to share their property by suitable partition without litigation or strife. With this intention and to this end he has first divided all his substance and movable goods ascertained to be in his treasure chamber on the day aforesaid in gold, silver and precious stones, and royal ornaments into three lots and has subdivided and set off two of the said lots into twenty-one parts, keeping the third entire. The first two lots have been thus subdivided into twenty-one parts because there are in his kingdom twenty-one recognized metropolitan cities, and in order that each archbishopric shall receive by way of alms, at the hands of his heirs and friends, one of the said parts, and that the archbishop who shall then administer its affairs shall take the part given to it, and share the same with his suffragans in such a manner that one third shall go to the church and the remaining two-thirds shall be divided among the suffragans. . . . the third lot shall be employed for the owner's daily needs as property which he shall be under no obligation to part with in order to the fulfillment of any vow, and this as long as he shall be in the flesh and consider it necessary for his use. But upon his death or voluntary renunciation of the affairs of this world, this said lot shall be divided into four parts, and one thereof shall be added to the aforesaid twenty-one parts; the second shall be assigned to his sons and daughters, and to the sons and daughters of his sons, to be distributed among them in just and equal partition; the third, in accordance with the custom common among Christians, shall be devoted to the poor; and the fourth shall go to the support of the men servants and maid servants on duty in the palace. It is his wish that to this said third lot of the whole amount, which consists, as well as the rest, of gold and silver, shall be added all the vessels and utensils of brass, iron and other metals, together with the arms, clothing, and other movable goods, costly and cheap, adapted to diverse uses, as hangings, coverlets, carpets, woolen stuffs, leathern articles, pack-saddles, and whatsoever shall be found in his treasure chamber and wardrobe at that time, in order that thus the parts of the said lot may be augmented, and the alms distributed reach more persons. He ordains that his chapel—that is to say, its church property, as well that which he has provided and collected as that which came to him by inheritance from his father—shall remain entire, and not be dissevered by any partition whatsoever. If, however, any vessels, books, or other articles be found therein which are certainly known to have been given to the said chapel by him, whoever wants them shall have them on paying their value at a fair estimation. He likewise commands that the books which he has collected in his library in great numbers shall be sold for fair prices to such as want them, and the money received therefrom given to the poor. It is well known that among his other property and treasures are three silver tables and one very large and massive golden one. He directs and commands that the square silver table, upon which there is a representation of the city of Constantinople, shall be sent to the Basilica of St. Peter the Apostle at Rome, with the other gifts destined therefor; that

41. Psalter, North France.

the round one, adorned with a delineation of the city of Rome, shall be given to the Episcopal Church at Ravenna; that the third, which far surpasses the other two in weight and in beauty of workmanship, and is made in three circles, showing the plan of the whole universe, drawn with skill and delicacy, shall go, together with the golden table, fourthly above mentioned, to increase that lot which is to be devoted to his heirs and to alms.

This deed and the dispositions thereof, he had made and appointed in the presence of the bishops, abbots, and counts able to be present. . . .

## KING ST. LOUIS

### Fra Salimbene degli Adami

In the year of our Lord 1248 around the feast of Pentecost or a little later I went down from the convent at Auxerre to that at Sens. The provincial chapter of France was to be held there and the lord Louis, King of France, was to come there. . . . The king was slender and elegant, a bit tall and thin; he had the face of an angel and a gracious mien. He came to the church of the Friars Minor not with royal pomp but in the costume of a pilgrim, bearing a pilgrim's staff and cloak that adorned his shoulders beautifully. He did not come on horseback but by foot. His brothers, three counts, followed him with the same humility and the same garments. The eldest was Robert and the youngest Charles who accomplished great deeds worthy of praise. One might have said in the words of the prophet: *Some trust in chariots and some in horses; but we will call upon the name of the Lord.* (Ps. 19, 8)

The king did not care to have a train of nobles, but preferred the prayers and suffrages of the poor. Thus he accomplished what was said in Eccl. 4, 7: *Make thyself affable to the congregation of the poor.* Truth to tell, one might rather take the king for a monk, considering his piety than for a knight trained in the profession of arms. When we were gathered together in chapter, the king spoke first of his own affairs. He recommended himself and his brothers, the queen, the queen mother and his whole retinue to them. . . .

After these Brother John of Parma, the minister general, upon whom the duty of replying fell because of his office, made a speech and said: Ecclesiasticus (ch. 32) teaches: *Speak, thou that are elder for it becometh thee, to speak the first word with careful knowledge.* Our king and lord, father and benefactor who makes himself *affable to the poor,* came to us in humility desiring us to be useful, courteous and kind. He spoke to us first, as was right. He does not ask for gold or silver; by the grace of God his treasury is sufficiently full; he asks the prayers and suffrages of the brothers for a project that seems highly laudable. The lord king has in truth undertaken this voyage and this crusade for the glory of the Lord Jesus Christ, to bring help to the Holy Land, to fight the adversaries of the faith and of the cross of Christ, for the honour of the universal church and for the Christian religion and for the salvation of his own soul and the souls of all who are to go across the sea with him. Wherefore seeing that he has been a special benefactor and defender of our Order, not only at Paris, but throughout his realm, and that he has come humbly to us with so worthy a company to ask the prayers of the Order for this enterprise, it is fitting and just that we respond to his kindnesses. And since the brothers of France are all disposed to undertake this and intend to do more than I know how to impose on them, I do not put any precept upon them. But since I have begun the visitation of the Order, I have decided to enjoin on each priest the obligation to say four Masses for the king and his companions. The first will be the Mass of the Holy Spirit, the second, that of the Cross; the third, that of the Blessed Virgin, the fourth, that of the Holy Trinity. . . .

Moreover the king paid the expenses that day and dined with the brothers. We ate in the refectory. There were present three brothers of the king, the cardinal of the Roman curia, the minister general, the archbishop of Rouen, Brother Rigaud, the minister provincial, the custodes, definitors and discreets and the guest brothers whom we call strangers. Since the minister general knew, therefore, that there was a noble and worthy company with the king, namely the legate and cardinal of the Roman church, the archbishop of Rouen, he did not wish to push himself forward, according to the word of Ecclesiasticus (ch. 11, 4): *Be not exalted in the day of thine honour.* Though he had been invited to sit by the side of the king, he preferred to practice the humility and courtesy Our Lord taught by the example he gave us. The Lord said (Luke 14, 8-11): *When thou art invited to a wedding, sit not down in the first place, lest perhaps one more honorable than thou be invited by him; And he that invited thee and him, come and say to thee: give this man thy place. And then thou begin with shame to take the lowest place. But when thou art invited, go, sit down in the lowest place, that when he who invited thee cometh, he may say to thee: Friend, go up higher. Then shalt thou have glory before them that sit at the table with thee. Because everyone that exalteth himself shall be humbled; and he that humbleth himself shall be exalted.* Another text, one from the Book of Proverbs (25, 6): *Claim no honor in the king's presence, nor occupy the place of great men.*

Brother John preferred, therefore, to sit at the table of the humble who were ennobled by his presence. Many of those at the banquet were more edified by this good example. And, just as a generous countenance ennobles a mean repast, so also the presence of a humble man who seats himself humbly at table lends dignity so much to a place that the table is enriched with magnificence. . . .

At dinner we had first, cherries, then bread that was very white, wine in abundance and of the best, worthy of a king's magnificence. And according to the custom of the French, there were many guests who were eager to invite and compel them to drink that were not willing. We then had fresh beans boiled in milk, fishes and crabs, eel pasties, rice cooked with the milk of almonds and cinnamon, eels baked with excellent sauces, tarts, new cheese and fruits. We had everything necessary in abundance and fittingly arranged. All was brought on with much ceremony and served with care.

The next day the king continued on his way. When the chapter ended it was easy for me to catch up with the king for he often turned aside from his main route to visit at the right or at the left a hermitage of the Friars Minor or of other religious to recommend himself to their prayers. He did this every day till he came to the sea and embarked for the Holy Land.

After I had visited with the brothers at Auxerre, the convent to which I belonged, I went on in one day to Vezelay which is a celebrated village in Burgundy where it is believed the body of Mary Magdalene is to be found. The next day was Sunday. Early in the morning the king betook himself to the brothers to ask their prayers, according to the word of Proverbs, (11, 27): *Well doth he rise early who seeketh good things.* The king left his whole escort in camp, therefore the brothers were very little disturbed. He took with him only his three brothers, and some servants to watch the horses. After they had made a genuflection and reverence before the altar, the brothers brought them seats and benches. The king sat on the ground in the dust; this I saw with my own eyes, for the chapel was not paved. . . . It was told him that Charles was still praying with fervor. The king was happy and waited with patience, without mounting his horse, for his brother to finish his prayers. I saw for myself with what fervor Charles prayed and how the king waited patiently outside. I recognized how true is the saying of Holy Scripture (Prov. 18, 19): *A brother that is helped by his brother is like a strong city.*

(from *The Chronicle*)

## *The Literary Image*

*This same sense of organic form permeates the great literature of the Middle Ages. After the Bible, the most-read works were* Roman de la Rose, The Golden Legend, *and* Reynard the Fox. *The latter has survived as a fable; such hagiolatry as the* Legend *has gone out of fashion while in the* Roman *the charm of the allegory has faded, leaving a wearying didacticism. But many works won enduring popularity and, without exception, they are characterized by meaningful structure. Early* chansons de geste *and folk epics, retold in courtly language, gave us such well-known legends as* Tristan *and* Parsifal. *From England came* The Canterbury Tales *of Geoffrey Chaucer, a fourteenth-century clerk of customs, protégé of John of Gaunt; his use of the vernacular instead of his customary polished Latin gave invaluable assistance to the growth of the English literary tongue. This collection of stories as told by a group of pilgrims en route to Canterbury constitutes a panoramic view of the life and society of his time.*

*The other towering literary work of the century is Dante's* The Divine Comedy. *A political exile from his beloved city of Florence, Dante Alighieri chose its Tuscan dialect for his masterpiece, the narrative of his journey through the darkness and despair of Hell, the calm and hope of Purgatory to the eternal light of Paradise. Although the journey through the lower regions is in the Roman tradition of poetry and the choice of Virgil as guide pays homage to that tradition, Dante himself is the medieval pilgrim par excellence. This travail is also the struggle of the soul from its self-centered beginnings through the spiritual adventure of becoming God-centered.*

*Dante is a true scholastic, expounding the teaching of the schools in his view of the cosmos and of the hierarchy of good and evil, and in his use of allegorical, tropological and anagogical meanings as well as literary. His Gothic love of form extends even to the rhyme scheme: terza rima, one stanza overlapping another with an unlimited succession of rhymes. And his worship of Beatrice is in the best style of courtly love. Dante's Paradise, peopled with unique personalities, all reflecting the light of glory, graphically illustrates the belief in a God imaged in His creation.*

# FROM THE DIVINE COMEDY

## DANTE ALIGHIERI

### Inferno: Canto I

In the middle of the journey of our life I came to myself in a dark wood where the straight way was lost.

Ah! how hard a thing it is to tell what a wild, and rough, and stubborn wood this was, which in my thought renews the fear!

So bitter is it, that scarcely more is death: but to treat of the good that I there found, I will relate the other things that I discerned.

I cannot rightly tell how I entered it, so full of sleep was I about the moment that I left the true way.

But after I had reached the foot of a Hill there, where that valley ended, which had pierced my heart with fear,

I looked up and saw its shoulders already clothed with the rays of the Planet that leads men straight on every road.

Then the fear was somewhat calmed, which had continued in the lake of my heart the night that I passed so piteously.

And as he, who with panting breath has escaped from the deep sea to the shore, turns to the dangerous water and gazes:

so my mind, which still was fleeing, turned back to see the pass that no one ever left alive.

After I had rested my wearied body a short while, I took the way again along the desert strand, so that the right foot always was the lower.

And behold, almost at the commencement of the steep, a Leopard, light and very nimble, which was covered with spotted hair.

And it went not from before my face; nay, so impeded my way, that I had often turned to go back.

The time was at the beginning of the morning; and the sun was mounting up with those stars which were with him when Divine Love

first moved those fair things: so that the hour of time and the sweet season caused me to have good hope

of that animal with the gay skin; yet not so, but that I feared at the sight, which appeared to me, of a Lion.

He seemed coming upon me with head erect, and furious hunger; so that the air seemed to have fear thereat;

and a She-wolf, that looked full of all cravings in her leanness; and has ere now made many live in sorrow.

She brought such heaviness upon me with the terror of her aspect, that I lost the hope of ascending.

And as one who is eager in gaining, and, when the time arrives that makes him lose, weeps and afflicts himself in all his thoughts:

such that restless beast made me, which coming against me, by little and little drove me back to where the Sun is silent.

Whilst I was rushing downwards, there appeared before my eyes one who seemed hoarse from long silence.

When I saw him in the great desert, I cried: "Have pity on me, whate'er thou be, whether shade or veritable man!"

He answered me: "Not man, a man I once was; and my parents were Lombards, and both of Mantua by country.

I was born *sub Julio,* though it was late; and lived at Rome under the good Augustus, in the time of the false and lying Gods.

A poet I was; and sang of that just son of Anchises, who came from Troy after proud Ilium was burnt.

But thou, why returnest thou to such disquiet? why ascendest not the delectable mountain, which is the beginning and the cause of all gladness?"

"Art thou then that Virgil, and that fountain which pours abroad so rich a stream of speech?" I answered him, with bashful front.

"O glory, and light of other poets! May the long zeal avail me, and the great love, that made me search thy volume.

Thou art my master and my author; thou alone art he from whom I took the good style that hath done me honour.

See the beast from which I turned back; help me from her, thou famous sage; for she makes my veins and pulses tremble."

"Thou must take another road," he answered, when he saw me weeping, "if thou desirest to escape from this wild place:

because this beast, for which thou criest, lets not men pass her way; but so entangles that she slays them;

and has a nature so perverse and vicious, that she never satiates her craving appetite; and after feeding, she is hungrier than before.

The animals to which she weds herself are many; and will yet be more, until the Greyhound comes, that will make her die with pain.

He will not feed on land or pelf, but on wisdom, and love, and manfulness; and his nation shall be between Feltro and Feltro.

He shall be the salvation of that low Italy, for which Camilla the virgin, Euryalus, and Turnus, and Nisus, died of wounds;

he shall chase her through every city, till he have put her into Hell again; from which envy first set her loose.

Wherefore I think and discern this for thy best, that thou follow me; and I will be thy guide, and lead thee hence through an eternal place,

where thou shalt hear the hopeless shrieks, shalt see the ancient spirits in pain, so that each calls for a second death;

and then thou shalt see those who are contented in fire: for they hope to come, whensoever it be, amongst the blessed;

then to these, if thou desirest to ascend, there shall be a spirit worthier than I to guide thee; with her will I leave thee at my parting:

for that Emperor who reigns above, because I was rebellious to his law, wills not that I come into his city.

In all parts he rules and there holds sway; there is his city, and his high seat: O happy whom he chooses for it!"

And I to him: "Poet, I beseech thee by that God whom thou knowest not: in order that I may escape this ill and worse,

lead me where thou now hast said, so that I may see the Gate of St. Peter, and those whom thou makest so sad." Then he moved; and I kept on behind him.

## Inferno: Canto V

Thus I descended from the first circle down into the second, which encompasses less space, and so much greater pain, that it stings to wailing.

There Minos sits horrific, and grins: examines the crimes upon the entrance; judges, and sends according as he girds himself.

I say, that when the ill-born spirit comes before him, it confesses all; and that sin-discerner

sees what place in hell is for it, and with his tail makes as many circles round himself as the degrees he will have it to descend.

Always before him stands a crowd of them; they go each in its turn to judgment; they tell, and hear; and then are whirled down.

"O thou who comest to the abode of pain!" said Minos to me, when he saw me leaving the act of that great office;

"look how thou enterest, and in whom thou trustest; let not the wideness of the entrancy deceive thee." And my guide to him: "Why criest thou too?

Hinder not his fated going; thus it is willed there where what is willed can be done: and ask no more."

Now begin the doleful notes to reach me; now am I come where much lamenting strikes me.

I came into a place void of all light, which bellows like the sea in tempest, when it is combated by warring winds.

The hellish storm, which never rests, leads the spirits with its sweep; whirling, and smiting it vexes them.

When they arrive before the ruin, there the shrieks, the moanings, and the lamentation; there they blaspheme the divine power.

I learnt that to such torment are doomed the carnal sinners, who subject reason to lust.

And as their wings bear along the starlings, at the cold season, in large and crowded troop: so that blast, the evil spirits;

hither, thither, down, up, it leads them. No hope ever comforts them, not of rest but even of less pain.

And as the cranes go chanting their lays, making a long streak of themselves in the air: so I saw the shadows come, uttering wails,

borne by that strife of winds; whereat I said: "Master, who are those people, whom the black air thus lashes?"

"The first of these concerning whom thou seekest to know," he then replied, "was Empress of many tongues.

With the vice of luxury she was so broken, that she made lust and law alike in her decree, to take away the blame she had incurred.

She is Semiramis, of whom we read that she succeeded Ninus, and was his spouse; she held the land which the Soldan rules.

That other is she who slew herself in love, and broke faith to the ashes of Sichaeus; next comes luxurious Cleopatra.

Helena see, for whom so long a time of ill revolved; and see the great Achilles, who fought at last with love;

see Paris, Tristan"; and more than a thousand shades he showed to me, and pointing with his finger, named to me those whom love had parted from our life.

After I had heard my teacher name the olden dames and cavaliers, pity came over me, and I was as if bewildered.

I began: "Poet, willingly would I speak with those two that go together, and seem so light upon the wind."

And he to me: "Thou shalt see when they are nearer to us; and do thou then entreat them by that love, which leads them; and they will come."

Soon as the wind bends them to us, I raised my voice: "O wearied souls! come to speak with us, if none denies it."

As doves called by desire, with raised and steady wings come through the air to their loved nest, borne by their will:

so those spirits issued from the band where Dido is, coming to us through the malignant air; such was the force of my affectuous cry.

"O living creature, gracious and benign; that goest through the black air, visiting us who stained the earth with blood:

if the King of the Universe were our friend, we would pray him for thy peace; seeing that thou hast pity of our perverse misfortune.

Of that which it pleases thee to hear and to speak, we will hear and speak with you, whilst the wind, as now, is silent for us.

The town, where I was born, sits on the shore, where Po descends to rest with his attendant streams.

Love, which is quickly caught in gentle heart, took him with the fair body of which I was bereft; and the manner still afflicts me.

Love, which to no loved one permits excuse for loving, took me so strongly with delight in him, that, as thou seest, even now it leaves me not.

Love led us to one death; Caïna waits for him who quenched our life." These words from them were offered to us.

After I had heard those wounded souls, I bowed my face, and held it low until the Poet said to me: "What are thou thinking of?"

When I answered, I began: "Ah me! what sweet thoughts, what longing led them to the woeful pass!"

Then I turned again to them; and I spoke, and began: "Francesca, thy torments make me weep with grief and pity.

But tell me: in the time of the sweet sighs, by what and how love granted you to know the dubious desires?"

And she to me: "There is no greater pain than to recall a happy time in wretchedness; and this thy teacher knows.

But if thou hast such desire to learn the first root of our love, I will do like one who weeps and tells.

One day, for pastime, we read of Lancelot, how love constrained him; we were alone, and without all suspicion.

Several times that reading urged our eyes to meet, and changed the colour of our faces; but one moment alone it was that overcame us.

When we read how the fond smile was kissed by such a lover, he, who shall never be divided from me,

kissed my mouth all trembling: the book, and he who wrote it, was a Galeotto. That day we read in it no farther."

Whilst the one spirit thus spake, the other wept so, that I fainted with pity, as if I had been dying; and fell, as a dead body falls.

## Purgatorio: Canto I

To course o'er better waters now hoists sail the little bark of my wit, leaving behind her a sea so cruel.

And I will sing of that second realm, where the human spirit is purged and becomes worthy to ascend to Heaven.

But here let dead poesy rise up again, O holy Muses, since yours am I, and here let Calliope rise somewhat,

accompanying my song with that strain whose stroke the wretched Pies felt so that they despaired of pardon.

Sweet hue of orient sapphire which was gathered on the clear forehead of the sky, pure even to the first circle,

to mine eyes restored delight, soon as I issued forth from the dead air which had afflicted eyes and heart.

The fair planet which hearteneth to love was making the whole East to laugh, veiling the Fishes that were in her train.

I turned me to the right hand, and set my mind on the other pole, and saw four stars never yet seen save by the first people.

The heavens seemed to rejoice in their flames. O Northern widowed clime, since thou art bereft of beholding them!

When I was parted from gazing at them, turning me a little to the other pole, there whence the Wain had already disappeared,

I saw near me an old man solitary, worthy of such great reverence in his mien, that no son owes more to a father.

Long he wore his beard and mingled with white hair, like unto his locks of which a double list fell on his breast.

The rays of the four holy lights adorned his face so with brightness, that I beheld him as we the sun before him.

"Who are ye that against the dark stream have fled the eternal prison?" said he, moving those venerable plumes.

"Who hath guided you? or who was a lamp unto you issuing forth from the deep night that ever maketh black the infernal vale?

Are the laws of the pit thus broken, or is there some new counsel changed in Heaven that being damned ye come to my rocks?"

Then did my Leader lay hold on me, and with words, and with hand, and with signs, made reverent my knees and brow.

Then answered him: "Of myself I came not. A lady came down from Heaven through whose prayers I succoured this man with my company.

But since it is thy will that more be unfolded of our state, how it truly is, my will it cannot be that thou be denied.

He hath ne'er seen the last hour, but by his madness was so near to it, that very short time there was to turn.

Even as I said, I was sent to him to rescue him, and no other way there was but this along which I have set me.

I have shown him all the guilty people, and now do purpose showing those spirits that purge them under thy charge.

How I have brought him, 'twere long to tell thee: Virtue descends from on high which aids me to guide him to see thee and to hear thee.

Now may it please thee to be gracious unto his coming: he seeketh freedom, which is so precious, as he knows who giveth up life for her.

Thou knowest it; since for her sake death was not bitter to thee in Utica, where thou leftest the raiment which at the great day shall be so bright.

The eternal laws by us are not violated, for he doth live and Minos binds me not; but I am of the circle where are the chaste eyes

of thy Marcia, who visibly yet doth pray thee, O holy breast, that thou hold her for thine own: for love of her then incline thee unto us.

Let us go through thy seven kingdoms: thanks of thee I will bear back to her, if thou deign to be mentioned there below."

"Marcia was so pleasing to mine eyes while I was yonder," said he then, "that every grace she willed of me I did.

Now that she dwells beyond the evil stream, no more may she move me, by that law which was made when I thence came forth.

But if a heavenly lady moves and directs thee, as thou sayest, no need is there for flattery: let it suffice thee that in her name thou askest me.

Go then, and look that thou gird this man with a smooth rush, and that thou bathe his face so that all filth may thence be wiped away:

for 'twere not meet with eye obscured by any mist to go before the first minister of those that are of Paradise.

This little isle all round about the very base, there, where the wave beats it, bears rushes on the soft mud.

No other plant that would put forth leaf or harden can live there, because it yields not to the buffetings.

Then be not this way your return; the sun, which now is rising, will show you how to take the mount at an easier ascent."

So he vanished; and I uplifted me without speaking, and drew me all back to my Leader, and directed mine eyes to him.

He began: "Son, follow thou my steps: turn we back, for this way the plain slopes down to its low bounds."

The dawn was vanquishing the breath of morn which fled before her, so that from afar I recognized the trembling of the sea.

We paced along the lonely plain, as one who returns to his lost road, and, till he reach it, seems to go in vain.

When we came there where the dew is striving with the sun, being at a place where, in the cool air, slowly it is scattered;

both hands outspread, gently my Master laid upon the sweet grass; wherefore I who was ware of his purpose,

raised towards him my tear-stained cheeks: there made he all revealed my hue which Hell had hidden.

We came then on to the desert shore, that never saw man navigate its waters who thereafter knew return.

There he girded me even as it pleased Another: O marvel! that such as he plucked the lowly plant, even such did it forthwith spring up again, there whence he tore it.

## Purgatorio: Canto II

Already had the sun reached the horizon, whose meridian circle covers Jerusalem with its highest point,

and night which opposite to him revolves, from Ganges forth was issuing with the Scales, that fall from her hand when she prevails;

so that fair Aurora's white and ruby cheeks, there where I was, through too great age were turning orange.

We were alongside the ocean yet, like folk who ponder o'er their road, who in heart do go and in body stay;

and lo, as on the approach of morn, through the dense mists Mars burns red, low in the West o'er the ocean-floor;

such to me appeared—so may I see it again!—a light coming o'er the sea so swiftly, that no flight is equal to its motion;

from which, when I had a while withdrawn mine eyes to question my Leader, I saw it brighter and bigger grown.

Then on each side of it appeared to me a something white; and from beneath it, little by little, another whiteness came forth.

My Master yet did speak no word, until the first whitenesses appeared as wings; then, when well he knew the pilot,

he cried: "Bend, bend thy knees; behold the Angel of God: fold thy hands: henceforth shalt thou see such ministers.

Look how he scorns all human instruments, so that oar he wills not, nor other sail than his wings, between shores so distant.

See how he has them heavenward turned, plying the air with eternal plumes, that are not mewed like mortal hair."

Then as more and more towards us came the bird divine, brighter yet he appeared, wherefore mine eye endured him not near:

but I bent it down, and he came on to the shore with a vessel so swift and light that the waters nowise drew it in.

On the stern stood the celestial pilot, such, that blessedness seemed writ upon him, and more than a hundred spirits sat within.

*"In exitu Israel de Aegypto,"* sang they all together with one voice, with what of that psalm is thereafter written.

Then made he to them the sign of Holy Cross, whereat they all flung them on the strand and quick even as he came he went his way.

The throng that remained there seemed strange to the place, gazing around like one who assayeth new things.

On every side the sun, who with his arrows bright had chased the

Goat from midst of heaven, was shooting forth the day,

when the new people lifted up their faces towards us, saying to us: "If ye know show us the way to go to the mount."

And Virgil answered: "Ye think perchance that we have experience of this place, but we are strangers even as ye are.

We came but now, a little while before you, by other way which was so rough and hard, that the climbing now will seem but play to us."

The souls who had observed me by my breathing that I was yet alive, marvelling grew pale;

and as to a messenger, who bears the olive, the folk draw nigh to hear the news, and none shows himself shy at trampling;

so on my face those souls did fix their gaze, fortunate every one, well nigh forgetting to go and make them fair.

I saw one of them draw forward to embrace me with such great affection, that he moved me to do the like.

O shades empty save in outward show! thrice behind it my hands I clasped, and as often returned with them to my breast.

With wonder methinks I coloured me, whereat the shade smiled and drew back, and I, following it, flung me forward.

Gently it bade me pause: then knew I who it was, and did pray him that he would stay a while to speak to me.

He answered me: "Even as I loved thee in the mortal body so do I love thee freed; therefore I stay: but wherefore goest thou?"

"Casella mine, to return here once again where I am, make I this journey," said I, "but how hath so much time been taken from thee?"

And he to me: "No wrong is done me, if he who bears away when and whom he pleases hath many times denied me this passage;

for of a just will his will is made. Truly for three months past he hath taken, in all peace, whoso hath wished to enter.

Wherefore I, who now was turned to the seashore where Tiber's wave grows salt, kindly by him was garnered in.

To that mouth now he hath set his wings, because evermore are gathered there, they who to Acheron sink not down."

And I: "If a new law take not from thee memory or skill in that song of love which was wont to calm my every desire,

may it please thee therewith to solace awhile my soul, that, with its mortal form journeying here, is sore distressed."

*"Love that in my mind discourseth to me,"* began he then so sweetly, that the sweetness yet within me sounds.

42. Rose window, Chartres Cathedral.

My Master and I and that people who were with him, seemed so glad as if to aught else the mind of no one of them gave heed.

We were all fixed and intent upon his notes; and lo the old man venerable, crying: "What is this, ye laggard spirits?

what negligence, what tarrying is this? Haste to the mount and strip you of the slough, that lets not God be manifest to you."

As doves when gathering wheat or tares, all assembled at their repast, quiet and showing not their wonted pride,

if aught be seen whereof they have fear, straightway let stay their food, because they are assailed by greater care;

so saw I that new company leave the singing, and go towards the hillside, like one who goes, but knoweth not where he may come forth; nor was our parting less quick.

## Paradiso: Canto XXXI

In form, then, of a white rose displayed itself to me that sacred soldiery which in his blood Christ made his spouse;

but the other, which as it flieth seeth and doth sing his glory who enamoureth it, and the excellence which hath made it what it is,

like to a swarm of bees which doth one while plunge into the flowers and another while wend back to where its toil is turned to sweetness,

ever descended into the great flower adorned with so many leaves, and reascended thence to where its love doth ceaseless make sojourn.

They had their faces all of living flame, and wings of gold, and the rest so white that never snow reacheth such limit.

When they descended into the flower, from rank to rank they proffered of the peace and of the ardour which they acquired as they fanned their sides,

nor did the interposing of so great a flying multitude, betwixt the flower and that which was above, impede the vision nor the splendour;

for the divine light so penetrateth through the universe, in measure of its worthiness, that nought hath power to oppose it.

This realm, secure and gladsome, thronged with ancient folk and new, had look and love all turned unto one mark.

O threefold light, which in a single star, glinting upon their sight doth so content them, look down upon our storm!

If the Barbarians coming from such region as every day is spanned by Helice, wheeling with her son towards whom she yearneth,

on seeing Rome and her mighty works—what time the Lateran transcended mortal things—were stupefied;

what then of me, who to the divine from the human, to the eternal from time had passed, and from Florence to a people just and sane,

with what stupor must I needs be filled! verily, what with it and what with joy, my will was to hear nought and to be dumb myself.

As the pilgrim who doth draw fresh life in the temple of his vow as he gazeth, and already hopeth to tell again how it be placed,

so, traversing the living light, I led mine eyes along the ranks, now up, now down, and now round circling.

I saw countenances suasive of love, adorned by another's light and their own smile, and gestures graced with every dignity.

The general form of Paradise my glance had already taken in, in its entirety, and on no part as yet had my sight paused;

and I turned me with rekindled will to question my Lady concerning things whereanent my mind was in suspense.

One thing I purposed, and another answered me; I thought to see Beatrice, and I saw an elder clad like the folk in glory.

His eyes and cheeks we overpoured with benign gladness, in kindly gesture as befits a tender father.

And: "Where is she?" all sudden I exclaimed; whereunto he: "To bring thy desire to its goal Beatrice moved me from my place;

and if thou look up to the circle third from the highest rank, thou shalt re-behold her, on the throne her merits have assigned to her."

Without answering I lifted up mine eyes and saw her, making to herself a crown as she reflected from her the eternal rays.

From that region which thundereth most high, no mortal eye is so far distant, though plunged most deep within the sea,

as there from Beatrice was my sight; but that wrought not upon me, for her image descended not to me mingled with any medium.

"O Lady, in whom my hope hath vigour, and who for my salvation didst endure to leave in Hell thy footprints;

of all the things which I have seen I recognize the grace and might, by thy power and by thine excellence.

Thou hast drawn me from a slave to liberty by all those paths, by all those methods by which thou hadst the power so to do.

Preserve thy munificence in me, so that my soul which thou hast made sound, may unloose it from the body, pleasing unto thee.

So did I pray; and she, so distant as she seemed, smiled and looked on me, then turned her to the eternal fountain.

And the holy elder said: "That thou mayest consummate thy journey perfectly—whereto prayer and holy love dispatched me,—

fly with thine eyes throughout this garden; for gazing on it will equip thy glance better to mount through the divine ray.

And the Queen of heaven for whom I am all burning with love, will grant us every grace, because I am her faithful Bernard."

As is he who perchance from Croatia cometh to look on our Veronica and because of ancient fame is sated not,

but saith in thought, so long as it be shown; "My Lord Jesus Christ, true God, and was this, then, the fashion of thy semblance?"

such was I, gazing upon the living love of him who in this world by contemplation tasted of that peace.

"Son of grace! this joyous being," he began, "will not become known to thee by holding thine eyes only here down at the base;

but look upon the circles even to the remotest, until thou seest enthroned the Queen to whom this realm is subject and devoted."

I lifted up mine eyes, and as at morn the oriental regions of the horizon overcome that where the sun declineth,

so, as from the valley rising to the mountain; with mine eyes I saw a region at the boundary surpass all the remaining ridge in light.

And as with us that place where we await the chariot pole that Phaëton guided ill, is most aglow, and on this side and on that the light is shorn away;

so was that pacific oriflamme quickened in the midst, on either side in equal measure tempering its flame.

And at that mid point, with out-stretched wings, I saw more than a thousand Angels making festival, each one distinct in glow and art.

I saw there, smiling to their sports and to their songs, a beauty which was gladness in the eyes of all the other saints.

And had I equal wealth in speech as in conception, yet dared I not attempt the smallest part of her delightsomeness.

Bernard, when he saw mine eyes fixed and eager towards the glowing source of his own glow, turned his eyes to her, with so much love that he made mine more ardent to regaze.

*The intellectual works of the period reveal the same emphasis on systematic organization. There was a feeling that if all knowledge on a given subject could be organized, all problems could be solved. The architectonic quality of medieval thought is most apparent in the number of summas. These summations of a subject or an area of knowledge are not encyclopedias, but a discussion of principles in their right order. The most comprehensive is the* Speculum *of Vincent of Beauvais, consisting of quotations from other writers on nature, doctrine and history. Its six thousand pages are a marvel of organization, and its wealth of Arabic learning a valuable contribution. Another summa-writer, Albertus Magnus, broke down philosophy into physics, mathematics and metaphysics, declaring that "it is our intent to make all the said parts intelligible to the Latins." Mightiest of all, however, is the twenty-one volume* Summa Theologiae *of St. Thomas Aquinas, a monumental work which touches on every aspect of theology from the application of reason to revelation to the standards of behavior for men and institutions and, in fact, all facets of men's existence. In explicating Christian truth by rational logic, he was bringing to a culmination the work begun by Abelard, and like Abelard, he met with opposition, although in time the Church accepted his system as the philosophy for the schools.*

# TREATISE ON THE DIVINE GOVERNMENT

## St. Thomas Aquinas

### Whether the World is Governed by Anyone

*We proceed thus to the First Article:*

*Objection* 1. It would seem that the world is not governed by anyone. For it belongs to those things to be governed which move or work for an end. But natural things which make up the greater part of the world do not move, or work for an end, for they have no knowledge of their end. Therefore, the world is not governed.

*Objection* 2. Further, those things are governed which are moved towards some object. But the world does not appear to be so directed, but has stability in itself. Therefore it is not governed.

*Objection* 3. Further, what is necessarily determined by its own nature to one particular course does not require any external principle of government. But the principal parts of the world are by a certain necessity determined to something particular in their actions and movements. Therefore the world does not require to be governed.

*On the contrary,* It is written (*Wis.* xiv. 3): *But Thou, O Father, governest all things by Thy Providence.* And Boethius says: *Thou Who governest this universe by mandate eternal.*

*I answer that,* Certain ancient philosophers denied the government of the world, saying that all things happened by chance. But such an opinion can be refuted as impossible in two ways. First, by the observation of things themselves. For we observe that in nature things happen always or nearly always for the best; which would not be the case unless some sort of providence directed nature towards good as an end. And this is to govern. Therefore, the unfailing order we observe in things is a sign of their being governed. For instance, if we were to enter a well-ordered house, we would gather from the order manifested in the house the notion of a governor, as Cicero says, quoting Aristotle. Secondly, this is clear from a consideration of the divine goodness, which, as we have said above, is the cause of the production of things in being. For as *it belongs to the best to produce the best,* it is not fitting that the supreme goodness of God should produce things without giving them their perfection. Now a thing's ultimate perfection consists in the attainment of its end. Therefore it belongs to the divine goodness, as it brought things into being, so to lead them to their end. And this is to govern.

*Reply to Objection* 1. A thing moves or operates for an end in two ways. First, in moving itself to the end, as do man and other rational creatures; and such beings have a knowledge of their end and of the means to the end. Secondly, a thing is said to move or operate for an end, as though moved or directed thereto by another, as an arrow is directed to the target by the archer, who knows the end unknown to the arrow. Hence, as the movement of the arrow towards a definite end shows clearly that it is directed by someone with knowledge, so the unvarying course of natural things which are without knowledge shows clearly that the world is governed by some reason.

*Reply to Objection* 2. In all created things there is a stable element, even if this be only primary matter, and something belonging to movement, if under movement we include operation. Now things need governing as to both, because even that which is stable, since it is created from nothing, would return to nothingness were it not sustained by a governing hand, as will be explained later.

*Reply to Objection* 3. The natural necessity inherent in those beings which are determined to a particular course is a kind of impression from God, directing them to their end; just as the necessity whereby the arrow is moved so as to fly towards a certain point is an impression from the archer, and not from the arrow. But there is a difference, inasmuch as that which creatures receive from God is their nature, while that which natural things receive from man in addition to their nature is something violent. Therefore, just as the violent necessity in the movement of the arrow shows the action of the archer, so the natural necessity of things shows the government of divine providence.

## Whether the End of the Government of the World Is Something Outside the World

*We proceed thus to the Second Article:*

*Objection* 1. It would seem that the end of the government of the world is not something existing outside the world. For the end of the government of a thing is that to which the thing governed is brought. But that to which a thing is brought is some good in the thing itself; and thus a sick man is brought back to health, which is something good in him. Therefore the end of the government is some good, not outside, but existing within the things themselves.

. . .

*Objection* 3. Further, the good of a multitude seems to consist in order and peace, which is *the tranquillity of order,* as Augustine says. But the world is composed of a multitude of things. Therefore, the end of the government of the world is a peaceful order in things themselves. Therefore the end of the government of the world is not an extrinsic good.

*On the contrary,* It is written (*Prov.* xvi. 4): *The Lord hath made all things for himself.* But God is outside the entire order of the universe. Therefore the end of things is something extrinsic to them.

*I answer that,* As the end of a thing corresponds to its beginning, it is not possible to be ignorant of the end of things if we know their beginning. Therefore, since the beginning of all things is something outside the universe, namely, God, as is clear from what has been said above, we must conclude that the end of all things is some extrinsic good. This can be proved by reason. For it is clear that good has the nature of an end. And so the particular end of anything consists in some particular good, while the universal end of all things is a universal good. A universal good is good of itself by virtue of its essence, which is the very essence of goodness; whereas a particular good is good by participation. Now it is manifest that in the whole created universe there is not a good which is not such by participation. Therefore that good which is the end of the whole universe must be a good outside the universe.

*Reply to Objection* 1. We may acquire some good in many ways: first, as a form existing in us, such as health or knowledge; secondly, as something done by us, as a builder attains his end by building a house; thirdly, as something good possessed or acquired by us, as the buyer of a field attains his end when he enters into possession. Therefore nothing prevents something outside the universe from being the good to which it is directed.

*Reply to Objection* 3. The end of the universe, namely, the order of the universe itself, is a good existing in it. This good, however, is not its ultimate end, but is ordered to an extrinsic good as to an ultimate end; just as the order in an army is ordered to the general, as is stated in *Metaph.* xii.

. . .

## Whether All Things Are Subject to the Divine Government

*We proceed thus to the Fifth Article:*

*Objection* 1. It would seem that not all things are subject to the divine government. For it is written (*Eccles.* ix. 11): *I saw that under the sun the race is not to the swift, nor the battle to the strong, nor bread to the wise, nor riches to the learned, nor favor to the skillful, but time and chance in all.* But those things subject to the divine government are not ruled by chance. Therefore those things which are under the sun are not subject to the divine government.

*Objection* 2. Further, the Apostle says (1 *Cor.* ix. 9): *God hath no care for oxen.* But he that governs has care for the things he governs. Therefore all things are not subject to the divine government.

*Objection* 3. Further, what can govern itself needs not to be governed by another. But the rational creature can govern itself. For it is master of its own act, and acts of itself; nor is it made to act by another, which seems proper to things which are governed. Therefore all things are not subject to the divine government.

*On the contrary,* Augustine says: *Not only heaven and earth, not only man and angel, but even the bowels of the lowest animal, even the wing of the bird, the flower of the plant, the leaf of the tree, hath God endowed with every fitting detail of their nature.* Therefore all things are subject to His government.

*I answer that,* For the same reason is God the ruler of things as He is their cause, because the same cause gives being that gives perfection; and this belongs to government. Now God is the cause, not of some particular kind of being, but of the whole universal being, as was proved above. Therefore, as there can be nothing which is not created by God, so there can be nothing which is not subject to His government. This can also be proved from the nature of the end of government. For a man's government extends over all those things which come under the end of his government. Now the end of the divine government is the divine goodness, as we have shown. Therefore, as there can be nothing that is not ordered to the divine goodness as its end, as is clear from what we have said above, it is impossible for anything to escape from the divine government.

Foolish was the opinion of those who said that the corruptible lower world, or individual things, or that even human affairs, were not subject to the divine government. These are represented as saying, *God has abandoned the earth* (*Ezech.* ix. 9).

*Reply to Objection* 1. Those things are said to be under the sun which are generated and corrupted according to the sun's movement. In all such things we find chance; not that everything is by chance which occurs in such things, but that in each one there is an element of chance. And the very fact that an element of chance is found in these things proves that they are subject to government of some kind. For unless corruptible things were governed by a higher being, they would tend to nothing definite, especially those which possess no kind of knowledge. So nothing in them would happen unintentionally; which constitutes the nature of chance. Therefore to show how things happen by chance and yet according to the ordering of a higher cause, he does not say absolutely that he observes chance in all things, but *time and chance,* that is to say, that defects may be found in these things according to some order of time.

*Reply to Objection* 2. Government implies a certain change effected by the governor in the things governed. Now every movement is the act of a movable thing, caused by the moving principle, as is laid down in *Physics* iii. Now every act is proportioned to that of which it is an act. Consequently, diverse movable things must be moved diversely, even as regards movement by one and the same mover. Thus, by the one art of the divine governor things are diversely governed according to their diversity. Some, according to their nature, act of themselves, having dominion over their actions; and these are governed by God, not only in this, that they are moved by God Himself, Who works in them interiorly, but also in this, that they are induced by Him to do good and to fly from evil, by precepts and prohibitions, rewards and punishments. But irrational creatures, which do not act but are only acted upon, are not thus governed by God. Hence, when the Apostle says that *God hath no care for oxen,* he does not wholly withdraw them from the divine government, but only as regards the way in which rational creatures are governed.

*Reply to Objection* 3. The rational creature governs itself by its intellect and will, both of which require to be governed and perfected by the divine intellect and will. Therefore, above the government whereby the rational creature governs itself as master of its own act, it requires to be governed by God.

## Whether Anything Can Happen Outside the Order of the Divine Government

*We proceed thus to the Seventh Article:*

*Objection* 1. It would seem possible that something may occur outside the order of the divine government. For Boethius says that *God disposes all by good.* Therefore, if nothing happens outside the order of the divine government, it would follow that no evil exists.

*Objection* 2. Further, nothing that is in accordance with the pre-ordination of a ruler occurs by chance. Therefore, if nothing occurs outside the order of the divine government, it follows that there is nothing fortuitous and by chance.

*Objection* 3. Further, the order of divine providence is certain and unchangeable, because it is in accord with an eternal design. Therefore, if nothing happens outside the order of the divine government, it follows that all things happen by necessity, and nothing is contingent; which is false. Therefore it is possible for something to occur outside the order of the divine government.

*On the contrary,* It is written (*Esth.* xiii. 9): *O Lord, Lord, almighty King, all things are in Thy power, and there is none that can resist thy will.*

*I answer that,* It is possible for an effect to happen outside the order of some particular cause, but not outside the order of the universal cause. The reason for this is that no effect happens outside the order of a particular cause, except through some other impeding cause; which other cause must itself be reduced to the first universal cause. Thus, indigestion may occur outside the order of the nutritive power by some such impediment as the coarseness of the food, which again is to be ascribed to some other cause, and so on till we come to the first universal cause. Therefore, as God is the first universal cause, not of one genus only, but of all being, it is impossible for anything to occur outside the order of the divine government; but from the very fact that from one point of view something seems to evade the order of divine providence considered in regard to one particular cause, it must necessarily come back to that order as regards some other cause.

*Reply to Objection* 1. There is nothing wholly evil in the world for evil is always founded on good, as was shown above. Therefore something is said to be evil because it escapes from the order of some particular good. If it escaped wholly from the order of the divine government, it would wholly cease to exist.

*Reply to Objection* 2. Things are said to be by chance as regards some particular cause from whose order they escape. But as to the order of divine providence, *nothing in the world happens by chance,* as Augustine declares.

*Reply to Objection* 3. Certain effects are said to be contingent as compared to their proximate causes, which may fail in their effects; and not as though anything could happen entirely outside the order of divine government. The very fact that something occurs outside the order of some proximate cause is owing to some other cause, itself subject to the divine government.

43. Tympanum showing thirty-one figures of the zodiac. West portal, Autun Cathedral.

*Other cosmic systems met with less favor. Abbot Joachim of Flora, for example, proposed a developmental history that found little acceptance outside the monasteries. Taking the Franciscan view that God is progressively at work in nature and in history, he outlined three ages: the age of the Father which had its highest point in Moses and then declined; the age of the Son beginning with Oziah and at its peak with Christ, but waning since that time; the age of the Holy Spirit, to begin in the year 1260 (the year recalls the 1260 days in Revelations that the Woman clothed with the Sun spent in the wilderness). The age of the Spirit would be the rule of the saints on earth—monks and hermits who practice asceticism as proof and as preparation of the Coming. All Scripture could be adapted to this scheme, Joachim believed. For example, on the third day of the festivities of the wedding at Cana, the bridegroom (the ecclesiastical hierarchy) and the bride (Christian believers in the second age) were in difficulties when Mary (the monastic orders) came to their rescue with Christ (the Holy Spirit who will substitute baptism by the Spirit for a baptism of water). Joachim skirted heresy, but many of his followers were less cautious and were condemned by ecclesiastics who were offended by the role assigned to them.*

*Even the* Summa *of Thomas Aquinas, although much admired, is not widely read today. To appreciate the medieval sense of structure at its best, we still look at the cathedrals. Aspiring as the people who built them, they sought the sky, but in no reckless manner. Like all the art of the age, they have an awareness of form—window follows window, telling its story; carving follows carving, leading to a climax. A rare combination of mathematics and inspiration, they remain the symbol of a people who lived by symbols.*

*Just as the aspiring structure and essential unity of the cathedrals reveal the nature of their builders, so, too, their asymmetrical design may be taken to typify some of the inner conflict of those natures. In many societies of antiquity man had suffered a sense of guilt, a belief that the gods must be appeased for some unknown transgression. Medieval man was spared this anxiety; though he knew his sin, the weight of his redemption, he believed, had been assumed by the Son*

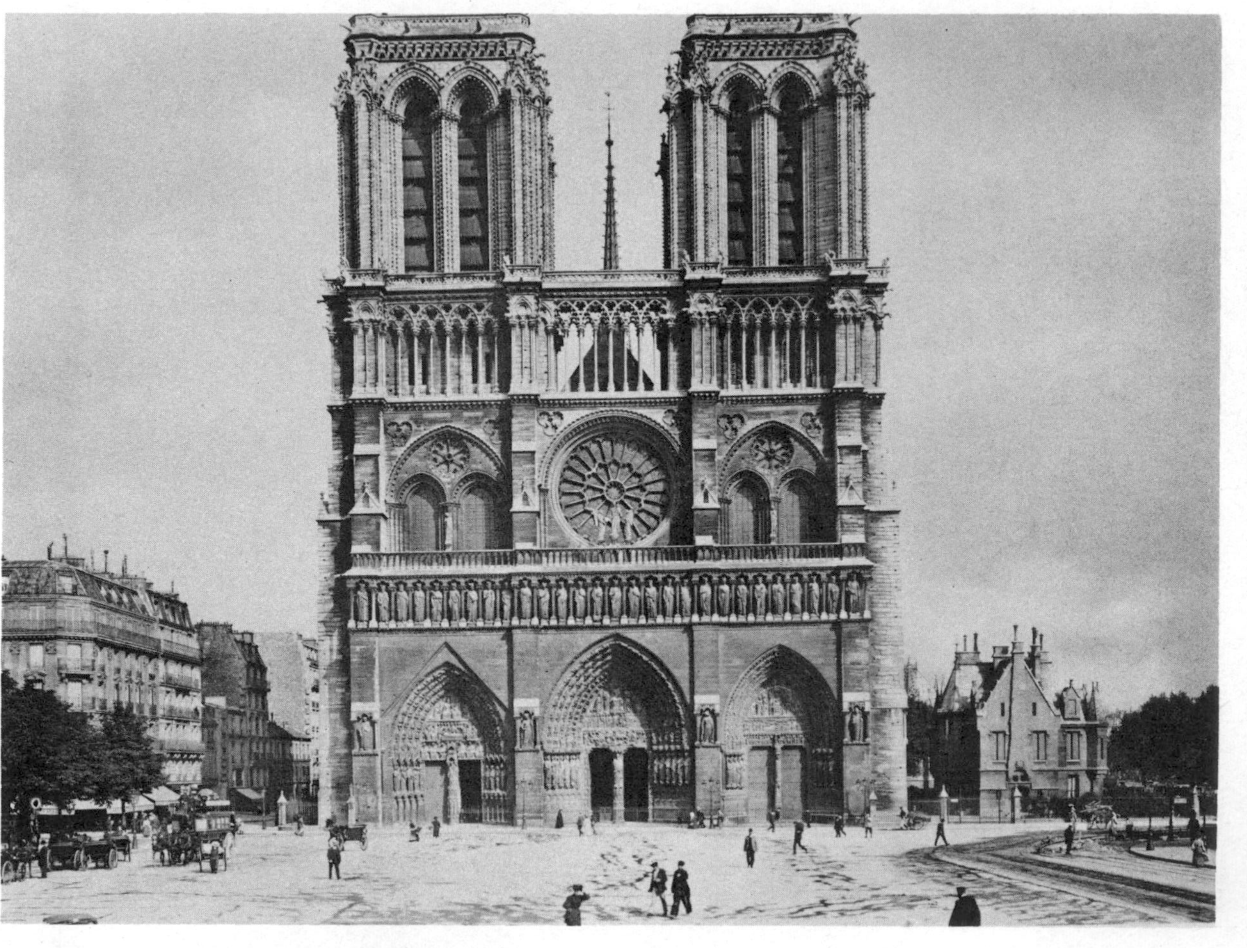

44. West façade, Cathedral of Notre-Dame, Paris.

*of God become incarnate to propitiate the Father. For him there was another problem. Full-blooded, lusty, sensitive, he loved life and he loved the earth in which he lived. "Lay up treasures in heaven, where moth and rust cannot consume," he was counseled in Scripture, but the treasures of earth were attractive as well. Citizen of the City of God, he still moved among the joys of the terrestrial city—political power, wealth, secular knowledge—which drew him from the contemplation of his proper goal.*

## DIES IRAE

### THOMAS OF CELANO (?)

Day of anger, that woeful day
Shall the world in ashes lay
David and Sibylla say.

What a trembling, what a fear
When the dread Judge shall appear
Strictly searching far and near.

Hark! the trumpet's wondrous tone
Through sepulchral regions blown
Summons all before the throne.

Death shall shiver, Nature quake,
When the creatures shall awake
Answer to their Judge to make.

Lo, the Book of ages spread
From which all the deeds are read
Of the living and the dead.

Now before the Judge severe
All things hidden must appear
Nought shall pass unpunished here.

Wretched man what shall I plead,
Who for me will intercede
When the righteous mercy need?

King of awful majesty,
Author of salvation free,
Fount of pity, save thou me!

Recollect good Lord I pray
I have caused Thy bitter way,
Me forget not on that day.

Weary, thou didst seek for me
Didst redeem me on the tree;
Let such toil not fruitless be.

Judge of righteousness severe
Grant me full remission here
Ere the reckoning day appear.

Sighs and tears my sorrow speak,
Shame and grief are on my cheek;
Mercy, mercy, Lord, I seek.

Thou didst Mary's guilt forgive
And absolve the dying thief,
Even I may hope relief.

Worthless are my prayers I know
Yet, o Lord, thy mercy show.
Save me from eternal woe!

Make me with the sheep to stand,
Far from thy convicted band,
Placing me at thy right hand.

When the damned are put to shame
Cast into devouring flame,
With the blest then call my name.

Suppliant at thy feet I lie
Contrite in the dust I cry,
Care thou for me when I die.

. . . .

Day of tears and day of dread
When arising from the dead

Guilty man awaits his doom;
God have mercy on his soul!

Gentle Jesus, Lord of grace,
Grant to them eternal rest.

*As the pace of living accelerated, the very factors that had caused the rise of medieval culture hastened its decline. The growth of commerce caused both prices and standards of living to rise, obliging the noble to exact more from his peasants, igniting the rebellion against feudalism. The enormous financial and political power of the church rendered it incompetent to stabilize the economic and civil order. Undue emphasis on involvement of the spiritual in the temporal led to the secularization of large segments of society; among those with a stronger religious orientation, the reduction of spiritual things to the natural level often seemed an identification of the two, resulting in vulgar devotions, theological pedantry, philosophic hair-splitting. Gradually, as the image of the City of God lost vitality, the culture based on it became stagnant—a vacuum awaiting the cultural Renaissance, the religious Reformation.*

# EPILOGUE

In the following centuries, medieval man was severely criticized for his otherworldliness; the delight of men in rationalism or in the god of reason or the god of scientific discovery pushed the medieval age backwards, as companion to the Dark Ages. Yet while the medievals lost touch with the wellsprings which had lent grace and greatness to their age, their vision of creative history is so organic that it continues to develop in our own time. Writes the twentieth-century paleontologist, Père Teilhard du Chardin:

> For reasons of practical convenience and perhaps also of intellectual timidity, the City of God is too often described in pious works in conventional and purely moral terms. God and the world he governs are seen as a vast association, essentially legalistic in its nature, conceived in terms of a family or government. The fundamental root from which the sap of Christianity has risen from the beginning and is nourished, is quite otherwise. Led astray by a false evangelism, people often think they are honoring Christianity when they reduce it to a sort of gentle philanthropism. Those who fail to see in it the most realistic and at the same time the most cosmic of beliefs and hopes, completely fail to understand its "mysteries." Is the Kingdom of God a big family? Yes, in a sense it is. But in another sense it is a prodigious biological operation—that of Redeeming Incarnation.
>
> As early as in St. Paul and St. John we read that to create, to fulfil and to purify the world is, for God, to unify it by uniting it organically with himself. How does he unify it? By

partially immersing himself in things, by becoming "element" and then, from the point of vantage in the heart of matter, assuming the control and leadership of what we now call evolution. Christ, principle of universal vitality because sprung up as man among men, put himself in the position (maintained ever since) to subdue under himself, to purify, to direct and superanimate the general ascent of consciousnesses into which he inserted himself. By a perennial act of communion and sublimation, he aggregated to himself the total psychism of the earth. And when he has gathered everything together and transformed everything, he will close in upon himself and his conquests, thereby rejoining, in a final gesture, the divine focus he has never left. Then, as St. Paul tells us, *God shall be all in all.* This is indeed a superior form of "pantheism" without trace of the poison of adulteration or annihilation: the expectation of perfect unity, steeped in which each element will reach its consummation at the same time as the universe.

The universe fulfilling itself in a synthesis of centres in perfect conformity with the laws of union. God, the Centre of centres. In that final vision the Christian dogma culminates.

# BIOGRAPHICAL NOTES

ABELARD, PETER (1079-1142) son of a minor lord in Brittany, famous teacher in the Paris schools of philosophy, died a monk in the abbey of Cluny.

ALCUIN (d. 804) Harrow-educated teacher in the schools of Charlemagne.

ALIGHIERI, DANTE (1265-1321) greatest Italian poet, political exile from Florence, writer of Latin and Italian prose treatises.

ANSELM, ST. (1033-1109) Italian-Norman, Archbishop of Canterbury, Doctor of the Church, outstanding theologian of his time, pioneer in scholastic philosophy.

AQUINAS, ST. THOMAS (1225-1274) the "angelic doctor," member of a noble family of Naples, greatest light of the Dominican Order, philosopher and theologian.

AUGUSTINE, ST. (d. 430) philosopher, bishop, religious founder, most influential and prolific writer of the Dark Ages.

BARTHOLOMEUS ANGLICUS, twelfth century compiler of information on all branches of knowledge.

BACON, ROGER (c.1214-c.1294) Franciscan friar at Oxford, pioneer in experimental science.

BENEDICT, ST. (d. c.543) patriarch of Western monasticism, founder of Benedictine Order at Monte Cassino.

BERNARD OF CLAIRVAUX, ST. (d. 1153) Cistercian abbot, mystic, Mariologist, papal adviser, prominent statesman, last of the Church Fathers.

BONAVENTURE, ST. (1221-1274) Italian philosopher, General of Franciscan Order, proponent of Platonic-Augustinian tradition in the Paris schools.

BONIFACE VIII, POPE (d. 1303) member of Gaetani family, diplomat, exponent of papal civil power.

CASSIAN, JOHN (360-435) monk and ascetic writer of southern Gaul, disciple of St. John Chrysostom, bridge between Eastern and Western monasticism.

CHAUCER, GEOFFREY (1340-1400) English poet, protégé of John of Gaunt, customs clerk, most important figure in English literature before Shakespeare.

DURANDUS, WILLIAM (c.1220-1296) priest, teacher, writer on canon law.

EINHARD (775-840) secretary to Charlemagne and his first biographer.

DE FRANCE, MARIE (d. 1185) French poet living in England, wrote verse from Celtic sources and spread custom of courtly love.

FRANCIS OF ASSISI, ST. (1126-1182) founder of Franciscan Order of mendicants, vowed to the "Lady Poverty" in the tradition of chivalry.

FORTUNATUS, VENANTIUS (d. c.600) last Gallic Latin poet.

FREDERICK II (1215-1250) German Emperor, king of Sicily, patron of learning and the arts.

GLABER, RODULFUS (d. c.1050) Benedictine chronicler.

GHIBERTI, LORENZO (c.1378-1455) Florentine sculptor.

HUGH OF ST. VICTOR (1096-1141) monk, mystical theologian, educational theorist.

JOHN OF SALISBURY (d. 1180) humanist, bishop of Chartres, secretary to Pope Adrian IV and also to Thomas à Becket.

LANGLAND, WILLIAM (c.1332-1400) probably an English parish priest situated near London, obviously well-educated.

KNIGHT DE LA TOUR LANDRY (13th century) French nobleman writing for the education of his daughters.

LULL, RAMON, Blessed (1235-1315) Majorcan soldier, devoted his life to conversion of the Saracens to Christianity.

OTTO OF FREISING (d. 1158) member of Hohenstaufen family, became Cistercian monk, bishop of Freising 1137-1158.

PATRICK OF ARMAGH, ST. (d. 461) Breton missionary bishop who spread Christianity through Ireland with astonishing success.

PETER THE VENERABLE (12th century) abbot of the monastery of Cluny.

POLO, MARCO (c.1254-1327) Venetian traveler to court of the Grand Khan.

RICHARD OF ST. VICTOR (d. 1173) disciple of Hugh of St. Victor, symbolist and mystical theologian.

ROGER OF WENDOVER (d. c.1418) monk of St. Alban's, one of the three great chroniclers of that abbey.

SALIMBENE DEGLI ADAMI (1221-1288) Franciscan chronicler.

THEOPHILUS (12th century) compiler of *Schedula diversarum artium,* a primary contemporary source of information on painting in the Middle Ages.

THOMAS OF CELANO (d. after 1247) Franciscan monk, first biographer of St. Francis, reputed author of the sequence *Dies Irae.*

DA TODI, JACOPO (d. 1306) Franciscan friar, political opponent of Pope Boniface VIII.